HUN

& THE HU

*

THE KE

HUNGARY
& THE HUNGARIANS

*

THE KEYWORDS

a concise

DICTIONARY

OF FACTS AND BELIEFS, CUSTOMS, USAGE & MYTHS

by István Bart

Second edition

CORVINA

Translated by Judith Sollosy

First published in 1999 by Corvina Books Ltd.
1051 Budapest, Vörösmarty tér 1., Hungary
E-mail: corvina@axelero.hu
http://www.corvinakiado.hu

Second edition, 2002

Jacket artwork by András Felvidéki

ISBN 963 13 5190 4

A Word in Advance

Language is not just words and grammar, it works by metaphors and allusions that make up (and also hide away) meanings wich are indecipherable without the knowledge of the culture code. Every student of any foreign language is painfully aware how this meta-language lurking behind even the simplest of turns can make reception of even everyday speech such a precarious affair. For there may be worlds in a word, not unlike the boxes within boxes within boxes of a Chinese puzzle. And bilingual dictionaries, constructed on the principle of equivalence, do not help here, because they do not try to invoke the thoughts, concepts and images that are invoked for the native speaker upon hearing the name of a town or a region, a festival, a form of address, a dish peculiar to his country or the lines of a song. For languages are made up of popular memories, myths and beliefs, customs and ever changing usage, words ring bells – and if our ears don't hear their toll, life is merely a silent movie.

This book was born out of innumerable futile efforts to explain to visitors what is behind a gesture or a melody, a name, an attitude. It is both a guide to the "secrets" of the Hungarians' code-language and a concise cultural encyclopaedia of Hungarianness.

A

ABC →**közért**

Ady Endre (pron. *aah–dee*); the greatest poet of the turn of the century (→*századforduló*), a condemned but seraphic figure, whose works elicit passionate responses from people to this day. His *New Poems*, published in 1906, are said to have brought Hungarian literature into the 20th century. →**Kerepesi úti temető; temetés; táltos**

Akácos út… '*Road with acacias…*' (lit.); the title and first words of the lyrics of one of the most popular and sentimental Hungarian songs (→*magyar nóta*) which continues: "…*when I stroll down your lane, / I remember a lovely old refrain: / it was a summer's eve, a bird sang up in the tree … stop Gypsy by the window / and play to make that beautiful girl weep …*"; this type of Hungarian song is known as a "courting song".

Akadémia, az *Academy, the;* the popular name for the Hungarian Academy of Sciences established in 1825 thanks to a generous donation by → *Széchenyi*, who hoped to foster the development of the Hungarian language (→*magyar nyelv*) and Hungarian literature (and thus the national consciousness) thereby; it soon became the centre for the great pioneers of the early 19th century Reform Age. Originally a chain of scholary societies for the elite in sciences, it was turned into a veritable "ministry of sciences" (with its own research institutes independent of the universities) and "brain trust" (under tight government control) only in the sixties (→*hatvanas évek*), until by degrees it once again became (more or less) independent of politics, thereby improving its reputation in the eyes of the public; however, during the time of the change in regime (→*rendszerváltás*), this fact made its members (along with independent writers and artists) much sought-after participants in public life, with the various political parties using them, directly or indirectly, with or without their consent, to ingratiate themselves with the Hungarian public, who continue to regard the Academy as one of the precious few national institutions deserving of unconditional respect.

alázatosan jelentem! '*I humbly report*' (lit.); the term used by all subordinates in the old Hungarian army (→*honvédség*) before addressing their superiors. Today, it is *tisztelettel jelentem* ('I respectfully report'). The formula for signalling understanding and acceptance is *értettem* ('I understand'), and *igenis* ('*aye*'). →**köszönés**

albérlő *subtenant*; still, the English expression cannot conjure up with sufficient force the image of the musty room of a crumbling apartment house (→*bérház*) giving out on the outer corridor (→*gang*) redolent of the smell of savoy cabbage (→*kelkáposzta*), which immediately comes to the mind of every native speaker. However, this does not mean that there are no other types of sub-tenancies. →**társbérlet**

Alföld (Nagyalföld) *The Great (Hungarian) Plain*; the wide expanse of lowlands which stretches from the Danube (→*Duna*) at the point where it turns south at →*Esztergom* to the mountains of Transylvania (→*Erdély*) to the east and south-east; it is further divided by the river →*Tisza*; since →*Petőfi*, who was born here, this "boundless", grassy prairie (→*puszta*) is considered a romantic terrain, the symbolic abode of "unfettered liberty" galloping on horseback, which the landscape painters of the 19th century turned, once and for all, into the quintessence of *the* Hungarian landscape, thereby making the galloping manes of the →*Hortobágy*, the whip-cracking wrangler (→*csikós*) and the incessantly "bobbing" draw-well an indispensable prop of the landscape; this is how the sparsely populated lowlands and the small, isolated farm or homestead (→*tanya*) – not to mention the storks nesting atop the chimneys – became the pictorial stereotype of all of Hungary which, the more outrageously outdated it became with time, was imbued with that much more sentimentalism, until it became confined to the realm of tourist propaganda and the maudlin lyrics of Hungarian songs (→*magyar nóta*). Still, the people of the Alföld's open spaces (less densely populated than Transdanubia), though they may not be more "Magyar" than the rest of the country's populace, really are different in many ways, not only because of their history but, first and foremost, because urbanization has not yet wreaked havoc with their lives. →**Hódoltság**; **Kúnság**; **Dunántúl**

Algopyrin the most popular pain killer found in every woman's purse, especially if she is prone to migraine; it is dispensed to fellow sufferers with a knowing little smile of sympathy.

alispán '*deputy steward*' (lit.), *Lord Lieutenant's Deputy*; historically, the principal elected official of the pre-1950s county (→*megye*) administration, who thus represented and embodied local interests (and historically, the autonomy of the local nobility or →*nemes* class), while his superior, the Lord Lieutenant (→*főispán*), was appointed by the government, and was more like a prefect or chief magistrate.

államosítás '*state-ification*' (lit.), *nationalization*; the term refers to the *blitzkrieg*-like *gleichschaltung*, or speedy and forceful levelling of the populace which, as part of the Communist takeover, confiscated every bit of property from everyone with no thought to compensation of any kind, from banks, mines and factories to hole-in-the-wall shoe-repair shops (not to mention every large and desirable apartment and house), thereby introducing the all-powerful economic system which became known as socialism (→*szocializmus*), the creation, in the blinking of an eye, of perfect social equality based on all-pervasive penury; worn out by the war and the German and Russian occupations, the majority of the people suffered it with apathy, while a minority – heads reeling with thoughts of a Communist utopia and fired to fever pitch by revolutionary fervor – enthusiastically endorsed it and drove it through; introduced in a matter of months, the new economic system almost immediately led to total chaos and poverty; as a consequence, reforms were implemented almost right away, but these could do precious little to improve the situation. Still, with periodic jump-starts and remissions (which caused a great number of political crises into the bargain), billed as a reform (→*reform*), the "experiment" lasted until the 1990 change in regime (→*rendszerváltás*). →**termelőszövetkezet; kárpótlás**

aludttej *'sleeping milk'* (lit.), *sour milk*, *butter milk*; also known as the Hungarian yogurt. In the countryside (and in some urban households as well), you can still see on many a window-sill a big mug of fresh (not boiled or pasteurized!) milk left over from the day before, standing out in the sun to "sleep"; in warm weather it turns into a deliciously sour, quivering, jelly-like substance consumed for breakfast, usually with a slice of bread (→*kenyér*). In today's households, it is often replaced by buttermilk made from pasteurized skim milk.

Amerika *America*; in Hungary, the term does not designate the entire continent, but only the United States (and of course, Canada). Since the turn of the century, when according to the common lore one and a half million Hungarians "staggered out" to America (as →*József Attila* wrote), it has been considered a pleasant, homey, welcoming sort of place, even though the majority eventually returned and bought land with what they earned there. Still, there was no end to the flood of Hungarian emigrants (→*kivándorló*), as each political upheaval sent yet another wave of hopefuls on their way; consequently, today there are approximately two million U.S. citizens who consider themselves of Hungarian origin, and many of whom still have relatives in Hungary. While the newspapers called the U.S. "imperialist" and "hostile", charity packages, or "love packages" (→*szeretetcsomag*) "arrived" from America (as if they had no senders), while music and much else that was "modern" (including fashion, science and technology) also "arrived" from there; the gifted as well as the poor dreamt of going to America, and the intelligentsia (→*értelmiség*) were learning English and reading American novels (seeing how they could never actually get there), while a lucky few were "helped out there" by their loving relatives. In short, going to America, whether to work or to visit, conferred an enviable status on the individual. →**disszidens**; **emigráns**; **külföldre szakadt hazánkfia; amerikai nagybácsi;**

amerikás magyarok; amerikai magyarok; amerikázni; mindenki magyar

amerikai magyarok *Hungarian Americans*; they are the Americans of Hungarian origin (→*magyar származású*), many of whom belong to the "expatriate sons of the nation" (→*külföldre szakadt hazánkfia*) category and may have been dissidents (→*disszidens*), but not emigrants (→*emigráns*). The expression refers to the generations of Hungarians who went to America before, during or after WW II and made good there, and who were better educated than the "Americanish" Hungarians (→*amerikás magyarok*); the former went with the express purpose of settling in the U.S. and were quick to assimilate (they live in the greatest numbers in New York and California), yet kept close ties with their Hungarian relatives, and when post-war détente finally set it, began visiting their native country with increasing daring and frequency. Lately, some of them (especially retired persons) have even opted to repatriate. Their children speak Hungarian poorly, if at all, and think of themselves as Americans.

amerikaiak, az *Americans, the*; seen from Hungary, the United States (→*Amerika*) was always the far-distant land of untold riches, particularly so during the fifties (→*ötvenes évek*), when the "Peace Camp" (→*béketábor*) was readying itself for war against it. Still, Hungarians never really understood the Americans, whom they saw "in bulk" for the first time as inmates of POW camps in Germany; they thought of Americans as "great big children", innocent and naive, and felt superior (adult) compared to them (though there's no denying, in some sense also inferior), a feeling which is still very much in evidence among most of the populace. They are seen first and foremost as practical, which some consider admirable, others vulgar; nonetheless, thanks to mass culture, "American" forms of behavior (or behavior that is considered American), along with the context that breeds them, is quickly gaining ground, a situation which, in the face of the resolute march of Americanization – and in order to protect "classical" European traditions – has already given rise to a Hungarian variant of anti-Americanism.

amerikás magyarok '*Americanish Hungarians*' (lit.), vulgarized grammar; the term refers to the approximately one and a half million Hungarian citizens who went to the United States (later Canada as well) between the 1880s and the outbreak of WW I; some were emigrants (→*kivándorló*), but the majority were poor though adventurous farmhands and peasants who traveled back and forth many times before they could save enough money to buy a bit of land back in Hungary. The mines of Virginia and the huge industrial centers of Ohio and Illinois drew them in great numbers; then, when the war broke out, many were stranded in the U.S., and though they never learned to speak English properly, they soon became naturalized American citizens whose descendants, on the other hand, no longer speak Hungarian. "*Csikágó*" (Chicago), the name of the ill-reputed seventh district of Budapest built at the turn of the century (→*századforduló*) in imitation of the regular "American-type" street plan is one of the lasting reminders of those times. →**amerikai magyarok; emigránsok**

amerikázni '*to americize*', '*to act/do like the Americans*' (lit.), *to play hockey;* this word, now considered near obsolete, was used to refer to loitering, i.e., staying out of school or work, and is a perfect example of what people (who obviously had never been overseas) thought about life in the United States (→*Amerika*); the still current expression, '*Itt van Amerika!*' ("This is America!"), comes to mind, used when Lady Luck comes knocking at the door.

Andrássy út 60. *60 Andrássy Avenue*; the infamous building situated on Budapest's loveliest tree-lined boulevard which during WW II served as the fascist Arrow Cross (→*nyilas [keresztes] mozgalom*) headquarters, then as the headquarters of the dreaded communist secret police (→ *ÁVÓ*). Those who survived the tortures and interrogations in its subterranean the prison cells were usually taken to prison camp at →*Recsk*. In the sixties (→*hatvanas évek*), the street, formerly named after Count Andrássy, Minister of Foreign Affairs during the Monarchy (→*Monarchia*), then rechristened first in honor of Stalin, then in honor of the Hungarian People's Republic (Népköztársaság útja), was given new house numbers in a futile attempt to obliterate the past. It is now once again Andrássy út.

angolok, az *English, the;* in an effort to look beyond the painfully familiar German culture sitting on their doorstep, since the early 19th century Hungarians have been turning to England for answers and inspiration (one of the first being count →*Széchenyi*); however, England and its way of life have remained distant and all too utopistic, and the Hungarians' sincere respect and admiration (their Anglophilia) has not been reciprocated; needless to say, this love of all things English is based on the romantic conception of English history, for few Hungarians have seen England first-hand, despite the fact that by the end of the 20th century English has become the most popular foreign language among the educated; when a Hungarian says "England", he or she means the British Isles as a whole.

Angyalföld '*Angels' Land*' (lit.); a former working class district of →*Pest* situated on both sides of →*Váci út* was one of the "Red" districts of the capital inhabited by the petit bourgeois, workers (→*munkás*) and the poor in general. Surrounded by bogus and maudlin proletarian romanticism mixed with equally bogus ruffian-romanticism, it was regarded as the "last bastion" of the working class even after its factories were being shut down in quick succession. Today it is characterized by prefab mass housing (→*panelház*), and its factories have been replaced by or turned into "business centers", shopping malls, and automobile showrooms. →**Csepel**; **Újpest**; **Kispest**

anya *mother*; besides the numerous holidays of the Hungarian Catholic Church (→*katolikus egyház*) held in honor of the Virgin Mary, the other indication of the existence of some sort of mother cult in Hungary is the fact that any mention of someone else's mother (*anyázni*, lit. '*to mention someone's mother*') while one is cursing (→*káromkodás*) or hurling profanities is a serious first step towards the escalation of hostilities, possibly leading to assault and battery; this is especially likely in the case of someone with a pathetic, heart-shaped tattoo on his hairy arm, and across it the words, "I love you Mom!" The fetishization of the word is especially striking among Gypsies (→*cigány*). In Hungarian, one's own mother is called *édesanya* (lit. '*sweet mother*'), and likewise one's own father *édesapa* (lit. '*sweet father*'), which helps avoid confusion and misunderstanding in the sea of metaphorical meanings. →**Anyák Napja**

Anyák Napja *Mothers' Day*; the only non-traditional holiday that has become a must in the recent past, perhaps in response to the disappearance of socialist-inspired Women's Day. Presenting a bouquet of fresh-cut flowers (invariably lilacs and tulips!) to one's mother and grandmother, regardless of one's own age, is everyone's bounden duty on Mother's Day, held in Hungary on the first Sunday (→*vasárnap*) in May.

anyu/apu *mom/dad*; childrens' expressions, the diminutive forms of *anya* ('mother') and *apa* ('father') respectively, and the most frequently used words to address parents (but only by the very young). The double diminutives *anyuka/apuka* ('*mommy*, *daddy*') are also reserved for use by the very young. "*Mama/papa*" ('*mom*, *pop*') are related forms of address (→*megszólítás*) used for the elderly, and not only relatives, and when used in this way, now carry a tone of condescension and disrespect, and are anything but loving.

anyukám '*my* (*little*) *mother*' (lit.), *mum/mommy*;children and grownups alike can address their mother in this way, while in an urban working class environment every older woman (including wives!) can be addressed in this manner, in which case, however, the word is both ingratiating and condescending at the same time. Sometimes the word *muter* (from German '*Mutter*') is used instead; *apukám* ('*my little father*', lit.) and *fater* (equally from the German) are equivalent forms of address for men. →**megszólítás**

április 4 *4 April* the day when (according to military historians, at any rate) hostilities ceased on Hungarian territory at the end of WW II, and therefore made into "Liberation Day" (*Felszabadulás ünnepe*). At first every year, then as the funds (not to mention the militant self-confidence) of the regime waned, less frequently, military reviews were held on the parade ground in front of the Stalin statue (→*Sztálin-szobor*) in Budapest, and the government handed out high State awards to the worthy. Though the end of the war had been a great relief to everyone, as time passed many forgot the former circumstances and insisted on regarding April 4th as the symbolic first day of a new (this time Soviet, instead of German) occupation, which hurt the sensibilities of those Jews (→*zsidó*), and non-Jews alike whose lives had been saved by the victory of the Red Army. The ill-conceived debate over this issue, which began at the time of the change in regime (→*rendszerváltás*) was naturally also about the reevaluation of the years of socialism (→*szocializmus*), even if this was never said in so many words. However, Hungarian society is far too busy right now transforming itself and worrying about the immediate future to occupy itself with an in-depth analysis of its past.

apu →**anyu/apu**

apukám →**anyukám**

ÁPV Rt '*State Privatization and Property Company*' (lit.), *privatization agency*; beginning with the early 90s, the State Privatization and Property Company and its legal predecessor, the State Property Agency (*Állami Vagyonügynökség*, ÁVÜ for short) passed nearly all assets of the Hungarian economy into private hands, thereby causing, within the short space of about 8 to 10 years, a number of major corruption scandals (the temptation, it seems, having been too hard to resist), this amid the loud disgruntlement of the beneficiaries and aggrieved parties alike, in other words, the nation as a whole; the ÁPV Rt, it seems, had no social, only pecuniary visions and considerations. →**privatizáció**

Aquincum the capital of the former Roman province of →*Pannonia*, comprising the area of today's Transdanubia (→*Dunántúl*); its ankle-deep ruins can be visited in what is now →*Óbuda*; its amphitheater was later used by the conquering Hungarians (→*honfoglalók*) as a fortification, while in the Middle Ages its stones, along with the stones of the *castrum*, or military camp, were incorporated into the walls of the nearby township.

Arad city in the southern Great Plain (→*Alföld*) annexed to Romania after the First War by the Peace Treaty of Versailles (→*Trianon*). It is remembered as the place where in the autumn of 1849 thirteen Hungarian army generals were hanged or shot in the head (as an act of clemency) by the Austrians in the courtyard of the local fortification after Austria (→ *Ausztria*) put down the Hungarian War of Independence (→*szabadságharc*) with Russian (→*orosz*) help. The death of the generals, whom the nation (→*nemzet*) came to regard as martyrs of the cause of liberty (the "Arad Thirteen", or the "Martyrs of Arad"), is remembered on October 6th (→*október 6.*) of every year, which is an official day of mourning. Throughout the years, the laying of wreaths at the local memorial of the Arad Thirteen has been an unending source of bitter Hungarian-Romanian conflict until a recent bilateral agreement conceded that the Hungarian State has a right to remember its heroes. →**Ferenc József**

Aranycsapat, az *Golden Team, the* the popular name for the Hungarian national football (→*futball*) team of the fifties (→*ötvenes évek*), who beat the invincible English team 6 to 3 (→*hat–három*) on home turf. It came very close to winning the 1954 World Championships as well, and when it did not, the general disappointment was so great that its fans (meaning the country as a whole) cried treason (→*árulás*) and foul play. Just as earlier they had regarded the triumph of "the boys with the legs of gold" as a compensation of sorts for their bitter national history, now people saw their defeat as a tragedy of national (→*nemzet*) proportions. Still, the "golden age" of Hungarian football lives on in the nation's memory, and even those born many years after the glorious victories of the Golden Team know the names of every team-mate by heart. →**Puskás Öcsi**

aratás (*grain*) *harvest;* thanks to its fundamental role in the economy, the wheat (→*búza*) harvest, which begins in late June, is a closely-watched event of national – one might say cultic – proportions, while its termination on the 20th of August (→*augusztus 20.*) is the biggest national and ecclesiastic holiday of the calendar year.

Arisztid és Tasziló *Aristides and Tassilon*; two characters with monocles and typical, very rare aristocratic-sounding first names who were the standard figures of innumerable popular jokes in the inter–war period (to be turned later into the tools of proletarian class–struggle), the punchlines of which invariably revealed the folly and foolishness of the "degenerate" aristocracy (→*arisztokrácia*), showing that people did not think very highly of them by then; in fact, nobody within living memory was bestowed these first names. →**vicc; Kohn bácsi**; **Móricka**

arisztokrácia *aristocracy*; during the turbulent course of Hungarian history, the Hungarian aristocracy was replaced about every two to three-hundred years, until by the early 20th century, Hungary's aristocracy was mainly of foreign origin. Having lost its leading role back in the 19th century, after WW II most of its memberst sought refuge under the protective wings of their Western European relatives. Today, an aristocratic origin is regarded as a mere curiosity, and owning up to it is thought of as a form of (pardonable) eccentricity. →**Y; Csekonics; Eszterházy, Széchenyi; nemesség; Arisztid és Tasziló**

Árpád (vezér) (*chieftain/prince*) *Árpád*; the head of the Magyar tribe, then elected leader of the alliance of the conquering tribes (→*honfogalók*). Though we know little about him except that for 400 years his descendants ruled the nation, during the Age of Romanticism in the 19th century, his legendary figure (along with the Conquest, or →*Honfoglalás* itself) became one of the symbols of national identity. →**Pusztaszer**

Árpád-ház *'House of Árpád'* (lit.), *the Árpád dynasty*; the descendants of the leader of the Conquest or Landtaking (→*Honfoglalás*) reigned in Hungary until 1301, when the male line of the family died out and was replaced by various families from abroad related through the female line as, starting with the first Christian king, St. Stephen (→*Szent István*), the Árpáds married into practically every European dynasty possible from Scotland through Kiev, and from Sicily and Catalonia through Byzantium.

áruló, az *traitor, the*; in the morality play of Hungarian history, tradition has assigned the diabolical role of traitor to General Artúr Görgey, the last commander-in-chief of the army of the War of Independence (→*Szabadságharc*). Being outnumbered by Russia's superior forces and soberly realizing the uselessness of further resistance in face of certain defeat, in August 1849 Görgey laid down arms; mourning its defeat with a vengeance, the nation went in search of a scapegoat, and quickly found it in Görgey, the "traitor", who played into their hands when, thanks to the intervention of the Russian Czar, he was not hanged along with the "Arad Thirteen" (→*Arad*), a circumstance which, in the eyes of the public, implicated him directly. In Hungarian historical mythology, Görgey is always coupled with →*Kossuth*; they are like light and shade, and so, taking the part of the one or the other is tantamount to taking a strong political stand, for to argue Görgey's case was just as surely a sign of "national conservatism" as arguing Kossuth's case was that of "irresponsible radicalism".

asszimiláció *assimilation*; it is their common history, culture and language (which expresses their common history and culture), and not their common origin that has welded the Hungarians into a nation (→*nemzet*). Throughout its history, Hungary has welcomed not only settlers, but whole peoples as well; in fact, ever since the tragic loss of its populace during the Turkish occupation in the 16th and 17th centuries, population growth has invariably been a result of the assimilation of new immigrants, while during the course of the 19th century, when Hungary developed into a modern nation, this process of assimilation took on such gigantic proportions and was so consciously supported, that Hungary (and not just its towns and cities) became a veritable melting pot of the peoples of the Carpathian Basin. →**kunok; ki a magyar; névmagyarosítás; zsidók; magyar nemzet**

asszony '*woman/wife*' (lit.); though formerly *asszony* simply meant 'woman', today it is generally used as a synonym for 'wife'. It is also used when referring to older (!) women of lowly social standing; though there is also such a thing as →*úriasszony* ('gentlewoman'), it has a quaint ring to it and can easily strike a pejorative note. →**asszonyom**; **hölgy**, **úrnő**, **néni**

asszonyom '*my woman*' (lit.); *madam*; the most frequently used courteous form of address in any situation for women of any age, and the exact equivalent of →*uram* ('sir').→**úrnő**; **úrhölgy**; **asszony**; **néni**

aszú '*shrunken (grapes)*' (lit.); *sweet Tokaji*; the Tokaji-Furmint grape, a dull yellow fruit with a thick skin, is left on the vine until late fall and is allowed to become overripe until some of the berries shrivel to the size of a raisin due to the 'noble rot' produced by the fungus Botrytis Cinerea; after harvesting, which may not occur until after the first snow has fallen, the thick liquid dripping out of the extra-rich, handpicked berries turnes into an extraordinarily syrupy, sweet, heavy, deep golden, perfumed essence of a fine liqueur-like oiliness which is added in various proportions to fermenting Tokaji (→*tokaji*) wine, labeled three, four, five, or even six (!) *puttonys* (buckets), depending on the amount of the concentration added to the barrel as the wine matures. →**szamorodni**

atilla a tight-fitting Magyar-style costume (→*magyaros ruha*); a jacket or coat with a high collar and toggle closures (instead of buttons) attached to braids, once (typically in the 19th century) worn mainly (but not exclusively) by men; it is differentiated from the name of the king of the Huns (→*Attila*) only by its spelling, but not by its pronounciation. →**bocskai**

Attila while worldwide, the frightful reputation of Attila the Hun (→*hun*), the Scourge of God, is rivaled only by that of Genghis Khan, in Hungary *Attila* has been a popular first name since the 1920s, when giving ancient Magyar (→*ősmagyar*) names (including that of →*Csaba*, Attila's son, or →*Árpád*) without parallels in Christian lore came into vogue. Attila as a historical figure has been popular since the late 18th century, when the nascent science of historiography discovered evidence of a Hun-Magyar relationship (→*hun-magyar rokonság*) in ancient legends about the Eastern origin of the Magyars, and though modern science has never given it serious credence, just as it later gave no credence to the 20th century pseudo-scientific theory of a Sumerian-Magyar relationship (→*sumér-magyar rokonság*), still, National Romanticism conceived of Atilla as the proud ancestor of a great Magyar empire that would one day rise, phoenix like, up out of its ashes; consequently, his heroic figure became a much used literary metaphor. →**atilla; Hunnia; hunok; turul**

augusztus 20 *20 August*; also known as St. Stephen's Day (for the first king of Hungary), in the Middle Ages it was the day, when the king administered judgement in person. It is the oldest and biggest Church holiday and national holiday in one; it is also the most popular folk (→*népi*) holiday, when the new bread (→*kenyér*) is traditionally cut, which also makes it into a harvest (→*aratás*) festival as well, which is often combined with a fair (→*vásár*), the best known being the one held at →*Hortobágy*, which in turn makes it an ideal time for politicians to address their countryside constituencies. Since it refused to go away, it remained a national holiday even under socialism, when it was called the "Festival of the New Bread", or later "Constitution Day" (for with great foresight it was used to have Parliament ratify the country's new, Stalinist constitution). When several years before the change in regime (→*rendszerváltás*) on account of the holiday King Stephen, the founder of the state, was "taken out of the mothballs" (while carefully avoiding any mention of his status as a saint), everyone had premonitions of great changes to come, and indeed, after the change in regime, the leaders of the nation once again began attending holiday Mass at St. Stephen's Basilica in Budapest, celebrated by the Bishop of Esztergom (the primate of Hungary; →*esztergomi érsek*) then joined in the procession of the "Holy Right" (hand) (→*Szent Jobb*) to follow, broadcast by State television for all the world to see. In the evening, after sundown, there is a spectacular half-hour display of fireworks from Gellért Hill, which is as much part of the holiday by now as the Fourth of July fireworks are in the U.S., and is attended by thousands of people who watch from the opposite bank of the Danube in Pest

Ausztria *Austria*; in the centuries-long struggle for Central-European (→*Közép-Európa*) hegemony, Austria was a rival of Hungary's during the Middle Ages; then, when following the 16th century battle of →*Mohács* the struggle finally ended in favor of the →*Habsburg* Empire, it became Hungary's inevitable fate and destiny for the next four hundred years. Still, while blaming Austria for all its woes, Hungary looked up to its stronger and more advanced western neighbor with envy (even if not unmixed with suspicion and distrust), which (needless to say) in its injured pride it denied, even when not engaged in armed rebellion against it. This relationship gained a modicum of emotional balance only after the Compromise of 1867 (→*Kiegyezés*), until in recent times the feelings of the two countries towards each other have become nothing if not cordial. None the less, a certain →*kuruc* song is still current in Hungary: "*Watch it, Hungarian, when a German calls you, whatever sweet words he* *should say…".* →**osztrákok; Bécs (Vienna); Monarchia, a; Erzsébet királyné; Osztrák-Magyar Monarchia; Habsburgok**

ÁVÓ '*State Security Department*' (lit.), *acronym of the secret police of the 50s;* though at first it was a department only within the Ministry of the Interior and a secret political police force within the regular police force, it soon became the *Államvédelmi Hatóság*, or State Security Authority, a veritable army in its own right whose very acronym, *ÁVH*, was enough to paralyze the heart of a nation with fear; the "fist of the Party" and the over-zealous and arrogant vehicle of the Communist reign of terror, it was fashioned after the Soviet Cheka, and struck such abject terror in the hearts of people, that there aren't even jokes (→*vicc*) about it. Though it was dissolved (in its original form, at any rate) in the mid-fiftites (→*ötvenes évek*) consequent to the fall of →*Rákosi*, the feeling of intimidation and fear is still alive in the national consciousness, and the noun →*ávós*, formed from its name, still sends shivers down the spines of the people of Hungary. →**három per három**; **Andrássy út 60.**

ávós '*from the ÁVÓ*' (lit.), *a member of the ÁVÓ*; the →*ÁVÓ*, or State Security Department, was a thing of the past, having been long since replaced by the much smaller and comparatively harmless "three per three" department of internal security (→*három per három*), when the common vernacular still labeled anyone suspected of being in touch with the Ministry of the Interior (which included the police) an *ávós*, in which case the individual in question soon found that people were unusually taciturn and hostile in his presence. → **belügyes**

Az a szép, az a szép … '*She is pretty, she is pretty who …*' (lit.); the first words of the most popular folksy (→*népies*) song which continues: "*… has eyes of blue / Mine are dark blue, / But my darling still won't have me …*"; of obscure origin, but certainly relatively new, it is a drinking song known by every Hungarian; all the same, it is considered so trite, that people break into it only after they have cast off their inhibitions, for instance, after a glass or two of wine or → *pálinka*, drunk to the accompaniment of a Gypsy band (→*cigányzenekar*). →**magyar nóta**

Az ember tragédiája '*The Tragedy of Man*'; →***Tragédia, a***

B

bá' →**bácsi**

bableves *bean soup*; the indispensible item on the menu of every Hungarian restaurant, and especially every roadside inn (→*csárda*), it is the favorite Hungarian one-dish meal, and is therefore usually well made even in the most modest of places. The recipe calls for onions, pinto beans, smoked pork, especially smoked butt or flank, and paprika (→*pirospaprika*), and is said to taste even better reheated than freshly made. Some people like to eat it with the addition of a spoonful of sour cream or a dash of vinegar, which is a real bone of contention between the "purists" and the "revisionists". When served at home, it is usually followed by a helping of poppy seed noodles (→*mákostészta*). →**büfé**

bácsi (bá') '(*little*) *older brother*' (lit.), *uncle*; an older male relation; also used amicably (by both men and women) as a form of deferential address to an older person unrelated by blood ("Uncle Tom"); children (of both sexes) address every male (at least ten years their senior) in this way; it is used with both first and surnames, depending on the nature of the relationship; the *bá'* form has survived mostly in addressing *cserkész* (Boy Scout) officers. →**bátyám**; **néni**; **megszólítás**

bajtárs '*companion in adversity*' (lit.), *companion in arms*, *comrade*; the traditional 18th century form of address used by soldiers and policemen among themselves; its closest equivalent is the German *Kamerad*. →**elvtárs**

bajusz *moustache*; wearing one has always been considered a *magyaros* (true Hungarian) thing to do, not to mention military; in fact, wearing one was compulsory for every 19th century Hussar (→*huszár*). There was a peasant (→*parasztos*) and gentrified version as well, the former thick and hanging down on two sides ("handlebars"), the latter thinner and twirled upwards (like a Vandyke or tile beard); there was also a bourgeois version which was shaved narrow, not to mention various transitions thereof; since in response to world fashion it has reappeared about two decades ago, nowadays the Hungarian moustache is mostly thick and brushlike. →**szakáll**

baka *private*; a soldier without rank in the (Hungarian) army (specifically, in the heavy-gaited infantry), who is really a sensible civilian forced into uniform (→*egyenruha*), and who suffers with patience and equinimity the inflexible, inviolate and arbitrary rules and regulations of army life; he has no greater ambition than to survive it, as a result of which he tries to outwit his officers; unfortunately, he is not as cheerfully serene as "the Good Soldier Švejk"; a close relative of the *tommy* and the *GI.*

→**honvédség**; **katonaság**; **őrmester**; **katonadal**

Bakony (pron. *bah-kony*); a wide expanse of wooded, sparsely populated mountainous region north of lake →*Balaton* and south of the Danube (→*Duna*); in the 19th century it was still a pathless wilderness and the haunt of famous highwaymen (→*betyár*), and is still considered wild and romantic to this day.

Balaton (pron. *bah-lah-ton*); though in the second half of the 18th century it was almost drained in order to gain farmland, by the early 19th century members of the aristocracy who owned land near the lake built themselves a medicinal bath at Füred. It was turned into a modern (major, busy) resort when the middle classes (having lost their own seaside after WW I), began vacationing around its shores, thereby giving new meaning to the romantic appellation, the "Hungarian sea" (→*magyar tenger*); they planted trees in orderly rows, put up villas, pensions and yacht clubs, especially along the shallow southern shore, which has always been easily accessible by rail, while the wine-producing, hilly northern shore remained a rustic, pseudo-romantic place thought more suited to excursions. It was later turned into an inexpensive and crowded holiday spot, veritably synonymous with summer vacations, with the introduction of free socialist trade union "passes" (*beutaló*) to company resorts (*üdülő*), until in the seventies the remaining beautiful old villas were crowded out too by the small and shabby houses of the new, →*Zsiguli* owning middle class. Even later, the lake turned into the playground of the moneyless youth of Central Europe (including the former GDR!), as well as the haven for families with small children, since the the shallow water of the lake is not only eminently suited for splashing around and is quick to warm up to a suitable temperature, it is also clean (and drinkable once again!), glitters like the purest gold, and the sand at its bottom is as soft and silky as the finest India cloth. →**víkendház**

Balkán, a *Balkan(s), the*; often used as the antonym of Europe (→*Európa*), it is not a geographical designation but a painfully and embarrasingly familiar cultural terrain which consists not so much of the ominous, bleak mountains lying at such (uncomfortably) close range to Hungary's frontiers, as of a certain historically based *angst* which – as experience has shown – can be best alleviated by moving closer to the West (→*Nyugat*); it is related to the concepts of backwardness, chaos, filth, unbridled and treacherous aggression and rampant corruption; accordingly, to think of Hungary as part of the Balkans is an even greater insult than to think of it as part of Eastern Europe (→*Kelet Európa*).

Ballag már a vén diák ... '*the old student is already wandering away*' (lit).; an old European student song which is sung in all high schools (*középiskola*) during the graduation parade (→*ballagás*), bringing tears to the eyes of all those who hear it; this melancholy song, bidding farewell to student life, ends with the words, "*filiszter leszek magam is*" (in loose translation, 'I will now be a simple citizen myself').

ballagás '*sauntering*', '*wandering*', '*strolling*' (lit.), *graduation parade*, *valediction*; inherited from old German colleges, this tradition goes back several centuries; through the years it has become increasingly common, and not limited to high schools (*középiskolák*); in the middle of May, on the last day of the last week of classes, graduating seniors (the boys in dark suits, the girls in sailor-blouses, or →*matrózblúz*) slowly march around the school from room to room, each decorated with flowers; they sing as they march in line, each student's right hand resting on the shoulder of the student in front, then they bid farewell to their school at a sentimental ceremony, with the juniors bidding farewell to them in turn, which touches the hearts of even the most indifferent teenager; the *ballagás* is attended by parents and other relatives, as well as former students and new girlfriends and boyfriends, all of whom bringing flowers, especially lilacs, which open at this time of year. The tradition of *ballagás* has become so popular, that ceremonies are now held even in kindergartens. →***Ballag már a vén diák …; Gaudeamus igitur…; szerenád, szalagavató bál***

Bánk bán '*Bánk, the Palatine*'; written by József Katona in 1815, *Bánk bán* was soon considered a symbol of nationalism and became the most frequently performed 19th century play. The hero of the story, which takes place in the 13th century and which, in its historical scope, at least, is reminiscent of Shakespearean drama (the language being that of contemporary translations of Shakespeare), is the *bán* or palatine of Hungary; seeing the rowdiness of the German Queen, a haughty and ambitious woman, and her knights, a rowdiness which is depleting the treasury and is bringing moral ruin to the country (all this in the king's absence, who is off fighting in the Holy Land), the *bán* is caught between his solemn promise to his sovereign and the love of his country; driven by moral considerations (albeit with a bad conscience, to be sure), he finally murders the Queen, then suffers the tragic loss of his young wife, gone mad after being seduced by the Queen's brother. József Katona's drama was the forerunner of the Hungarian literary tradition whereby the writer (→*író*) wraps his thoughts on contemporary issues in historical garb and language; for their part, Hungarian audiences, used to reading between the lines, have always been highly adept at deciphering such texts; for instance, *Bánk bán* was performed at the National Theatre on the eve of 15th of March (→*március 15.*), 1848 upon the insistance of the "Revolutionary Youth", while the opera based on it and composed by →*Erkel Ferenc* is so revered, that to be asked to sing in it is considered a sign of great honor, especially when it is performed at the Budapest Opera House, which invariably includes it in its program on major national holidays.

barackpálinka '*apricot pálinka*' (lit.), *apricot brandy*; though →*pálinka* can be distilled from many kinds of fruit, the most noble, aromatic and smooth brew comes from carefully picked, undamaged, fresh apricots, especially those grown in the orchards of Kecskemét; this, of course, also makes it the most expensive Hungarian brandy. →**szilvapálinka**; **kisüsti**

Bartók Béla (pron. *bahr-towk*); not only a great composer but a great moralist as well, Bartók has continued to be idolized by the Hungarian intelligentsia (→*értelmiség*), despite the fact that they are just now getting used to the sound of his music; apart from his original compositions, his most valuable contribution to Hungarian culture is the "discovery", notation and adaptation – and thus the preservation! – of folk music (→*népzene*), done with the collaboration of Zoltán Kodály at the twenty-fourth hour, just before its disappearance and replacement by modern music.

Bartók Rádió for years the only FM station in Hungary, it had the best quality sound, but also the smallest transmission area of any domestic radio station. It broadcast a lot of classical music as well as programs of interest to the intelligentsia (→*értelmiség*), and since it was not much in the public eye, prior to the change in regime (→*rendszerváltás*) its 10 p.m. news (in which, as a sign that the regime was at odds with itself, at times things could be heard that could not be heard elsewhere) was the most informative news program on radio. →**Kossuth Rádió**

bassza meg '*fuck it*' (lit.); the most wide-spread obscenity which, however, has lost none of its force and is therefore often shortened to *zamek* or *bameg* even in today's world, it's use in public is taboo, though it is really an expletive used like the related →*fene egye meg* ('the pox take it'). →**káromkodás**

bátyám '*my elder brother*' (lit.), *uncle*; term of address used by (for example) younger male (never female) colleagues when talking to dignified elderly gentlemen (especially among lawyers and doctors); it has a patriarchal ring to it, especially in the form of *urambátyám* and *bátyámuram* (lit. '*my lord and brother*') it is respectful, yet suggests a degree of intimacy since it is always used along with the informal form of address, the →*tegezés* (just like the term *öcsém* i.e., '*my younger brother*', used by older men when addressing younger men); in a similar situation, women might use the term →*bácsi*; furthermore, young men past adolescence (who have stopped using the childish →*kezicsókolom* ('*I kiss your hand*') but are not yet old enough to say →*jónapot* ('*good day*') use it (in conjunction with the informal →*tegezés*) when addressing friends of the family they had formerly addressed as →*bácsi*: "*Tiszteletem, Józsi bátyám. Hogy vagy?*" ('My respects, Uncle Joe. How do you do?') However, the latter is quickly becoming quaint and outmoded. →**megszólítás**

Bécs *Vienna*; for centuries, the traditional first stop for Hungarians headed for the West (→*Nyugat*), an all too familiar, admired, envied and despised city, seen as arrogant and supercilious, but also the tempting source of all things luxurious and aristocratic, the embodiment of the world "outside", barely a day's carriage ride on a dusty highway, yet a distant and unreachable ideal for Hungarians stuck outside the gates in the confines of their penurious existence, but (for centuries) also the burial ground of the country's hopes; then, when during the Dual Monarchy (→*Monarchia*), Budapest became the distant co-capital of the proud Imperial City, Vienna suddenly went from an ideal to a rival, a sister city and the nearby home of relatives, where one would "go up" for a short weekend visit; later, the Iron Curtain turned it into the hopelessly distant city of one's dreams, where only a lucky few could go who (provided that a miracle happened) and they did not defect (missing the rare chance to go abroad) but came back with incredible stories of a cornucopia of riches, elegance and modern technology; to this day →*Budapest* still continues to compare itself to Vienna (believing that it is much more lively and interesting, and intellectually more stimulating than its neighbor, which has become too staid, *petit bourgeois* and provincial due to the good life, not to mention annoyingly conceited); still, while Vienna is no longer the yardstick of real success, but New York, when they hanker after something special, Hungarians still go to Vienna to shop. →**osztrákok**; **Ausztria**

befőtt '*cooked fruit*' (lit.), *canned* or *bottled fruit*; it can be made of any fruit, but usually peaches, apricots, cherries, sour cherries and plums are used to "put away" for the winter months; *befőtt* is distinguished from stewed fruit by the addition of lots of sugar and preservatives as well as the painstaking preparations which require a full day (!) of work; until recently, the shelves of pantries (→*éléskamra*), especially in the countryside, were lined with jars of bottled fruit and jam (→*lekvár*), though the canned fruit industry is making rapid headway in Hungary, too; all the same, when serving industrially canned fruit, Hungarian housewives do so with a bad conscience, apologizing for their "laziness".

beigli (*walnut/poppy seed*) *roll*; the butter dough is rolled out and spread generously with a creamy walnut or poppy seed cream filling (with lots of raisins!), then it is rolled up very carefully (so the cream will not come out at the ends); no Easter (→*Húsvét*) or Christmas (→*Karácsony*) is complete without it, and a "taste" of it is often sent by proud housewives to neighbors and relatives, though it is increasingly bought at pastry shops (→*cukrászda*), too, where it must be ordered sometimes weeks in advance; years of experience have shown that while men (and boys) tend to prefer poppy seed *beigli*, inexplicably, women would rather eat *beigli* filled with walnuts. →**sütemény; mák**

bejárónő '*the woman who comes in*' (lit.), *cleaning lady*; →**cseléd**

bekecs (pron. *beh-ketch*), *a jump*; the fur-lined (sheepskin) short, sleeveless coat worn by people working outside in the cold, because it does not restrict their movements; it is also worn by men (and women) along with a fur hat (→*kucsma*) or kerchief tied around the head when they have to run outside to the yard to open the gate or to take care of some other hasty business.

béketábor '*peace-camp*' (lit.); a historical term by now from the language of fifties propaganda (→*ötvenes évek*) to refer to the entirety of the (unwilling) allies of the Soviet Union (→*Szovjetunió*); according to an unforgettable mass song (→*tömegdal*) "*the Peace Camp is invincible, and the road to peace is a secure road*"; it is included here only as an admirable example of newspeak (though there was also a *békeharc*, or '*peace-war*'), and because it has survived as part of the jocular warning: "*Akkora pofont kapsz, hogy kirepülsz a béketáborból*" (lit. '*You'll get a slap that'll send you reeling out of the Peace Camp.*')

belügy, a '*domestic affairs, the*' (lit.), *home office, Department of the Interior*; when they hear the word, which stands for the Ministry of Interior Affairs (*Belügyminisztérium*), people still do not think of the Ministry but of the political police, which until the change in regime (→*rendszerváltás*) was part of it; consequently, a "*belügyes*", someone working for the *belügy*, was not a humble civil servant, but a secret policeman or an informer (*besugó*, lit. '*whisperer*'), whose identification was often a matter of concern to people, especially at the work place, since it was taken for granted that there had to be one. →**ÁVO**; **három per három**

Belváros, a '*Inner City, the*' (lit.), *downtown*; the term refers exclusively to the section of →*Pest* formerly surrounded by a city wall and situated between Szabadsághíd (*Liberty Bridge*) and the Chain Bridge (→*Lánchíd*) relatively untouched by 19th century city planning frenzy, and which, after it outgrew its city wall was closed off by a semicircular boulevard (today Károly körút) built concentric to the old wall; the last fifty years have made its buildings look a lot worse for wear, and its inhabitants, too, are predominantly older people, but since life has returned to the area, Inner City addresses have once again become desirable; consequently, the former apartments and the houses themselves are increasingly occupied by shops, offices, and banks. →**Vörösmarty tér**; **Váci utca**

bérház *'rental house'* (lit.), *apartment house;* stucco-decorated buildings with two or three storeys, often with hanging corridors (→*gang*) built in the central areas of Hungarian towns and cities over the last 100 to 150 years (before *Bauhaus* took over), which by now have grown old along with their tenants; their unadorned versions, found on the outskirts of towns, with usually just one small room and kitchen, built for workers (→*munkás*) and other poor people, were called *bérkaszárnya* (*'rent-barracks'*), while the more spacious and ornate "bourgeois" houses (such as the edifices along Budapest's →*Andrássy út*), were called *bérpalota* (*'rental palaces'*), until the lamentable state of affairs that characterized life in Hungary after 1948 made this expression politically embarrasing as well as de facto ridiculous. →**albérlet; társbérlet; lichthóf; öröklakás; panel**

bérkaszárnya *'rent-barracks'* (lit.); →**bérház**

bérpalota *'rent-palace'* (lit.); →**bérház**

betlehem *'Bethlehem'* (lit.), *manger; Nativity scene;* at Advent time the Nativity scene is set up in front of the church altar; comprised of various life-like images made of plaster (the Infant in his manger, Mary and Joseph, not to mention the shepherds, donkey, cow and sheep), it is displayed for the children, though sometimes the children make *betlehems* themselves (or at least, used to) by populating a box, often made out of cardboard, with Biblical figures made out of paper, with the Infant placed in the center, surrounded by animals, shepherds and the Three Magi, with lit candles at the two sides of the miniature "stage", which after sundown they take around the towns and villages. →**betlehemesek**

betlehemesek *'Bethlehemers'* (lit.), *Nativity players*; dressed as (Hungarian) shepherds in high fur hats (→*kucsma*), short sheepskin coats (→*bekecs*) turned inside-out, with painted mustaches (→*bajusz*) and big sticks, on evenings during Advent time the Nativity players, mostly children, go from house to house with their manger (→*betlehem*), performing a short, playful traditional pastoral (even in the cities, in the yards of 'rent-houses' or →*bérház*) in which one of the shepherds, who is "old" and deaf, misunderstands everything he hears; "Can we chant for you?" sounds the question on the doorstep, then they will sing the carol →*Mennyből az angyal* in exchange for small gifts (money).

betyár (pron. *beh-tyahr*); *outlaw, highwayman*; a thief (and a murderer) in actual fact, the national imagination has raised the Hungarian *betyár*, the character of countless folk ballads with tragic overtones, not to mention 19th century art and literature, in which he appears as a noble savage – into a romantic hero; the *betyár* was seen as a desperate *szegénylegény*, or 'poor lad' (the two are synonyms) rebelling against his fate and chosing to live the unfettered life of a

Robin Hood out in the Hungarian prairie (→*puszta*) and the woods of the →*Bakony* mountains, despoiling the rich and helping the poor; in the stories made popular by 19th century chap books sold at country fairs, a *betyár* invariably has a handsome steed and a pretty country lass for a lover (mostly the wife of the local innkeeper), he always outwits the *pandúrs* (local police force) chasing him; in real life the *betyárs* were driven out of existence by the gendarmes (→*csendőrség*) who after the Compromise of 1867 (→*Kiegyezés*) were set on improving the safety of the Great Plain (→*Alföld*); in familiar (→*népies*) usage the word denotes a wily man or artful dodger, especially one who can wrap a young woman (→*menyecske*) around his fingers.→**Rózsa Sándor; Sobri Jóska**

bicska *jacknife*; until recently, every Hungarian male had a knife on him (especially in the countryside), something which today is restricted to the plaything of adolescent boys; the *bicska* itself is a large pocket knife with a wooden handle which opens up (without springs!), and which can still be bought from knife-vendors at fairs (→*vásár*), but it is actually too big, too long and wide-bladed and has too many uses to be considered a real jackknife or pocket knife; rather, it is the traditional (often lethal) weapon of hot-blooded young men (→*legény*) used when fighting breaks out in a tavern (→*kocsma*), traditionally in areas such as Somogy County; when someone is outraged at something, people say that "it makes the *bicska* open in his pocket".

bikavér *'bull's blood'* (lit.); a dark heavy red wine which tends to be mildly dry and can attain a luscious velvety depth; actually a kind of cuvée, it has fire in it, and is probably the best known Hungarian red wine, perhaps because of its name. It is made in a lot of places, but the best known *bikavér* comes from →*Eger*. →**bor**

birka *sheep*; in Hungary it is not something you eat (unless in the form of →*pörkölt*), but something you sheer for its fine wool.

bisztró *bistro*; →**büfé**

Boci boci tarka ... *'Spotted calf, little spotted calf ...'* (lit.); a simple little tune, like *Chopsticks*, about a mottled little calf with no ears and no tail that any child can learn to play on the piano, and usually does; the ditty goes on: "*... got no tail and got no ear, I will go and live where milk can be found for sale.*"

bocsánatot kérek *'I beg your pardon'* (lit.); this courteous form of apology (which, just like in English, can be said in such a way that it will sound more like an indignant exclamation or demand) is often shortened to *bocsánat*, even *bocs* (!), especially when we step on someone's feet or have to force our way through the crowd on a bus); a related expression is *elnézést kérek* (*'I ask [you] to look the other way'*), i.e., *excuse me.*

bocskai (pron. *bawch-kah-yee*), *tunic*; the 20th century version of a Hungarian-style tunic (→*magyaros ruha*) which received its name from the 16th century Transylvanian (→*Erdély*) prince István Bocskay, maybe because he managed to keep it independent despite the →*Habsburg* and Turkish (→*törökök*) threats, as a consequence of which – and in the wake of the century's repeated disillusionments and historical debacles suffered by the nation – he became a symbol of Hungary's independence and Hungarian self-determination, i.e., the (often Xenophobic) "third alternative"; consequently, after WW I, nationalistic movements adopted the *bocskai* as a veritable uniform (→*egyenruha*).

bocskai-sapka '*Bocskai hat*'(lit); a kind of '*kalpack*' or hat worn with the →*bocskai*, often adorned with a crane feather or the feather of some other undomesticated bird (as may be seen on portraits of Prince István Bocskay); peaked in front, it is snug in the back (not unlike a glengarry bonnet), with a tight-fitting, turned-up brim (held together with braiding if it has slits in it); it also used to be worn by secondary school (→*gimnázium*) students, and after 1990 became once more part of the Hungarian →**honvéd** uniform. →**egyenruha**

Bodri (pron. *bowd-ree*), '*Curly*' (lit.); until contrived, aristocratic sounding names came into vogue, *Bodri* was a popular name for dogs, many of which, as the word implies, were →*pulis*.

bogrács *kettle*; if there is any cooking on an open fire (which these days is restricted to special occasions when there are a lot of mouths to feed), it is always done in this black kettle; whatever is made in it, →*halászlé* (fish-soup), →*gulyás* or →*paprikás*, the ingredients are added in layers and are not stirred while cooking, but at most gently moved around or loosened; there is no danger of anything burning to the bottom, since the shape insures the proper distribution of the heat from the bottom up, which is the secret of the unmistakeable flavor and aroma of *bogrács*-cooked foods.

Boldogasszony anyánk ... '*Our Mother (you) Holy Lady*' (*lit.*), *Our Mother Mary*; an 18th century hymn to the Virgin Mary still sung in Catholic churches today; it continues: "*... our great, heavenly patron, / being in great need, our country now calls you, / Hungary, our sweet homeland, / do not forget us, poor Hungarians ...*"; it is a prayer and supplication in one to the Virgin Mary, the patron saint of Hungary (seen on banners and coins) ever since king St. Stephen (→*Szent István*) offered up his country into her protection; before the birth of the National Anthem (→*himnusz*) – in the country's Catholic (→*katolikus*) half at any rate – it served as the "national song" and is still considered today a "second national anthem", and so it was song by the crowds at Imre Nagy's re-burial (→*temetés*) in 1989.

bor *wine*; situated at the northern edge of the European wine-producing region, Hungary has traditionally been a producer of an impressive variety of high quality wines; it is a wine-consuming country, though in the past couple of decades there has been a marked growth in preference for beer (→*sör*) and brandy (→*pálinka*), probably because socialist (→*szocialista*) agriculture produced few quality wines. Thanks to privatization (→*privatizáció*), Hungarian wines have quickly regained their former reputation; still, people in villages prefer to drink the wine of their own making, even in areas not suited to wine production; furthermore, not every small producer knows the secret of making a good wine, and so, it is advisable to be circumspect when one is offered a glass (or two or three); dry white wines are especially excellent, among which the wines produced from the volcanic soil along the northern shore of Lake Balaton (→*Balaton*) being unparalleled; red wines, most of which are also dry, are best, though, when they come from their traditional growing area (→*Eger*, Villány, Szekszárd, →*Sopron*); among the most famous Hungarian wines the white Tokaji (→*tokaji*) is renowned for its rich density and bouquet (owing to the moulds covering the ancient wine cellars which reach deep into the lap of the Tokaj mountains); in some areas, the small houses ("press houses") built above the wine cellars lining the hilly outskirts of villages form veritable little "villages" of their own which come alive on Sunday afternoons when the men gather to taste each other's wines under the walnut trees in front of the green doors, sized so the full barrels can be rolled out unhampered between the posts. →**szürkebarát; bikavér; must; kadarka; borozó**

borozó '*winery*' (lit.), *Weinstube* (Germ.); originally, establishments usually found in basements accessed from the street where men in towns and cities would show up for a glass of wine, and are thus also called "wine tasters" (*borkóstoló*); their standard, just like the quality of the wine they offer (check before you drink or buy to take away!), ranges over a wide scale, and almost the only thing they have in common is the dinginess and lack of seating, as a result of which they are jocularly referred to as *talponálló* (lit. '*where you stand on your feet*'); lately, many of these cheap establishments have been given a face lift and have reemerged as respectable pubs, taverns or restaurants, and their old customers are now enjoying their wine, beer or brandy (→*pálinka*) in taprooms (→*kocsma*), few of which are left in the respectable, regentrified parts of towns. →**bor; kocsma**

borravaló '(*money*) *for wine*' (lit.), *tip*; tipping is a must in just about all areas of the service sector (from the barber and mailman to the gas station attendant), regardless of the quality of the service rendered; in shops, too, people will often leave the change at the cashier ("*Keep the change!*"), a throwback to (all too recent) times when in one way or another, everyone was state employed (and therefore underpaid, undermotivated and grumpish) and (it being a shortage economy) there was a shortage of goods, a state of affairs which placed anyone in charge of distributing (selling) anything whatsoever in a position of superiority, which meant that their "good will" (including the sale of a pair of shoes or a decent cut of meat) had to be courted; this sort of tipping, however, is not to be confused with bureaucratic-level corruption, which was given renewed impetus with the privatization (→*privatizáció*) that followed the change in regime (→*rendszerváltás*) when, having nothing else to sell, clerks, civil servants and other public officials capitalized on their government (and other) positions; nor does it have anything to do with →*hálapénz* (lit. '*gratitude money*') slipped into the pockets of underpaid (and overworked) nurses and physicians.

búcsú *parish feast*; on the name day of the saint to whom the local or parish church is dedicated (or on the anniversary of the consecration of a church) besides the religious celebrations (Mass, pilgrimage) a fair (→*vásár*) is traditionally held where there is a lot of eating, drinking and dancing, especially because those who have moved away from the village traditionally go home for such occasions.

Buda (pron. *boo-dah*); today the part of →*Budapest* surrounded by hills on the right bank of the →*Danube*, at one time it was the royal residence which lay in the Castle District (→*Vár*) and the hillsides of the Castle area; even at the time of the unification of →*Budapest*, only a good hundred years ago, it was still a humble baroque-style town (despite the fact that it was nominally the capital city of Hungary) with a predominantly German-speaking population (who, being conservative and Catholic, as well German-speaking, vehemently protested against unification with noisy and vulgar Pest); its character began to change only at the turn of the century (→*századforduló*), when the grand bourgeoisie got rid of the vineyards on the slopes of →*Rózsadomb* to build themselves villas, while the petit bourgeoisie moved into the new apartment houses (→*bérház*) that sprang up along the wide roads in the seams of the valleys; in the sixties (→*hatvanas évek*), the face of Buda changed once again when the (then) young intelligentsia (→*értelmiség*), whose life-style was gradually improving, built co-ops (→*társasház*) on the hillsides facing the →*Danube*; there is also a small town in Iowa that used to be called New Buda, founded by the emigrant (→*emigráns*) followers of Lajos Kossuth (→*Kossuth Lajos*). →**Pest; Óbuda**

Budapest (pron. *boo-dah-pesht*); Budapest, which became the capital of Hungary in 1873 with the unification of →*Pest*, →*Buda*, and →*Óbuda*, in no time at all turned from a provincial-type center with a combined population of only 200 thousand into a cosmopolitan,

European-style metropolis which strove to become the worthy sister-capital of Vienna (→*Bécs*) in the Dual Monarchy (→*Monarchia*); however, this incredibly quick change in size and character cut Budapest off from the rest of the country, which regarded it as a "sinful city", and resented it, too, for it attracted the country's talent and money to itself like a magnet (and indeed, those whose forebears had lived in Budapest, like themselves, are still in the minority); it was mockingly referred to as *vízfej* (lit. hydrocephalus or '*waterhead*', i.e., '*pumpkinhead*'), and following the Peace Treaty of Versailles (→*Trianon*) after WWI., it did grow disproportionately large compared to the rest of the country (today one out of five Hungarians live here); the people of Budapest, on the other hand, insist that near and far (within and without the country's borders) it is the only real city (where money, pluck, spirit, brains and talent converge, even if they do not always meet), and they won't hear of living anywhere else; they are even proud of the scandals, which in their eyes are proof of the city's big-city character, and are convinced that everyone in the country envies their status; of course, with the rapid pace of development elsewhere in the country, especially in the towns of Transdanubia (→*Dunántúl*), this is no longer the case. →**Pest-Buda**; **Pest**; **Buda**; **Óbuda**

Búj-búj zöld ág, zöld levelecske... '*Pass, pass, green bough, little green leaf...*'; first line of a children's song which continues: "*... the golden gate is open, go pass through!*"; the children (especially girls) stand up and form a double file, making a "gate" with their arms under which the last pair tries to run through, but from time to time the "gate" is closed, the children lower their arms, and take the couple "captive".

bukta *Danish*; an ill-reputed dessert (→*édesség*), staple in high school and college canteens (→*menza*); a heavy and filling pastry which looked and felt like a piece of brick the size of a fist, it was (theoretically) made from buttered dough with a bit of jam for stuffing (→*lekvár*), poppy seeds (→*mák*), or sweetened cottage cheese (→*túró*); it is rarely made at home. →**étkezde**

burgonya *potato*; the "official" name for →*krumpli* as it appears on the menus of restaurants.

búza *wheat*; still one of the major crops produced in Hungary, where the climate is ideal for its cultivation; the wheat harvest (→*aratás*) continues as an important national event (going to a harvest and personally taking up a scythe is compulsory for politicians), and people are anxious to read about the yield, for even today, a plentiful harvest and high export prices can save the economy; Hungarians believe that their wheat is the best in the world, and love the soft, snow-white bread (→*kenyér*) baked from it, especially when fresh, and preferably retaining the heat of the oven; traditionally, the first loaf made from the harvested wheat is cut up on St. Stephen's Day (→*Szent István*) within the framework of Church celebrations, folk celebrations, country fairs (→*vásár*), and political rallies held for voters in the countryside; every harvest celebration is also attended by one VIP or another, where young girls dressed in folk costume (→*népviselet*) present him with a huge, big-bellied, "blonde" loaf of bread tied round with the national colors (→*nemzetiszín*), at the very sight of which TV audiences feel an irrepressible urge to eat some themselves. →**rozs**; **zab**

büfé *buffet* (lit.), *snack bar*; the generic term for a variety of inexpensive eateries which have in common only the counter separating the customers from the staff; the term is used also for the ground-floor conversation areas of public institutions where the clerks go to drink coffee (→*kávé*), have a mid-morning snack (→*tízórai*), or buy French salad (→*francia saláta*) and croissants for lunch; it is also the name for the decrepid self-service restaurants (→*önkiszolgáló*), also known as "bistros" (→*bisztró*), but called "the House of Lords" in the ironic language of their regulars, where the poor people of the city spoon up their bean soup (→*bableves*) standing by a tall counter; today, these are being replaced by Pizza Huts, McDonalds ("*makdodó*" in the vernacular) and other fast food places, as a consequence of which the poor must "frequent" the municipal soup kitchens. →**étkezde**; **kifőzde**; **fasírt; főzelék**

C

cekker (*from German*), *shopping bag*; →**háló**

cifra szűr '*elaborate/ornate felt* (*coat*)' (lit.); →**szűr**

cigány *Gypsy* (*Gipsy*); though Gypsies have been living in Hungary since the Middle Ages, they began making an impact on the popular consciousness only in the 18th century; until the early 20th century they were on the one hand itinerant, on the other, they engaged in traditional crafts such as tub-making, adobe-making and nail-making (blacksmithing), not to mention the many excellent Gypsy musicians; in 19th century literature the Gypsy was treated either as a comic figure or else the romantic symbol of freedom; today, the romantic conception of Gypsies, who make up the largest minority in the country (and who are mostly unskilled, uneducated and increasingly jobless), has been replaced by images of crime and poverty; they have lost not only their traditional professions and language, but as they moved into the big cities, their traditional social structure as well; police reports refer to them by recourse to the politically correct expression: "suspects with strikingly dark skin", while the expression *cigányútra ment* (lit. 'has gone the Gypsies' way'), used to describe the highly unpleasant moment when a person swallows and the food goes down the wrong way (down the larynx, or at least, it feels like it), speaks volumes about what people used to think about the Gypsies. →**cigányzenekar**; **roma**

cigányozás '*Gypsying*' (lit.); to let your hair down and have a darned good time enjoying a drink or two (in a →*kocsma* or restaurant) as a Gypsy band (→*cigányzenekar*), or even a single Gypsy violinist, plays familiar Hungarian tunes (→*magyar nóta*) while you sing along (with or without your friends) at the top of your lungs, that's *cigányozás*; the entertainment, however, is not complete without you asking the Gypsy band to play your favorite song (meaning your favorite Hungarian song, such as:"*Hey, Gypsy, hey Gypsy, / Play my song! / The string snaps in hundred threads ...!*"); this custom is especially *de rigeur* at the house of newlyweds when a wedding feast is held (→*lakodalom*), in which case you're supposed to pin a banknote on the strings of the *prímás* (the leader of the Gypsy band) with a gesture of →*betyár* abandon, or once the festivities are well into the night, to stuff the money inside the double-bass; it is a rural, small town custom which is wearing thin but not wearing out; just like the serenade (→*szerenád*), it was originally part of the world of the late 19th century gentry (→*dzsentri*); today, it is considered boorish and is quickly losing its social status, although when the republic (→*Köztársaság*) was declared in

1918, it was still a joyful Gypsy band (though in jackets, and not →*huszár*-type uniforms), who played the *Internationale* in front of Parliament (→*Parlament*), and even today no New Year's Eve television broadcast is complete without the most popular actors '*Gipsying*,' that is singing Hungarian songs to the accompaniment of a Gypsy band.

cigányzene *Gypsy music*; abroad (including the neighboring countries) it is often confused with Hungarian folk music (→*népzene*), a mistake made even by Franz Liszt (→*Liszt Ferenc*) because by the early 19th century Gypsy bands (→*cigányzenekar*) were so popular in Vienna and elsewhere in Europe, that the *prímás* János Bihari, the most famous of the popular Gypsy band leaders, was called the "*ungarischer Beethoven*" by his contemporaries, whereas "Gypsy music" is as far removed from the music of the Hungarian peasantry (→*parasztság*) as it is from original Gypsy folk music, since the songs played by Gypsy musicians are mostly Magyar songs (→*magyar nóta*); this is the variant of "Gypsy music" that (having lost ground elsewhere) can still be heard in a number of restaurants. →**cigányozás**

cigányzenekar *Gypsy orchestra* (lit), *Gypsy band*; the members of the band (at least one viola, one double bass and one zymbalon player headed by another violinist, or *prímás*), often wearing Magyar-type costumes, are generally from "musical Gypsy" families who form a caste of their own, and being real "entertaining musicians", they will play anything on request, giving whatever they play a "Gypsy" mood, i.e., they like to show off their virtuosity on the violin; at the end of the century (→*századvég*) they were as popular as pop musicians are today, though their popularity has almost completely faded along with the social prestige of the Magyar songs (→*magyar nóta*) they play; still, no self-respecting Hungarian restaurant is without its Gypsy band, playing soft music for the diners, who often ask them to play their favorite song. →**cigányozás**; **cigányzene**; **Dankó Pista**

címer *coat of arms;* after the country's humiliating, Soviet-type coat of arms used under socialism (→*szocializmus*), called popularly "the cabbage" (after its shape) the present symbol of Hungarian statehood is once again comprised of elements reaching back to the Middle Ages; the red and silver right-hand field with seven lines across it was originally the coat of arms of the Árpád Dynasty (→*Árpád-ház*), while the patriarchal cross in the left-hand field (standing above a mysterious "three hill" formation) harks back to the Apostolic kings of Hungary, and is thus the symbol of royal power; after heated Parliamentary debates following the change in regime (→*rendszerváltás*), and in order to emphasize the continuity of Hungarian statehood – and in keeping with tradition – the Holy Crown (→*Szent Korona*) was also included in the Hungarian coat of arms, even though both previous Republics (→*Köztársaság*) had removed it from theirs.

corvina the name for the illuminated codices of the famous library (*Bibliotheca Corviniana*) of the powerful Renaissance ruler King Matthias (→*Mátyás király*), also known as Mathias Corvinus; comprised of approximately 16,000 volumes, it was founded in 1464, but after the king's death and the battle of →*Mohács*, its priceless volumes were dispersed all over the world; in Hungary, the word *corvina* is synonymous with the fine art of book making.

cukrászda *confectioner's*, *pastry shop*, *sweetie shop*, *tuck shop*; the classical Central European (→*Közép-Európa*) alloy of an ice cream parlour, a tea shop and a coffee house whose humble, new variants have managed to retain some of the genteel charm of their predecessors thanks (first and foremost) to the delicious cakes (→*torta*) and pastries (→*cukrászsütemény*) prepared according to recipes perfected and handed down by generations of bakers; people come to these establishments, some 100 years old or even older, and still furnished with their original furnishings, not only to enjoy a piece of cake, to chat or to meet friends, but also to buy cake for Sunday lunch, or to take to someone's house when invited for coffee. Every town – and in Budapest, every district – has a *cukrászda* the locals will swear by, and no wonder, because it brings back childhood memories by the taste of their *gateaux*. →**Gerbeaud**

cukrászsütemény '*confectioner's/baker's cake*' (lit.), *pastry*; the name refers to those cakes and pastries (→*torta*) which because of their intricate recipes and ingredients are best left to the expertise of professional bakers; since they are rarely made at home, people go to a confectioner's (→*cukrászda*) to buy them by the slice. →**Zserbó**; **dobos torta**; **rigójancsi**; **krémes**; **zserbó-szelet**

Csaba (pron. *chah-bah*); according to legend, the son of →*Attila* the Hun who after his father's death was defeated in battle by his Goth brothers, and so, accompanied by some of his (surviving) warriors, he fled to his grandfather, the Greek emperor, while the other survivors stayed behind in Transylvania (→*Erdély*) to become the ancestors of the →*székelys*, who will always be helped if in need by Prince Csaba and his horsemen coming down to battle on the "Road of Warriors", otherwise known as the Milky Way. →**hun-magyar rokonság**

Csak egy kislány van a világon... '*There is only one girl in the world...*"; the first line of one of the best known old Magyar songs (→*magyar nóta*) which continues: "*... and she's my very own sweetheart*"; its dreamy melody, which suits the bitter-sweet lyrics offers the Gypsy *prímás* of many a Gypsy band (→*cigányzenekar*) a splendid opportunity to show off his virtuosity on the violin; this must have been the reason why, at the end of the century, the Spanish composer Sarasate used it as the main motif of his romantic violin piece entitled "*Zigeunerweiser*".

családi ház '*family house*' (lit.), *family home*; a one-storey (stone) house built by the petit bourgeoisie on the outskirts of towns and cities easily distinguishable from the tall apartment buildings (→*bérház*) of the inner town cores and the 'rental barracks' (→*bérkaszárnya*) of the working class districts, and in more recent times, the so-called →*panel* (prefab) housing, not to mention the pompous villas of the nouveau riche on *Rózsadomb*. The fruits of a long life of labor and frugality, these family homes, which stand on small plots surrounded by even smaller gardens, possibly with a fruit tree or two, have been lining the streets of towns since the turn of the century (→*századforduló*); usually standing on their own, plain and lacking in architectural invention, they are just big enough (two or three rooms, bathroom, kitchen, possibly some sort of tool shack in the back and a free-standing garage put up with the help of friends) to serve as the scenes of the humble lives of its occupants; since the seventies, when villages began to turn away from farming, similar houses have been replacing the lovely, traditional (though not necessarily healthy or comfortable) peasant houses – this is the spirit of becoming 'citified' and 'middle class'.

csángók, a (pron. *tshahn-gow*); the "lost tribe" of Hungarians living in poor, scattered villages of Moldova (Romania) outside the cusp of the eastern Carpathians who are in most likelihood the later-day descendants of the Szeklers (→*székely*) who emigrated from Transylvania (→*Erdély*) in several waves beginning with the Middle Ages; despite repeated attempts at forced assimilation and the absence of Hungarian-language schools, or priests, many still speak Hungarian, albeit archaic and hard to understand; they have also preserved their Catholic (→*katolikus*) religion (which in an Orthodox environment is one of their main links to their Hungarian origin), not to mention their treasury of ancient folk songs (→*népdal*), and customs.

csárda (pron. *tshahr-dah*), '(*wayside*) *inn*'; they used to stand along the road near small towns and villages, or else on their outskirts, where a weary traveler could spend the night.

csárdás (pron. *tshahr-dahsh*), '(*the dance*) *of the csárda*' (lit.); the national dance created in the age of national (→*nemzeti*) awakening in the first part of the 19th century, from the paired dances of various regions of the country; by mid-century it became the rage of the upper classes, too, and after the War of Independence (→*Szabadságharc*), it served as one of the symbols of resistance to the Habsburgs, though its original, rural variants also continued to be danced; in its simplest form, the man holds the woman's waist with both hands, while the woman puts both her hands, arms outstretched, on the man's shoulder, then they take two crisp steps to the right, and two to the left; it has several popular variants, including the "*csendes*" (slow), the "*friss*" (fast), the "*forgó*" (quick-turn), the "*rezgő*" (short-step), and so on, including one where the man and the woman dance separately; middle-aged Hungarians can still do the *csárdás*, having learned it in school, while young people learn it in dance houses (→*táncház*); it is also still danced at country weddings (→*lakodalom*), especially by older people. →**magyar nóta**

Csárdáskirálynő, a *The Csárdás Princess*; the quintessential operetta (→*operett*) written by Imre Kálmán in 1915 which is still as popular as ever; its characters, as played by celebrated actors, have taken on unchangeable shape in theatergoers' imaginations, while its lyrics and musical numbers written to emulate the then highly popular Hungarian songs (→*magyar nóta*), have practically become part of Hungarian folklore.

cseh *Czech*; used in combination with other words and as part of expressions, all of which have one thing in common – they refer to something unpleasant; for instance, "*csehül állunk*" (lit. '*a Czech state of affairs*') means "we're in (deep) trouble", while a '*Czech number*' is a number whose figures have gotten mixed up (e.g. 782 instead of 872). →**francia**

csehek, a *Czechs, the*; today, Hungarians see the Czechs as sober-minded, beer-drinking and somewhat dull people (not so in more sanguine centuries, when they came to Hungary as mercenaries); in the 19th century, they settled in Hungary in large numbers to work in factories and to fill positions as clerks of the Imperial government; in the 20th century, the Czech nation was often Hungary's political rival, which led to mutual national (→*nemzeti*) dislike to be relieved only by the mutual experience of Soviet occupation, and the fact that due to the isolation from the West, the intelligentsia (→*értelmiség*) of the two countries mutually discovered the value in each other's art and literature.

Csekonics gróf *Count Csekonics*; though at one time there really was an aristocratic family (→*arisztokrata*) of south-Slav origin by this name, their memory has survived only as the synonym of great wealth, as in the saying, "Who do you think I am? Csekonics?", the equivalent of saying, "I'm no Rockefeller!"

cseléd *servant*; originally the name for every man and woman employed around the house, including agricultural hands and day laborers (it shares the same root with the word '*család*' – family), it later became the name, in both towns and villages, of those (usually young) women who lived in the maid's room (→*cselédszoba*) and helped the lady of the house with her chores, or did all of them herself (unless there was a cook and a ladies' maid as well); before the

Second World War every middle class family and every well to do landowner had a live-in domestic servant who usually came from a village (either to escape poverty, or else to learn the tricks of running a home before they got married); conjuring up the helplessness and often bad treatment of servants living in a strange household, the word carries bad connotations; today, there are only 'women who come in' (*help*) for the day, usually just once a week, to do the cleaning, washing and ironing for citified white-collar and professional middle class families, for the wife (having a career of her own) is too busy working to attend to domestic chores.

cselédlépcső '*servant's stairs*' (lit), *back stairs*; before WW II apartment houses (→*bérház*) with hanging corridors (→*gang*) were built with two staircases, a spacious and elegant one for the tenants and their visitors, accessible from the main entrance, and a narrower, plain one, usually in the shape of a spiral staircase, for servants (and repairmen) who, in theory at least, were supposed to restrict their movements to it; the trash was taken out through these stairs, and so were the carpets, which were freed of dust downstairs in the courtyard; today it is distinguished from the main staircase only by the fact that due to nearly half a century of city council (→*tanács*) neglect, it is in an even worse state of disrepair.

cselédszoba '*servant's room*' (lit.), *maid's room*; before WW II just about every apartment in an apartment building (→*bérház*), even if it had only two rooms, would generally have a small separate room (which opened from the kitchen and with a small window opening onto the outdoor corridor (→*gang*) for the live-in maid (→*cseléd*), though many tenants could not afford to hire one; since the war the maid's room is usually occupied by adolescents and teenagers as their first stop on the way to independence. →**lichthóf**

csendőr '*guardian of silence*' (lit.), *gendarme*; the Royal Hungarian Constabulary (*Magyar Királyi Csendőrség*) was a famously effective police force organized along military principles to keep the peace outside of the towns and cities; it functioned until 1945, when the Constabulary, infamous for its blind discipline, was disbanded; today they are remembered for the ominous looking, quivering tall feather (tail feathers of a cock) stuck in their hats and the fear their appearance struck in people's hearts. →**rendőr**

Csepel (pron. *cheh-pel*); the largest island on the Danube (→*Duna*), the size of a small county, stretching toward the south from Budapest; in popular usage, its name is restricted to mean the northernmost tip of the island which belongs to the capital; by WW I it was one of the centers of heavy industry (it produced machine tools, "Csepel" trucks, motorcycles, bicycles, even aircraft); being a militant working class area, it was known as "Red Csepel", and had been regarded as a citadel of sorts by the Communists (→*kommunisták, a*), though when they were in power, they were also suspicious and wary of it (as a consequence of which there was meat in the shops here even when there was none to be had anywhere else); today, the huge shops of the once large plants are occupied by small workshops and warehouses. →**Angyalföld**; **Újpest**; **Kispest**

csikós *'colts' man'* (lit.), *horse-herd, wrangler;* besides the →*betyár*, the *csikós* is the main component of the romantic image of Hungary and Hungarians which still prevails (mainly) in German-speaking countries; he is seen as a wild and fierce figure keeping an equally wild and fierce herd of horses in check with his long ornate whip (*karikásostor*) as he rides tall and secure on his swift-footed steed on the plains (→*puszta*) which is his home (and which makes him a distant relative of the cowboy); though by the 19th century horses were no longer used for riding, tourist PR has kept his image vibrantly alive to this day. →**lovasnemzet**; **Alföld**; **Hortobágy**

csípős (étel) *hot* (*food*); though paprika (→*pirospaprika*) is the most often used spice in Hungarian cooking (→*magyar konyha*), Hungarian foods are not nearly as hot as foreigners think, nor is paprika, which comes in various degrees of "hot", and in both dried (crumbled) and pulverized form; only a couple of dishes are made with really hot paprika (red pepper), such as fisherman's soup (→*halászlé*), which is served with dried and crumbled red hot pepper in a separate little bowl to be added to the soup at the table; dried red pepper (→*paprika*) is also sometimes added to pickled vegetables (→*savanyúság*) to make them "hot".

csizma (*knee*) *boots*; once a necessary part of Hungarian costume (→*magyaros öltözet*), by the 20th century it was worn only by village folk (both men and women) in a tall and narrow hard-top variant and being expensive and highly prized, it was handed down from generation to generation; in "co-op" agriculture, these gave way to black rubber boots worn with blue overalls, which took the place of traditional folk costume (→*népviselet*), while in recent years green and yellow "recreation boots", the Hungarian variant of *green wellies*, have come into vogue among sportsmen (hunting, fishing), who consider it a kind of status symbol; in the army (→*honvédség*), their use was restricted to the cavalry and officers, until only officers would wear them (when in ceremonial uniform); the rest of the army wear short boots with clasps known as 'sapper boots', while the long brown *birgerli* boots, which tied up on the sides, were typically worn by the stewards of large estates; today, these conjure up images of the Arrow Cross (→*nyilaskeresztes mozgalom*) who (for some mysterious reason) took a special liking to it. →**paraszt**

Csodaszarvas, .a *Miracle Stag, the* (lit.); according to the ancient legend of the origin of the Huns and Magyars (→*hun-magyar rokonság*), it was when two brothers and their men went for a hunt, that Hunor and Magor, the two sons of King Nimród chasing a stag, came upon the daughters of King Dul in the marshes of Meotis (the delta of the river Don, from where the conquering Hungarians settled in the Carpathian Basin), whom they abducted, then became the fathers of the Huns and Magyars.

csók *kiss*; →**kézcsók**; **puszi**

csókolom '*I kiss you*' (lit.); the shortened form of →*kezicsókolom* (lit. '*I kiss your hand*') used mostly by children when addressing adults.

Csontváry Kosztka, Tivadar (pron. *chont-vah-ree*); this solitary genius who never attended art school was "discovered" in the 1960s (almost half a century after his death) and made into the cultic personification of modern Hungarian art, partly because of his brilliant colors, huge canvases and spectacular pictures, and possibly also because of his overriding obsession verging on madness. →**Munkácsy**

csusza →**túróstészta**

D

Dankó, Pista (pron. *dahn-koh pishtah*); legendary Gypsy *prímás* (violinist) and composer who lived at the turn of the century (→*századforduló*) and who even played at Court; his melancholy song, "*My violin is broken, she will not sing …*" about a broken violin, lovingly called 'Rózsi', after his sweetheart, is still sung today. →**cigányzenekar**; **magyar nóta**

Debrecen (pron. *deh-breh-tsen*); the largest city of the eastern part of the country and lately a veritable "second capital", made into an important town by its well-to-do, independent-thinking, Calvinist landowners (→*gazda*), as well as its Calvinist college, which has given Eastern Hungary its best intellectuals (→*értelmiség*) for centuries; in 1849, during the War of Independence (→*Szabadságharc*), the House of Representatives, having fled Pest, gathered in the huge local Calvinist church to declare the dethronement of the →*Habsburgs*, thereby making the city the symbol and seat of Hungarian self-determination; in 1944, the temporary National Assembly also convened here.

Debrecenbe kéne menni … '*We should go to Debrecen …*'; the first line of the tune, whose popularity, despite the silly lyrics, does not seem to wane, is sung to entertain very small children as, holding their hands, the grownup plays horsey with them; it continues: "*…and buy a turkey cock, / take care, driver, the wicker cage has a hole, / the turkey cock will jump out of it.*"

délibáb '*noon(time) witch*' (lit.), *fata morgana, mirage*; the mirage that could sometimes be seen on blistering summer days on the →*Hortobágy* and the →*Kúnság* until the plains (→*puszta*) fell under cultivation; this ethereal phenomenon indigenous to the prairie frequently appears in Romantic poetry and is usually described in the shape of a church seen in reverse, with its steeples touching the ground; though the *délibáb* no longer graces the skies, it has survived as the metaphor for daydreaming and self-delusion (ostensibly two characteristic blemishes on the Hungarian national character), and also in sayings such as "*délibábot kergetni*", chasing a mirage (pipe dream).

Délvidék '*the southern parts*' (lit.); not the southern counties of today's Hungary, but the →*Vajdaság* in northern Serbia which, along with its Hungarian population, was annexed to the new Yugoslav kingdom after WWI. by the Peace Treaty of Versailles (→*Trianon*). →**Újvidék**; **Erdély**; **Felvidék**; **Kárpátalja**

díszmagyar '*ornate Hungarian (dress)*' (lit.); as the name suggests, the *díszmagyar* is the ornate verson of traditional Hungarian dress (→*magyaros ruha*) and as seen on the society paintings from the turn of the century (→*századforduló*), it was also an evening dress and Court dress (on invitations from Emperor and King Francis Joseph gentlemen were asked to attend in tails or *díszmagyar*); by the inter-war years it was already considered anachronistic, though the ministers of the various new governments still wore them for their official group portraits. The English writer Patrick Leigh Fermor witnessed a group of Hungarian aristocrats in →*Esztergom*, in front of the cathedral, preparing for Easter church festivities in the year of 1934, all of them clad in their '*ornate Hungarian*': "*They were clad in dark, sumptuous and variously coloured doublets of heavy silk – or occasionally of velvet – fastened with chased buttons the size of gold hazelnuts and edged with brown fur at the cuffs and the throat and over the shoulders. Some wore knee-length over-tunics, furred likewise and open down the front and frogged with gold lace; others wore them slung across their backs with careful abandon, or askew over one shoulder like swinging dolmans. Tight breeches, stiff with embroidery, ended in Hessian boots which were black, scarlet, blue or rifle-green; gold braid edged their notched tops and gilt spurs were screwed into their heels. One or two had gold or silver chains about their necks and all of them wore kalpacks of light dark fur … plumed with white aigrettes or heron's feathers that burst from their jewelled clasps like escapes of steam. Carried nonchalantly under their arms or the crooks of their elbows or with points touching the flagstones when stationary and hands resting lightly on the cross-hilts, their nearly semi-circular scimitars were sheathed in green or blue or plum-coloured velvet and mounted in gold and adorned with jewels at intervals along the scabbards.*" →**kacagány; magyaros ruha**

disznó *pig, swine, hog, pork* (*meat*); though hogs fatted to 150 to 200 kilos for their thick layer of fatty bacon (→*szalonna*), have been replaced in most farmyards by animals with more meat on them, most villagers still fatten hogs, for most Hungarian meat dishes are still made from pork with pork fat (→*zsír*) being an indispensible ingredient in the recipes. →**disznóölés**

disznóölés *pigkilling*; the word conjures up images of dawns in purple and farmyards blanketed in pristine snow, a pleasant sense of anticipation, playful tomfoolery, mouthwatering smells and flavors, and a shot of brandy (→*pálinka*) in the early morn, gulped down on an empty stomach right after awakening; the slaughter of the fattened pig (→*disznó*) is usually done by a hired "pigsticker" (it takes not only great physical strength but know-how, too), while processing the animal is left to family and friends, who spend the entire day doing it. While the scorching of the skin is in progress out in the yard, in the kitchen the blood is fried with lots of onions which, with everyone busy seeing to their chores, is just about the only thing consumed until evening; first they carve out the ham which will be salted, cured and smoked (a craft in itself!) so it will stay fresh until Easter

(→*Húsvét*), when it is cooked and eaten (it being an indispensable part of the holiday cheer); next, the meaty bacon (→*szalonna*) is stripped off and hung up to be smoked, which is followed by the rendering of the lard (→*zsír*) and the tasting of the fresh cracklings (→*töpörtyű*); meanwhile, the women clean out the guts which next they clean, then fill it (it is hard work!) with seasoned ground meat for sausage (→*kolbász*), and also liver and blood filling to make liver and blood sausage (→*hurka*); the stomach is also cleaned and stuffed with chopped and cooked meat, ears, skin and gristle to make head cheese (→*disznósajt*); when all is done and it is late afternoon, the children take a plateful of the fresh →*disznótor*(*os*) for friends to taste (after all, every family swears by their own recipe). Pigkilling is still practiced today, for where there are pigs, they get slaughtered, one for the family, and one for relatives in town; what's more, since most households have refrigerators, the practice is no longer restricted to the winter months.

disznósajt '*pig cheese*' (lit.), *head cheese*; ears, tails, cheeks, hearts, kidneys together with other parts of the pig are cooked in well seasoned liquid with lots of garlic and paprika (→*pirospaprika*), then the meat is chopped fine and used to fill the cleaned stomach, which is then placed between two boards and pressed down with the use of heavy weights, then lightly smoked; like all "pig-killing" (→*disznótoros*) delicacies, this too is made according to individual house recipes, even in meat processing plants, and so buying head cheese always comes with a surprise; in its appearance it is something like *haggis*, except thanks to the *paprika* and the smoking process, it is reddish-brown in color. →**disznóölés**

disznótor '*pig's funeral feast*' (lit.); as the name indicates the *disznótor* is held to bid farewell to the slaughtered pig and is thus part of the pig-killing (→*disznóölés*) held in winter; it is usually held with many people around, and when the →*hurka*, sausage (→*kolbász*) and head cheese (→*disznósajt*) are ready, some of it is always sent to neighbors and family, even if they live at a distance and the meat needs be sent by mail. →**kocsonya**

disznózsír '*pork fat*' (lit.), *lard*; traditionally, Hungarian cooking relied heavily on pork fat, or lard; women who wished to run a household they could be proud of rendered the lard (→*zsír*) themselves from greasy bacon (which, once cooked, turns into cracklings or →*töpörtyű*), let it cool and solidify, then transferred it into a cone-shaped enamel container made specifically for this purpose, and stored it in the pantry (→*éléskamra*), where it would last for up to a year; during the last decade or so, however, it has gradually been replaced by oil in Hungary, too, which has resulted in the disappearance of many old flavours.→**disznóőlés**

disszidens '*dissident*' (lit), *emigré*; this

word, which today sounds strange, even ridiculous, was officially used during the years of Communism to designate persons who were "residing abroad unlawfully", i.e., they left the country illegally.

dísztávirat '*ornate telegram*' (lit.); the most prevalent and courteous form of greeting or congratulating someone, and also of sending one's condolence, is still the sending of a telegram, which is done by pasting the message onto an ornate sheet (with a drawing or painting on it) chosen from what is available at the Hungarian Post Office; these telegrams are holding their own while greeting cards have not yet caught on.

Doberdo one of the bloodiest battle fields of WW I where, among the rocks of the Italian Dolomites, where the Italian and Imperial (→*Monarchia*) forces, made up mostly of Hungarian soldiers, slaughtered each other for months during the year of 1917; the terrible barrage left such an indelible mark in Hungarian privates (→*baka*) souls, that several authentic 20th century folk songs (→*népdal*) have Doberdo as their subject.

dobos torta '*drum torte*' (lit.); the many-tiered Hungarian chocolate or cocoa filled torte made of Génoise (dessert roll) dough and topped with delicious clear caramel glaze as hard as a drum, hence the name *dobos* ('*drummer*') for this perennial favorite; in fact it is called after its inventor, József Dobos, a confectioner.

doktor úr '*mister doctor*' (lit.); the form of address used for doctors (who even when "Comrade" was the norm were not called "Comrade doctor"), while lady doctors are called *doktornő*, (lit. '*woman doctor*'). →**úr**; **megszólítás**

dolgozó '*he, who labors/works*' (lit.), *worker*; the word, irrevocably linked with the old Communist (→*komunista*) regime, was coined because a common term of denomination was needed to signify the mythical, larger than life worker (→*munkás*) *and* the peasant (→*paraszt*) who "joined forces to build socialism", i.e., it was used to designate blue collar (physical) laborers in general (especially in contrast to anyone holding a leading position of any kind; "the people" (→*nép*) was an even more positive synonym for *dolgozó*, which could only be outdone by the term "the working people" (*dolgozó nép*) which, according to the tenets of current ideology, was supposed to be in charge (the →*munkás* a little more so than the →*paraszt*); the word is still used today, but now it simply means '*employee*'.

Don-kanyar '*the bend of the river Don*' (lit.); →**Voronyezs**

Duna (pron. *doonah*), *Danube*; though it is on the plains of Hungary that the Danube becomes a really big river which cuts the country in two (until the construction of the Chain Bridge or →*Lánchíd* quite literally, producing two very distinct areas which have kept some of their individual character to this day), the Danube does not play an appreciable role in the Hungarian imagination, perhaps because its role in the economy (except for the ample fish in its waters which made for a fabulous catch until the last century), was negligible until→*Széchenyi* made it navigable, and the wheat (→*búza*) could be shipped from the south-eastern part of the country, where it was grown, to the mills in Vienna (→*Bécs*) and →*Pest*, but even this did not make Hungarians into a real sea (or river) faring nation, and to this day the traffic is slight on the river, which in the local imagination conjures up mighty floods and, of course,→*Budapest*, whose breathtaking, spectacular panorama has been bestowed on it by the Danube. →**Tisza**

Duna-Tisza Köze '*between the Danube and the Tisza*' (lit.); just barely one hundred years ago, this part of Hungary was still a veritable sweltering desert or sandy prairie (→*puszta*) with mirages (→*délibáb*) since the devastation caused by the Turkish occupation (→*hódoltság*), where only the hardy sheep (→*birka*) could survive, and the people of the farms (→*tanya*) just barely, until as a result of far-seeing, well planned agriculture (forestation and irrigation) made the area one of the richest yielding in the country; not only is it a major producer of vegetables and fruit, but also of light table wines, even though its roads still run as straight as an arrow, and the ground is as flat as the top of a table; this is where the horizon is greatest, where →*Petőfi* was born, and where→*Pusztaszer* is located. →**Alföld; Dunántúl**

Dunakanyar, a *Danube Bend, the*; at →*Esztergom*, the Danube (→*Duna*), which enters Hungary from the west, runs up against mountains, and making a hair-pin turn, heads south; the river as it surges between the mountains is an awesome sight, and its right bank, from Esztergom to→*Buda*, was the center of the Medieval kingdom; today, this part of the river is a popular holiday resort which until recently was threatened by plans for a gigantic power plant at →*Visegrád*, until a grass roots movement, which saw in it not only a danger to the environment but also the symbol of the regime, in 1989 got rid of both one and the other.

Dunántúl '*beyond the Danube*' (lit.), *Transdanubia*; the part of the country which lies to the west of the Danube (→*Duna*); with its string of quaint little towns, pleasant hills and ample waters, formerly it was the province of →*Pannonia* and thus part of the Roman Empire, whose remains (buried towns, villas and treasures) are still coming to light today, not to mention the stones used by the Roman legionaires to build roads; obviously, this is the country's more advanced half, whose life has always been influenced by the Western regions adjacent to it, as opposed to the much more sparsely populated, poorer and defenseless plains which lay to the east of the frontier of the Roman Empire. →**Alföld; Hódoltság; Duna-Tisza köze**

Dunaújváros '*new town on the Danube*' (lit.), (pron. *doonah-ooy-vah-rosh*); situated half-way between the capital and the southern frontier of the country on the shore of the Danube, *Dunaújváros* was originally the Roman fortification of Intercisa, then a village (→*falu*), which in the fifties (→*ötvenes évek*) had to make way for a bleak and dismal city until 1961 called Sztálinváros (*Stalintown*), conceived as the home of the people working in the new, oversized ironworks; though it quickly became the symbol of the forced industrialization of the country with brought economic ruin, contemporary propaganda continued to refer to it proudly as a "socialist city", even after its name was changed; during the revolution (→*forradalom, 1956*), this is where Soviet troops came up against the most desperate resistance, and this is where the fighting lasted the longest.

dupla '*double*' (lit.); *espresso* (*coffee*); originally this is how they called the small amount of coffee (→*kávé*) served in small cups or glasses in cafés (→*eszpresszó*), this because there was an even smaller portion that could be ordered, called the *szimpla* ('*single*'); with time, however, the single portion disappeared, and today there is only the *dupla*. →**fekete**

dzsentri *gentry*; this English loanword was used to designate the large numbers of the (lesser) nobility (→*nemesség*) living in the provinces who lost all of their real social influence along with their fortunes by the turn of the century (→*századforduló*), but continued to live an outdated, antebellum (sort of) and self-destructive life style of its landowning fathers on which (especially its outward marks) it insisted to the very last (and was finally swept away by the outbreak of WW II); having long since become operetta-like (→*operett*) and romantically archaic, the style nevertheless outlived the gentry, first infecting unrefined, but snobbish functionaries (→*funkcionárius*), then after the change in regime (→*rendszerváltás*), even the *nouveau riche*. →**sírva vigad a magyar**

E

ebéd *lunch*; →**vasárnap**

ebédlő '*lunching room*' (lit.), *dining room*; being small in size, most Hungarian homes do not have a separate dining room, and so the dining table (if there is one), is generally placed in the living room, which is thus sometimes referred to as the dining room; however, there is often a dinette (→*étkező*), especially in the pre-fab (→*panel*) apartments, which is really just a narrow, windowless adjunct of the kitchen or pantry.

Eger (pron. *eh-gher*); a small baroque town and archiepiscopal see situated at foot of the northern mountain range; it invariably conjures up images of the 16th century battles against the Turk (→*törökök*) fought on the shifting borderlands, of which the town became the symbol, for this is where the Hungarians fought one of their rare, triumphant battles against the Turkish forces who in 1552 laid siege to the town in far superior numbers; the highly popular novel for young people, *The Stars of Eger* (→*Egri csillagok*), was written about this siege and those who heroically fought in it.

Egmont-nyitány *Egmont Overture*; during the revolution (→*forradalom, 1956*) Kossuth Radio (→*Kossuth Rádió*) broadcast from a small, temporary studio, where the editors had only a handful of musical recordings at their disposal, which they had to play again and again to fill in the time between news broadcasts; Beethoven's tragic *Egmont Overture* was the only classical piece of music among the operetta (→*operett*) selections, and so it quickly became the musical emblem of the revolution, which it has remained to this day.

Egri csillagok *The Stars of Eger*; a children's literature classic written at the turn of the century (→*századforduló*) by Géza Gárdonyi which has lost none of its wild popularity; through the adventures of an adolescent youth who matures into a brave soldier, it illustrates how Hungary fought the conquering Turkish (→*török*) Empire from →*Mohács* to the successful defense of the fortress of Eger (→*Eger*) in 1552; Hungarian children learn their history by reading this novel, not to mention patriotism, for practically speaking, every school child gets to read it (some more than once), and ends up identifying with its attractive heroes. →***Pál utcai fúk***

egyenruha *uniform*; uniforms in general, just like the military (→*katonaság*) and of course the police (→*rendőrség*), do not enjoy real respect and popularity among Hungarians; these days not only school children are unwilling to wear uniforms (not even school caps), but even the postal workers and railroad workers have demanded new uniforms that bear the least possible resemblance to classical (military) uniforms; even the rank and file enlisted men (→*honvéd*) need to wear their uniform only when on duty, and even then their greenish uniform hardly differs from that worn by soldiers anywhere in the world, except, perhaps, for the fact that insignia are once again (traditionally) worn on the collar; the tailoring and color of the ceremonial uniform, however, is once again, i.e., since the change in regime (→*rendszerváltás*), traditional and bears a resemblance to the so called, coffee-brown →*atilla* worn during the War of Independence (→*Szabadságharc*) which originally inspired it; the foreign, Russian and German-type of flat headgear (nicknamed: *plate*), too, has been replaced by the familiar (sometimes shielded) →*bocskai* hat, which is worn even by officers. →**katonaság**; **hajdú**; **bocskai**; **huszár**

Egyszer volt, hol nem volt ... *'once there was, once there wasn't'* (lit.), *once upon a time*; →***Hol volt, hol nem volt ...***

éléskamra *'food chamber'* (lit.), *larder, pantry*; even small (and modern) apartments usually have a pantry of some sort to store non-perishable foodstuffs, a habit people retained (from traditional lifestyles) in response to the shortages produced by socialism (→*szocializmus*) and which they have not yet abandoned, albeit now they tend to keep their frigidaires and deep freezes in them; traditional, cool and spacious larders where sausage (→*kolbász*), fatty bacon (→*szalonna*) and cured bacon (→*sonka*) is hung in rows from the hooks, while jars of jam (→*lekvár*) and stewed fruit (→*befőtt*) line the shelves to bursting, and dozens of eggs lie in baskets on the floor, can be seen only in some country households.

Életünket és vérünket! '*(We shall give) our lives and blood!*' (lit.); it was with this Latin cry (*Vitam et sanguinem*) that the Hungarian nobility (→*nemesség*) pledged their support to the young Queen Maria Thesesa at the estates' assembly convened at Bratislava (→*Pozsony*) when the Empire and her crown was in dire need, though they were supposed to have added, *sotto voce*, "but no oats", i.e., anything but taxes; the phrase is still often quoted, albeit in trivial situations and in a humorous way.

ellenforradalom *counter-revolution*; the perfidious and deceitful word used by the nomenclature for the revolution of '56 (→*forradalom 1956*), which (probably) even János Kádár (→*Kádár János*) himself refrained from using in private conversation; naturally, the majority of the people considered the Kádár regime itself the "counter-revolution", and so, in order to avoid having to use the shameful designation "counter-revolution" (seeing how at the time they could not very well call '56 a "revolution"), people began referring to it simply as "fifty-six" (→*ötvenhat*). This term, at least, was neutral. →**sajnálatos események**

előszoba '*antechamber*' (lit.), *hall*; the older an apartment building or family house is, the larger its antechamber, where coats are hung on hooks and where the huge, old (inherited) garderobe stands in which outerwear is kept (while the family's suitcases are perched on top); the water closet and kitchen usually open from this generally dark and windowless small room, and from the kitchen the maid's room (→*cselédszoba*) and pantry (→*éléskamra*), and often also the bathroom.

elvtárs '*companion in principles*' (lit.), *comrade*; along with *szaktárs* (*colleague*; lit., '*companion in trade*', not to mention '*companion is sports*'(!), all of which have happily gone out of use), the word was coined by the Social Democrats of the end of the century after the German *Kamerad* as a form of address and referral; the Communists (→*kommunisták*) inherited it from them, and made good use of it by making it refer to just about everyone, except doctors (→*doktor úr*) and teachers (→*tanár úr*); the appellation was so ubiquitous, not to say compulsory, that if someone was addressed as "sir" (→*úr*) nonetheless, it was a sign of great respect. After the collapse of the socialist (→*szocialista*) regime, the word became the sarcastic and derogatory synonym for ex-functionaries (→*funkcionárius*).

Ember küzdj, és bízva bízzál! *Man, I have spoken: strive on, trust, have faith!*; the Lord's unequivocal advice at the end of *The Tragedy of Man* addressed to Adam after he'd become disillusioned with the future of mankind (i.e., lost faith in Creation itself); it is still quoted today in conversation, but only tongue-in-cheek. →***Tragédia, A***

emigráns *emigré*; ever since the defeat of the War of Independence (→*Szabadságharc*), this expression was used to refer to those "voluntary exiles" who left the country for political reasons – especially →*Kossuth*, and following him thousands of soldiers and civilians. (In an earlier age, →*Rákóczi* and his fellows were called "men in hiding"). Many of the *emigrés* who fled from the threat of incarceration and death on the gallows and survived participation in the American Civil War, the many and sundry South American uprisings, or the battles fought for the reunification of Italy, decided to return to their home country after the Compromise (→*Kiegyezés*) with →*Austria*, thereby solidifying the figure of the triumphant repatriate whose actions are justified by history, and who keeps reappearing on the stage of 20th century Hungarian politics again and again. Many politicians who emigrated during the Communist (→*kommunista*) takeover of 1948 and the refugees who fled the country in 1956 also repatriated, though they found the experience partly disillusioning; the Communists (→*kommunisták*) who fled to Moscow in 1919 after the fall of the short-lived Hungarian Republic of Councils (→*Tanácsköztársaság*) had also returned (provided they survived Stalin's purges, of course), to become the supreme lords of the country once again for a number of years, forcing others to emigrate in turn. The emigrés of '56 themselves were not blind to the depreciatory, insulting connotation of the word, and called themselves "Hungarians living abroad", with many even refusing to take up foreign citizenship; it is a sign of changing times that today these people are generally called simply "Hungarians abroad" (*külföldi magyarok*), the local term for expatriates. →**kivándorló**; **disszidens**

Erdély *Transylvania*; during the Middle Ages a domain "beyond the woods" (hence its name), and in Antiquity the Roman province of Dacia (for a short period), it was a distant and isolated duchy of the Hungarian kingdom alternatively ruled by crown princes and →*vajdas* (a *vajda* being something like a marquis), until the Turks (→*törökök*) occuped the central parts of the country, as a result of which the unoccupied eastern counties (→*vármegye*) of the Great Plain (→*Alföld*) and Transylvania proper organized themselves into an independent principality, electing a prince (but not a king!) to rule over them, who appeased as best he could the two great warring empires, the →*Habsburgs* (i.e., the legitimate kings of Hungary!) and the Turkish Sultan (to whom they paid taxes); in this way, for a hundred and fifty years Transylvania became "lesser Hungary", until, with the defeat of the Turkish forces, the Habsburgs inherited it, but without uniting it with the mother country, and it continued as a separate principality until the Compromise (→*Kiegyezés*); the Peace Treaty of Versailles (→*Trianon*) annexed not only the counties predominantly inhabited by Romanians, but also → *Székelyföld*, which to this day is almost exclusively Hungarian-speaking – not to mention the western part of the principality (also predominantly Hungarian-speaking at the time) – to Romania (which together are greater in area than present-day Hungary), as a result of which, even after hundreds of thousands fled Transylvania, two million Hungarians were turned into Romanian citizens, while Transylvania itself became a kind of mythical Atlantis of the "mainland" Hungarians. →**Kolozsvár**; **székelyek**; **szászok**; **románok**

érettségi '*maturity test*' (lit.), *graduation*; the expression is used to refer to the final examinations taken by 18-year-olds before their high-school graduation; several days in duration, they comprise both written and oral tests, and are the precondition for any further study; though by now these final examinations have lost much of their former status, when it was a real ordeal, they are still something to be reckoned with; despite all attempts at modernization, girls still go to take their finals in white sailor's blouses (→*matrózblúz*) and dark blue pleated skirts, and the boys in 'graduation suits' (dark colors only!) bought specially for the occasion; once everyone in class has taken their finals, there is a traditional banquet in a restaurant where the teachers are also invited so that they can now greet each other as mature adults and peers; the class reunions, usually held every five years, also take the form of dinner at a restaurant of choice; →**érettségi tabló**; **szalagavató bál**; **ballagás**

érettségi tabló '*graduation tableau*' (*lit.*), *graduation photo*; a typical turn-of-the-century (→*századforduló*), small-town tradition which held its own even after the expansion of towns into cities; the framed, formal group photo of a graduating class with the teachers on top (or the middle) and the portraits of the students below (or encircling them), is placed on display in the shop window of a busy store for everyone to see, and indeed, passers-by often stop, searching for a familiar face, while the graduation tableaux of former classes are hung in school corridors to gather dust until someone comes along ten or twenty years later, and removes them down to the basement.

Erkel Ferenc (pron. *ehr-kel*); the first director of the Budapest Opera, the "father" of Hungarian national (→*nemzeti*) opera, and the revered composer of the National Anthem (→*Himnusz*). →***Bánk bán***

értelmiség, az *intelligentsia, the*; in today's parlance, the intelligentsia is being increasingly identified with the professional classes (which in Hungary today is predominantly made up of first-generation college graduates), as well as the intellectual elite; be that as it may, the intelligentsia of Hungary – and generally of Eastern Europe (→*Közép Európa*) – have always felt an urgent sense of social responsibility, i.e., it felt obliged to carry out its moral obligation of providing leadership, defining national (→*nemzeti*) goals and "representing" the nation, in the flesh, if need be, regardless of professional experience; however, with the rise in the number of those engaged in professional endeavours, not to mention the professionalization of politics, the traditional role of the intelligentsia has become increasingly restricted to the activities of writers (and historians) who, as the self-appointed conscience of the nation, have raised their voices in moments of crisis; not only did writers help ignite the various political movements of the 19th century and consequent revolutions, they also played a prominent role in fifty-six (→*ötvenhat*) as well, not to mention setting the stage for the change in regime (→*rendszerváltás*); in short, the role of the intelligentsia has been (of necessity) political in nature; no wonder that so many writers (→*író*), historians, philosophers and scientists participate in contemporary Hungarian politics. →**Széchenyi**

Erzsébet királyné *Queen Elizabeth*; the heroine ("Sissi") of a dozen bitter-sweet Austrian films and the politically active, free-spirited and rebellious wife of Emperor Francis Joseph (→*Ferenc József*), the figure of Queen Elizabeth has been surrounded by an aura of devotion and gratitude for the open sympathy she expressed as a young empress towards Hungary at the time when her husband defeated the Hungarian half of the Habsburg Empire (→*Habsburg Birodalom*) in the War of Independence (→*Szabadságharc*); called "an angel of a woman" by →*Széchenyi*, and also "the handsomest woman in Europe", she even learned to speak Hungarian, and when a weakened Austria (→*Ausztria*) was forced into negotiations with the Hungarian opposition, she acted as the political go-between for the preparation of the Compromise (→*Kiegyezés*); after the change in regime (→*rendszerváltás*), her statue was put up again at the Buda end of the Elizabeth Bridge, which bears her name.

esküvő *wedding*; the official, administrative procedure held at the registrar's office at the local city hall is becoming shorter and simpler with time, while the "real" ceremony for which guests receive official invitations, is held in churches again; time-honored customs accompanying peasant weddings (→*lakodalom*) are disappearing (for example, carrying the bride's bed and bedding to the groom's house and putting the bride's hair up in a bun), with only the "lads' farewell" (→*legénybúcsú*) and the best man (→*vőfély*) remaining in most places, plus the wedding procession, in which the wedding guests, lead by the best man, conduct the young couple to the groom's house (or the local cultural center, if the wedding lunch is held there), accompanied by a Gypsy band (→*cigányzenekar*), though the wedding feast (for which the dishes are now rented from a restaurant instead of being borrowed from neighbors) often still features the traditional chicken soup with noodles, though it is usually followed by various German-type fries (*rántotthús*), and the home-made milk loaves (→*kalács*) have been replaced by cakes (→*torta*) bought from the local pastry shop (→*cukrászda*); at the same time, the bride's dance (→*menyasszonytánc*) is holding its own (it often brings in the full cost of the wedding feast), even if the young people do not dance the →*csárdás* and the Gypsy band (→*cigányzenekar*) plays "wedding rock" (→*lakodalmas rock*) tunes; some new customs have also appeared, though (mostly in the countryside), the custom of the groom throwing the bride's garter behind him, and throwing rice (in imitation of American films), being among them; in the towns and cities, weddings have turned into catering affairs in which everything, from the bride's long wedding dress, white veil and bouquet of flowers, not to mention the groom's black tuxedo, are rented, and everything happens in accordance to the general European prescription.

Esterházy (pron. *es-ter-hah-zee*); this fabulously wealthy family of counts and princes were the mightiest land-owners first of the Monarchy (→*Monarchia*), including Hungary, then of Central Europe (→*Közép-Európa*) as well, with holdings the size of small countries in Austrial, Bohemia, and Hungary, until everything of consequence that anyone owned fell victim to nationalization (→*államosítás*).

eszpresszó *coffee shop*; in Hungary, this is not the name for a certain type of coffee (→*kávé*), but the place where it is brewed and consumed; in place of the old cafés (→*kávéház*), which disappeared along with the bourgeois style of life, there appeared (generally) small, "Italian-type" places with small tables and small cups in which they serve the (theoretically) strong ("like poison") espresso coffee; the *eszpresszó* is an important venue of city life, a favorite meeting place for city-dwellers, where they gather to chat; even in villages the sign over many a tavern (→*kocsma*) has been changed to *eszpresszó*, though this has done precious little to alter the character of these drinkeries thereby. →**dupla**

Esztergom (pron. *es-ter-ghom*); the town by the Danube to the north of Budapest and the seat of the archbishop of the Catholic Church (→*katolikus egyház*) of Hungary, whose status is more or less that of the Archbishop of Canterbury; here, in the former Carolingian frontier town, from the 9th century the seat of the Hungarian princes, was St. Stephen, the first king of Hungary, born. →**Szent István**

étkezde *eating-place* (lit.), *eatery*, *canteen*; a dire place where for fifty years Hungarians ate their ubiquitous vegetables cooked with roux (→*főzelék*) accompanied by meatloaf (→*fasírt*), the infamous offering of socialist workplace canteens; served at counters by sour-faced (sometimes sweet-tempered) women, the food was ladled out of gigantic aluminum cauldrons upon the relinquishing of one's lunch ticket, printed on poor-quality paper, after which it was then taken to the oilcloth-covered tables on plastic trays, and eaten off of plastic plates with aluminum knives (blunt) and forks, a state of affairs which continued up until the demise of the big nationalized (→*államosítás*) companies, and with them their adjunct, the institution of "mass alimentation" (*közétkeztetés*). Today, the tradition lives on only in university cafeterias (→*menza*). →**kifőzde**, **büfé**, **önkiszolgáló**

etnikai kisebbség *ethnic minority* (lit.); the official, politically correct name for the Gypsies (→*cigány*) which, however, went out of use so quickly that today it almost has a sarcastic ring to it. →**roma**

Európa *Europe*; far from being a geographical designation, in Hungary the word is used a stamp of approval, conjuring up images of a civilized, bourgeois way of life as opposed to life in the uncivilized Balkans (→*Balkán*).

Ez elment vadászni ... *'This went hunting...'*(lit.); the popular nursery rhyme used to teach very small children to count; "*This went hunting* ... (and we bend the child's thumb into his palm), *this shot it* ... (and we bend his index finger), *this took it home, this cooked it, this little one ate it all ...*" (we say faster and faster, and after we have counted the child's pinky, too, we draw little circles in his palm), then we say even faster than before, *...little circle, little button, where has the little rabbit gone?*", ending the game by quickly nudging the child in the belly with our finger, which he tries to prevent with a wholehearted, gleeful laugh. The nursery rhyme which begins "*This little piggy went to market...*" is its English equivalent.

F

falu *village*; the distant sound of barking dogs, bright-red orchards, grandmothers (→*nagymama*), peace and tranquility, the buzzing of the bumble-bees, substantial noontime meals, the sonorous peeling of church-bells, pig killing (→*disznóölés*) and a full pantry (→*éléskamra*), home-distilled brandy (→*kisüsti pálinka*), cool, dry, white wines (→*bor*), snowy landscapes, sweltering hot summers, juicy pears, the smell of hay, the crowing of the cock, the dull clanking of cow-bells, all of these appear in the mind's eye in conjunction with this word. Needless to say, villages come in many shapes and forms, but the most characteristic is probably the ribbon-type settlement lying along a main road and consisting of just two or three long streets (lately covered with a hard surface) with a market place plus a public building or two adjacent to it – usually the town hall and school (and just behind it the granary); there is also the yellow Catholic church (mostly with Medieval foundations, but rebuilt in baroque–style) with a porched and trellised priory, and at some distance from it, the Calvinist church (though sometimes it's the other way around, and the former is at the lower end of the village, while the latter at the upper end), and also in a small, shaded park, the fenced in, distantly Palladian, neo-classical manor houses of the former land-owning families with their proud, pillared porticos, which the villagers call "mansions", and most of which were turned into the headquarters of farmers' co-operatives (→*termelőszövetkezet*). Formerly, village houses came with large farm-yards (with styes and stables), as well as gardens out back stretching down to the distant stream, and the structure of a village was a faithful reflection of the lives of the couple of hundred or thousand people who lived in it; today (now that the villagers are no longer engaged in agriculture but have gone off to work), the houses are bigger, but the plots smaller. During the course of the last century, towns grew out of the wealthy, gentrified villages (provided there was a railroad nearby), while preserving their former village-type structure; those that remailed villages socialism (→*szocializmus*) transformed into large agricultural estates, thus destroying the peasant (→*paraszt*) way of life, which received the kiss of death with the appearance of cars and television; the villages that survived are now either developing into small towns, or are the helpless victims of abject poverty, and instead of peasants working the land, are inhabited by roaming Gypsies (→*cigányok*) with no work and too much time on their hands.

falvédő '*wall guard/protector*' (lit.), *wall hanging*; it is known in two version, one meant for the wall next to the kitchen table (which today can be seen only in the homes of elderly village folk), made of linen and embroidered in colored thread and bearing some sweet banality of the "Home sweet home" type along with a rustic scene illustrating the saying (the expression, "I haven't come from off the wall hanging" thus means "I am not naive"); the second type is used to protect the wall of the bedroom (→*hálószoba*), so the paint won't wear off or the wallpaper get dirty with time as the person sleeping on the bed pushed up against the wall twists and turns during the night; it usually looks like a fluffy, hooked rug (possibly made by the lady of the house in her younger days), and it usually has some pattern on it that is supposed to be "modern".

Farkasréti temető (pron. *for-kosh-rey-tee*) *cemetery*; the largest cemetery in →*Buda*, which because many well-known artists, actors, writers and other celebrities have been buried here during the past couple of decades, has become a national (→*nemzeti*) Pantheon of sorts. →**Házsongárdi temető; Kerepesi úti temető; Kozma utcai temető; Újköztemető**

fasírt *ground meat loaf or patties*; patties the size of a small fist usually made from (cheap) ground pork (well seasoned with garlic); it is eaten hot or cold (it keeps well), as a mid-morning snack, a mid-afternoon snack, or as part of the main meal of the day, and is found in the cooler of every snack bar (→*büfé*), where it is served with vegetables (→*főzelék*); "*Combine the ground meat with eggs, rolls soaked in milk, salt and pepper; shape into patties, and fry in ample fat or oil until golden brown. Note! For us mammals it is better if we grind the meat, instead of the meat grinding us.*" (I. Örkény: *One Minute Stories*)

Fasori gimnázium *gymnasium on the avenue* (lit.); the popular name for the secondary school (a "gymnasium") founded by the Lutheran Church at the end of the last century, situated on Városligeti fasor in Pest, perhaps the best school of all times: three (American) Nobel Prize winners came from the ranks of its graduates, not to mention von Neumann and Edward Teller; it is now a parochial school again. →**Sárospatak; Pannonhalma; Piaristák**

fehér ló *white horse*; according to the legend (myth) of the Conquest (→*Honfoglalás*), Chieftain →*Árpád* made a present of a white horse to the Slav prince reigning over the territory of later-day Hungary, slyly asking for earth, grass and water in exchange, thereby making the prince symbolically hand his country over to the Magyars, which they, now considering it as their own, proceeded to settle.

fekete '*black*' (lit.), *coffee*; when he says he wants a *fekete*, every Hungarian means strong espresso (→*eszpresszó*) coffee, not (American-style) coffee without milk. →**kávé; dupla; eszpresszó**

fekete macska *black cat*; one of the most widespread superstitions around:

if a black cat runs across in front of us on the street, it means bad luck, and should it actually happen, some people will even turn back; it is also a sure sign of bad luck to walk under a ladder, and if the salt shaker toples over on the table, it signifies that an argument is in the offing. →**kéményseprő**

feketepiac *black market*; though today it is a part of history, everyone still remembers it vividly; the moment something disappeared from the shops (or there wasn't enough to go around, including beer, light bulbs, English textiles and →*Trabant* cars), it sprang up, as if by magic, on a geographically inditerminate, alternative marketplace; since it was considered (along with the corruption which was part and parcel of it) a natural adjunct of socialism (→*szocializmus*), those who offered their wares for sale (including housewives who engaged in a bit of smuggling to make ends meet) did not fall under public censure. →**lengyel piac; vám**

feles '*halfer*' (lit.), *tumbler*; in Hungary, hard drinks (spirits) are consumed half a deciliter at a time (without water or ice added), this is what people order, then quickly gulp down; smaller glasses or shots are usually not available in taverns (→*kocsma*), even though (in theory) there is such a thing as a 3 centiliter drink (the "small" cognac), but it is considered coffee shop (→*eszpresszó*) fare, and is generally ordered only by the ladies.

Felszabadulás *Liberation* (*Day*); →**April 4.**

Felvidék, a '*Highlands, the*' (lit.), *Upper Hungary*; the mountainous region of "historical Hungary" (→*történelmi Magyarország*) to the north of the Danube (→*Duna*), those fortunate counties (→*vármegye*) which were never occupied by the Turks (→*törökök*); today, the *Felvidék* is Slovakia proper (though the populace along the narrow southern lowlands is predominantly Hungarian-speaking), and Slovaks (→*szlovákok, a*) sorely resent their country being called its old Hungarian name. →**Délvidék; Kárpátalja; őrvidék; Erdély; Trianon**

fene '*gangrene*' (lit.), *bane*, *pox*; the name for various ugly ulcerous and festerous diseases which "feed on" the body; perhaps originally *fene* was some sort of wicked demon (like the →*manó*); today it is the most frequently used expletive which does not even count as cursing, as in " the pox take it!" (*a fene egye meg!*); strangely enough, the Hungarian for *enfant terrible* is "*fenegyerek*" (lit. bane child). →**franc(nyavalya)**; **bassza meg**; **káromkodás**

Ferenc József *Francis Joseph*; during his 68 years of reign over the →*Habsburg* Empire (including Hungary), he became the veritable emblem for his declining realm (which survived him by only two years), and so he lives in public imagination as an old man with a bald head and gray beard; he assumed his throne (1848), when the Hungarians were fighting a War of Independence (→*Szabadságharc*) against Austria (→*Ausztria*), and by the time he died (1916) as an old man, everyone knew that the Monarchy (→*Monarchia*) had lost WW I and was going to collapse, a fact which most of his subjects (who for many long years blamed his first fatherly then grandfatherly figure for everything that was good and bad, but in whose eyes he guaranteed the working order of all the institutions of the Empire) didn't mind very much, though he had spent his entire unhappy (one might say tragic) life as "the first public servant of the Empire", working hard and conscientiously for its upkeep (as far as his humble talents would allow); though the sociable Hungarians called him *Ferencjóska* (lit. Frankie-Joe), they could never forgive him for the deaths of the Martyrs of Arad (→*Aradi vértanúk*); on the other hand, the *redingote* was also called *ferencjóska*. →**Erzsébet királyné; Kiegyezés**

fiatalasszony '*young woman*' (lit.), *young lady*; today used only as the more courteous form of address for a woman (→*asszony*); it is the way a concierge (→*házmester*) or the stall-keeper at the market will address women (of a certain age); in the villages, they use the expression →*menyecske* instead. →**kisasszony**; **fiatalúr**; **megszólítás**

fiatalember *young man*; the courteous form of address for men from the ages of 16 to 50 whom one does not know (the equivalent of →*kisasszony*, or "little lady"); used to address someone under 16, it is a sign of jocular intimacy (but only when used by an older man to address a younger acquaintance).

fiatalúr '*young lord/gentleman*' (lit.), *young gentleman*; the term, now antiquated, was used by servants to address the son of the "master of the house"; it has a strong feudal sound to it, and is thus the equivalent of the term →*kisasszony* (young lady), rather than →*fiatalasszony* (young woman). →**úr**; **megszólítás**

finn-ugor rokonság *Finno-Ugric family (of languages)*; even though there is no Finno-Ugric language of which even one word (in its present form) would be comprehensible to a Hungarian, most linguists insist that the Hungarian language (→*magyar nyelv*) belongs to this family (by virtue of its syntax, at any rate); on the other hand, as opposed to the Finn connection (mockingly called "smelling of fish"), which many consider distant and alien, the number of those who opt for an Ugric (ancient Turkic) relationship is, if anything, growing (especially among laymen); while they also appeal to the science of linguistics, their arguments are often passionately voluble, fired by (among other things) the romantic sentiments they feel for their belligerent, equestrian ancestors who once roamed the *steppes*, though the most adamant champions of national pride, who don't care a jot for linguistics, have been insisting for over a century now that the true ancestor of Hungarian is the Sumerian (→*sumér*) tongue. →**hun-magyar rokonság**; **Honfoglalás**

foci *football, soccer*; →**futball**

forradalom, 1848 *revolution, 1848;* the historical upheaval when the modern, unified Hungarian nation (→*magyar nemzet*) was born, specifically, the War of Independence (→*Szabadságharc*) which errupted six months after the momentous day of March 15 (→*március 15*) and which, despite its defeat, remained in the national consciousness as something illustrious (which it was), and which →*Jókai* (who participated personally) called "times that changed one's soul"; it is such an unequivocally uplifting and ceremonious occasion in the history of Hungary, that every government, regardless of persuasion, has tried to turn it to its advantage by interpreting it to meet its own ends. →**Kossuth**; **Petőfi**; **Nemzeti dal**; **Világos**

forradalom, 1918 *revolution, 1918*; as a consequence of the defeat they suffered in WW I, in the autumn of 1918 every nation of the crumbling Austria–Hungary (→*Osztrák-Magyar Monarchia*) rushed to declare its independence from the Dual Monarchy (even – paradoxically – the Germans of Austria), including the Hungarians (bringing up the rear), and the politicians, who acted as the voice of the soldiers returning by the thousands from the front, declared the Republic (→*köztársaság*); this act became known as the "Michaelmas Daisy Revolution" (*őszirózsás forradalom*), because the soldiers stuck Michaelmas daisies, the flowers of All Souls' Day (→*Halottak Napja*) in their caps in place of the cap buttons with the crown on them; in the spring of 1919, in the midst of an increasingly hopeless and chaotic political and military situation, the communists (→*kommunisták*) took power, – most of them POWs returning from Russia with the dream of world revolution firing their breasts –, and declared the country (which by then was under partial foreign occupation) a Republic of Councils (i.e. *soviets*), and set up the dictatorship of the proletariat which was soon defeated (in turn) by the Romanian and Czech troops who were occupying the country with the consent of the western powers. →**Trianon**

forradalom, 1956 *revolution, 1956*; the bitter, desperate uprising against the Soviet Empire was one of the few events in the history of Hungary that was also of importance to the history of the world as a whole; the euphoric experience of the precious few days of freedom that followed the rapid, overnight collapse of an oppressive regime could never be forgotten, despite the forty-year-long, strict taboo against any mention of it; its defeat left an equally deep mark on the nation's consciousness, as did the painful realization that Hungary's fate was decided by the Great Powers, and not by the bloody fighting on the streets of Budapest; none the less, the events that led to the change in regime (→*rendszerváltás*) became irreversible (with every Hungarian citizen realizing this full well) when it was openly declared that what had happened in Hungary in 1956 was a revolution, and not a "counter-revolution" (→*ellenforradalom*). →**sajnálatos események**; **ötvenhat**; **Kádár János**; **Szabad Európa Rádió**; **szakáll**

forralt bor '*boiled wine*' (lit.), *mulled wine*; a tricky drink made by boiling (cheap) table wine with the addition of sugar and spices (especially cloves); it is consumed after long winter walks (and at ice skating rings) "to warm the spirits", as well as at home in the villages, and at unheated railroad stations. →**kalapkúra**

főispán '*main steward*' (lit.), *Lord Lieutenant* (*of a county*); formerly, the government-appointed overseer of a Hungarian county (→*megye*), and therefore, something like a prefect.→**alispán**

főzelék '*cooked* (*vegetable*) *dish*' (lit.), *vegetable roux*; garden vegetables (marrow, green peas, green beans, spinach, kohlrabi, etc.) are traditionally not eaten as salads (→*saláta*), nor prepared by stewing, but are cooked with the roux mixed in near the end of the cooking time to thicken the vegetables; the roux is made by lightly browning flour in fat (→*zsír*); without the roux the *főzelék* is considered "empty", and a poor man's dish; still, children usually eat it only under duress, especially savoy cabbage (→*kelkáposzta főzelék*). →**fasírt**

fradi (pron. *frah-dee*); short for the →*FTC* association football club; it was derived from *Franzstadt*, the German name of Ferencváros (an old industrial district of →*Pest*, the 9th, which was formerly inhabited mostly by German factory hands); sociologists consider its old rivalry with the →*MTK* club as the manifestation of the "competition" between the German (→*sváb*) and the Jewish (→*zsidó*) workers (→*munkásság*) and petit bourgeoisie of →*Pest*, in the late XIX. century race to assimilate (→*asszimiláció*); in order to lessen its poularity and (because its fans were considered anti-Semitic) to take the wind out of its sails, in the fifties (→*ötvenes évek*) it was renamed, but this did nothing to dampen the spirits of its enthusiastic fans, which was also true for the followers of the likewise renamed MTK: this was the extent of the tacitly approved freedom of the people, while the rivalry between the two teams has remained what it was to this day, even though the original spring and source of it has long since dried up.

franc(nyavalya) '*French* (*disease*)' (lit.), *bane*, *pox*; originally, the Hungarian name for syphilis (lit. *French bane*); the once dreaded curse, "May the pox – *French bane* – take it!) has, however, by now become an innocuous, frequently heard cry of despair; its use is the same as →*fene*. →**káromkodás**

francia *French*; the first component of many complex words, each of which refers to something surprising (possibly absurd) and out of the ordinary; for instance, a "French window" reaches down to the floor with only a narrow balcony railing in front of it; a "French cube" is a standing rectangle which, when it comes in the form of a notebook, is used by accountants to make their reckonings; a "French key" is one whose round sides (teeth) can be changed; and "French salad" is a kind of salad (→*saláta*) which has no *saláta* (Hungarian for "lettuce") in it at all, but has plenty of cooked green peas (and possibly →*párizsi*, or Bologna), swimming in mayonnaise instead. →**cseh**

franciák, a *French, the*; through the course of history, Hungarians have considered the French, whom they have only know from a distance, the idealized opposites of their all too familiar neighbors, the Germans (→*németek, a*) – i.e. Austrians -, whom they have known to be brawny, aggressive and narrow-minded, while the French have appeared to be refined, light hearted, easy going, and generous of spirit; though Hungarians have been visiting France since the Middle Ages, and in the 19th century Paris became the first stop of all political emigrés, there are only superficial stereotypes of France to this day, and few speak the language; on the other hand, fed by cultural currents and fashion trends, there is an appreciable amount of "francomania" among the Hungarian intelligentsia (→*értelmiség*), especially since, at the end of the last century, Hungarian modernism was inspired and influenced by French art and literature. →**angol; orosz; cseh; lengyel**

fröccs (pron. *frowtsh*), *spritzer*; onomatopoeic word which imitates the explosive, bubbly sound of the soda (seltzer) water forced into a glass of wine; the custom of adding soda water (sometimes mineral water or "wine water") to dry white (sometimes red) wine, thereby obtaining a refreshing bubbly brew which is consumed less for its alcoholic content than as a thirst-quencher on a hot summer's day, and also at meals (→*pörkölt*, →*zsíroskenyér*), is a Hungarian-Austrian tradition; depending on the size and the ratio of wine to soda, there is also such a thing as a "small spritzer", which is 1 dl. wine to1 dl. soda, and a "big spritzer", which is 2 dl. wine to 2 dl. soda, a "long step" or "big stride", which is 1 dl. wine to 2 dl. soda), and there is even a "concierge" (→*házmester*), which is 3 dl. wine to 2 dl. soda.

FTC an old and ever-popular association football team based in Budapest (*Ferencvárosi Football Club*) nicknamed the →*Fradi*, it is known today for its unruly fans, the Hungarian counterparts of English football hooligans ("*If you love Fradi, you'll be happy in life, / If you hurt Fradi, you'll be dead, / You must love Fradi, and hail the boys with us, / But if you hurt them, you'll be killed by us*"); its colors are green and white, which (according to their marching song) makes them "the green eagles". →**futball**

funkcionárius *functionary*; the official (though rarely used) name for Party (→*Párt*) bureaucrats; when used as part of the nomenclature, its shortened form *funkci* suggests a smug familiarity, while its use by an "outsider" is a sign of contempt and disdain, just like *elvti*, the unnatural, "endearing" form of →*elvtárs* (comrade), which had an even more hair-raisingly intimate form of endearment, *elvtikém* ("my little *elvti*").

futball *football, soccer*; its colloquial name is *foci*, which has pretty much taken the place of its official name; in Hungary only soccer is played, no other form of football is known. It was already wildly popular at the turn of the century (→*századforduló*), soon becoming the favorite sport of the petit bourgeoisie and the workers (→*munkásság*) – a state of affairs which has changed only to the extent that the concept of the petit bourgeoisie and the worker has changed. During the fifties (→*ötvenes évek*), when the Golden Team (→*Aranycsapat*) enjoyed its brief moment of glory, football became the one consolation of the entire nation (→*nemzet*), and the huge new *Népstadion* (*People's Stadium*) was the only place where people could let out their frustration at the top of their lungs (with the least fear of reprisal). Hungarian football fans have never forgotten the euphoria that the "boys with the golden legs" brought them; consequently, though for many years now the People's Stadium has not been filled to overflowing with spectators, the Hungarian national team can't play badly enough to discourage people from sitting in front of their television sets, hoping against hope for another miracle. →**MTK**; **FTC**; **Puskás Öcsi (vagy egy sorral bővíteni)**

függőfolyosó (körfolyosó) '*hanging corridor*', '*circular corridor*' (lit.); the official name for the →*gang*.

G

gang (függőfolyosó) *'hanging corridor'* (lit.), (pron. *ghaahngh*) *outside corridor, gallery, balcony*; until WW II, the majority of apartment houses (→*bérház*) in Hungarian towns and cities were built to form blocks around (generally rather small) interior courtyards; the cheaper apartments were accessible only from the outside corridor which runs around the insides of these houses and looks down on the yard, one on each floor. As opposed to the landlord's (the builder's) apartment, the largest in the house and situated on the first floor up, as well as the apartments that could be entered from the main stairway (i.e., which were "street-front" apartments), these "corridor apartments" were cheaper (most came with just one room and a kitchen, with the shared toilet down the end of the corridor), and the lives of their tenants, closely watched (and lorded) over by the concierge (→*házmester*), centered around the badly lit courtyard, which served as the playground for the children; the "climate", too, was different, for the air of the outdoor corridors was perpetually filled with the smell of (cheap) food coming from the kitchens, while the silence was continually broken by the sound of altercations, and so these apartments, and the outdoor corridors themselves, became synonymous with poverty. Naturally, the quality of such housing (and thus the social standing of the tenants) varied greatly; still, the majority of the populace lived in these poorer accommodations, which characterized old →*Budapest*, and most of which stood in ruins after WW II, and what remained just went from bad to worse after the nationalization (→*államosítás*) instituted by socialism (→*szocializmus*) – indeed, many still bear the marks of the war; at the same time, the larger apartments were first turned into co-tenancies (→*társbérlet*), then were actually divided up, and the only reason they did not turn into slums is because (almost) everyone was poor to begin with; then in the seventies, when large differences in income first began to divide the population, slummification, too, reared its ugly head, with everyone who could afford it moving into newly built apartments. →**albérlet**; **cselédlépcső**; **panel**

Gaudeamus igitur *Let us be merry...* (lit.); old Latin student song lauding the praises of student life (*"Let us be merry, while young we are..."*), which is sung at every graduation (→*ballagás*) in Latin (!) by the graduating class.

gazda *owner* (lit.); *farmer, husbandman*; generally meaning "landowner", or simply "owner", after decades of socialist "ownership", the term has acquired a new world-view, and is now used to refer to a person who manages what is truly his (mostly land) independently and with a sense of responsibility; the opposite of the "wage slave", he is the embodiment of the utopistic *citoyen.* →**paraszt**

Gellért-hegy *Mount Gellért;* →**Szent Gellért; augusztus 20.**

Gerbeaud *Gerbeaud's*; people call it *the* "Zserbó" (pron. *zher-bow*), a sign (*cf.* the definitive article and the hungarianized pronounciation) that the city regards it very much as its own. It is a renowned, hundred and fifty year old pastry shop (→*cukrászda*) on →*Vörösmarty tér*, which has retained its name (among the populace, at least, for under socialism, it was officially called →*Vörösmarty*, after the 19th century poet), and its original furnishings into the bargain (which, considering the recent, stormy history of the country is tantamount to a miracle); it has also kept up the quality of its cakes and pastries, though its regular customers, the old bourgeoisie of Pest, have long since been replaced by tourists, and elderly ladies (most widows) showing each other photographs of the children of their emigré (→*disszidens*) children, sitting at one of the minuscule tables as if left there by history, have become a rare sight, indeed. →**Gundel**

gimnázium '*gymnasium*' (lit.), *secondary school*; in today's school system, children go to gymnasium from 14 years of age, and take their finals when they graduate (→*érettségi*); though a student can go on to an institution of higher education after graduating any type of secondary school, only the gymnasium counts as a real "pre-college" institution of learning, especially if one wishes to enter upon a prestigeous course of study such as law or medicine.

gittegylet '*putty club/gang*' (lit.); in his early work, the novel for young people entitled *The Paul Street Boys*, the playwright Ferenc Molnár tells the story of two groups of adolescent boys living in Pest who fight each other for a vacant lot in the city (→*grund*) where they can play; one of the two gangs forms a self-important, bumptious club or society (which, in imitation of grown-ups, has a president, a treasurer, a seal, a records book, etc.) in order to collect as much putty as possible, which they get by scratching it out of the freshly glazed window frames of their school; the main activity of the club is to make sure that the putty remains soft, which they achieve by taking turns chewing it non-stop to prevent it from drying out; consequently, *gittegylet* has come to mean an organization with no real power or influcence busying itself with matters of little or no concern, and to say that the people at a meeting are just "chewing putty", means that there's a lot of talk (hot air), but no action. →**nemecsek ernő**; **Pál utcai fiúk, A**

góbé →**székely**

gombfoci '*button soccer*' (lit.), *table soccer*; the table game of adolescent boys (and adolescent-spirited men) played for want of the real thing; in the course of the game coat buttons are the "players" and a small button (from the fly of a pair of slacks) is the "ball", and the "players" are activated by giving a coat button a nudge with the nails of the thumb and index finger, which are brought and squeezed together, hoping that by sliding it across the "field" it will drive the "ball" into the goal; given the small size of apartments, it is/was usually played on the kitchen table, and there are regular "championships" organized, too; today the game (a kind of tiddly-winks) is being pushed out by electronics.

gombóc (*ball*) *dumpling*; a legendary home-made pastry made from dough worked together with boiled potatoes which is rolled out and filled with plums or peaches (on occasion jam, →*lekvár*), shaped into large-size dumplings and cooked in boiling water; it is served sprinkled with cinnamon sugar, and children and grown-ups alike can't wait to pierce it with a fork to see what is inside; everyone, in fact, has memories of some unforgettable *gombóc* or crepe (→*palacsinta*) eating contest from childhood. →**mákostészta; túróstészta**

Görgey Artúr (pron. *gowr-geh-yee*); →**áruló, az**

grund '*vacant lot* (*in a city*)'; according to Hungarian soccer (→*futball*) lore, the greatest football players have come from the ranks of proletarian children (→*proligyerek*) who played ball all day long on vacant city lots, as a result of which the sad decline of the game has consequently been attributed to the disappearance of these lots, in and out of Budapest; in Ferenc Molnár's perennial adolescent favorite, *The Paul Street Boys* (→*Pál utcai fiúk*), two gangs fight each other for possession of just such an empty lot, except, seeing how the story takes place at the turn of the century (→*századforduló*), the boys are not playing soccer yet, just war. In Molnár's own words, "*to the children of Pest the grund is open country, grassland and the Great Plains. It is a spell of freedom and boundlessness, this plot of ground that is hedged about by a rickety fence on one side, and by rearing walls stabbing skywards on the others.*" →**gittegylet**; **nemecsek ernő**

gulyás *goulash*; this dish is one of the few authentic contributions of Hungarian gastronomy to international cuisine, and even so, it usually resembles a stew, whereas it is supposed to be more like a soup. It is a traditional herdsmen's food (*gulya* = "herd", hence the name *gulyás*) as cooked by them; it is prepared with the beef cut into cubes, placed in a kettle (→*bogrács*) and cooked a blanc on a slow fire for about 2-3 hours with lots of water, onions and paprika (→*pirospaprika*), and is served with potatoes cut into cubes or small-size noodles (*csipetke*) added near the end of the cooking time; the fact that the name for a traveling canteen in the military is called a "goulash cannon" speaks volumes about the status of this well-known dish.

gulyáskommunizmus *goulash communism*; this expression, coined in the seventies by Western journalist in response to the relatively humble well-being of Hungarians and their (relative) easy lives became a trite cliché almost the moment it appeared on the scene; still, the humorous expression the Hungarians themselves came up with to characterize this same period in their history is not only more ironic, but also more to the point: "Hungary is the merriest barrack in the camp", a bitter play on words, with *láger*, or camp, referring not only to the Peace Camp, the name for the satellite nations of the Soviet Union (→*Szovjetunió*), but also to the (concentration) camps of WW II.

Gundel *Gundel's*; this renowned restaurant and Gerbeaud's (→*Gerbeaud*) were the two bright stars of the world of the bourgeoisie of Budapest; like Gerbeaud's, it too bears the name of its 19th century founder; in the post-war years it lost most of its lustre, but after the change in regime (→*rendszerváltás*), it was revived and is once again one of the best restaurants in Central Europe (→*Közép Európa*), though (again, just like Gerbeaud's), it too has lost its old clientele, who could never even pay for a humble meal here any more.

gyász *mourning*; in Hungary, too, black is the color of mourning, though except for elderly widows (who never take off their mourning clothes), black is worn only for a brief time, while a veil is only worn at funerals, if at all; requiems and the tradition of holding a (humble) wake following the funeral are, however, still holding their own. →**temetés**

gyászhuszár *'grief-hussar'* (lit.), *pallbearer*; this unusual pairing of words did double duty; originally (from the mid-19th century onwards), the expression was used in reference to those who assisted at funerals (but not the gravediggers!), because these ceremonial occasions called for the wearing of black hussar-type (→*huszár*) uniforms (during the 19th century, the hussar uniform served as the prototype for just about every non-military uniform); through the years its meaning was expanded, and today it is generally used teasingly in reference to anyone who acts, as the English saying goes, as a "wet blanket". →**ravatal**, **sír(emlék**; **temetés**

gyia! (pron. *dyee-ah*): the equivalent of *giddyup* or *giddap*, this is the sound to make a Hungarian horse get moving; if we want to stop the cart or wagon, we have to say *hőő* (pron. *huuw*).

Győr (pron. *dyowr*); the largest industrial center of Transdanubia (→*Dunántúl*) and an episcopal city in baroque; the town is situated half-way between Vienna (→*Bécs*) and →*Budapest* at the confluence of the Danube (→*Duna*) and →*Rába* rivers; one of its dubious claims to fame is the fact that it was here that in 1809 Napoleon's army beat the Hungarian army of nobles (→*nemes*); today it has become one of the main headquarters of the multi-national companies (→*multik*) operating in Hungary.

H

Habsburgok, a *Habsburgs, the*; in Hungary, when people refer to "the Habsburgs", they generally mean the Central-European empire they ruled (and not the dynasty itself), almost as if Hungary had not been a part of it (which it was until its defeat and post-war dissolution in 1918); this use of the word also shows the ambivalent relationship of the Hungarians to their Viennese (→*Bécs*) king, who wore several crowns besides the crown of Hungary, and against whose domination the Hungarians fought for 350 years, knowing full well at the same time, that for their country, seen from Vienna, as a distant ("Asiatic") and dangerous, alien land, the Empire provided a lifeline to Europe (→*Európa*), and also protected them (with various degrees of success) from the Eastern powers in exchange for its political independence, as a consequence of which the relationship between Austria (→*Ausztria*) and Hungary was like a badly conducted yet necessary and indissoluble "marriage of convenience". →**Kiegyezés**; **labanc**; **kuruc**; **Ferenc József**; **Szabadságharc**

hagyma *onion*; →**vöröshagyma; kékhagyma**

hajdú (pron. *hoy-doo*), *irregulars, liveried attendant*; today a popular family name; originally it referred to ill-reputed light cavalry irregulars of the 17th century recruited from among cowherds and desperados of dubious nationality, who populated in great numbers the frontier lands between warring Austria and Turkey i.e., they were the Central-European (→*közép-európa*) equivalent of the Cossack; in the early 18th century they were settled into the depopulated middle area of the Great Plain (→*Alföld*), which became knows as the Hajdúság, or "land of the Hajdús" (which today is part of Hajdú-Bihar County stretching to the eastern border of the country); in the 19th century, the *hajdú* were the law enforcement officers of the old county (→*megye*) governments who wore uniforms (→*egyenruha*) similar to the hussars (→*huszár*), and when they also went the way of history, the name was used for (liveried) office clerks, door keepers and janitors. →**bocskai**

Hajdúság →**hajdú**

hal *fish*; Hungarian housewives generally do with fish, on the rare occasion that they serve it, what they do with everything else: they either broil it or serve it breaded and fried, or else quick-cook it with onion and →*paprika*, with all other methods of preparing it being considered the task of a master chef; though there are a hundred types of fish in the rivers and lakes, of the domestic catch usually only carp (→*ponty*) is available at the markets, and even that is eaten in large quantities only at Christmas (→*Karácsony*), when it is the must-have fare. →**halászlé**; **keszeg**; **süllő**

hálapénz '*gratitude money*' (lit.), *tip, gratuity*; for decades Hungarian doctors were so badly paid by the government, that it became the custom to "thank" the doctors for their services with a gift of money (or some other form of gratuity), until it became part of a physician's regular income (after which now he must pay taxes); though there is no official "schedule of charges", it has even been given a chaste and medically sounding Latin name (*parasolventia*); though experience has shown that even without "gratuity money" a doctor will do the best he can for his patients, all efforts at stopping such donations (including a rise in doctor's salaries) has come to naught.

Halászbástya '*Fishermen's Bastion*' (lit.); the neo-Romanesque lacy stone backdrop for the Matthias Church (→*Mátyás-templom*) in Buda's Castle area which is unlike anything else anyone has ever seen; it was built at the end of the 19th century in place of a medieval bastion which was supposed to have been defended during sieges by the Fishermen's Guild; though architects have always been annoyed by this unabashedly spectacle-oriented complex, people like it, and during the one-hundred years of its existence, it has become an organic part of Castle Hill, though possibly our eyes have simply become accustomed to it.

halászlé '*fishermen's brew*' (lit), *fish soup*; the only food made from fish which is considered authentic enough and is thought highly enough of even for men to make it (of course, mostly fishermen), what's more, they are convinced that women don't really know how to cook it properly, and so there is usually no female participation in the *halászlé* contest held yearly at the riverside town of Baja on the →*Danube*; the *halászlé* from →*Szeged* is supposedly the best (perhaps because of the →*paprika*); be it as it may, it should be prepared over an open fire in a kettle (→*bogrács*) with many kinds of fish and (according to real gourmands) in fresh river water. →**hal**; **ponty**; **Karácsony**

háló '*net*' (lit.), *shopping bag*; today the word conjures up images of poor, old, unfortunate ladies toddling along with their shopping, but until the recent advent of plastic shopping bags and other forms of packaging, when someone went shopping he or she took something with them to carry what they bought; indeed, for many long years people would always carry some sort of bag with them which took up little space, in case blind luck would help them find something worth buying as they trod the streets of the city; the most popular form of shopping bag was the so-called *net* (also called →*cekker* and *szatyor*, or bag), an object of convenience made from string (or plastic filament) that would take up the shape of whatever was placed inside, until the plastic bags brought back from trips to the West (or received at airport Tax Free shops) and carefully preserved until they were literally worn to shreds from use (and also to show that its owner had seen the world), forced them out of existence; the jocular expression "old bag" (*vén szatyor*), used to refer to old women, has come into use probably because of the wrinkles on these old-type "net" bags.

hálószoba *bedroom*; the bedroom of a Hungarian (or any Central-European) worker (→*munkás*), petit bourgeois and peasant is furnished with a bed placed in the middle of one wall with a big, cheap holy picture hanging above it (in Catholic households, at any rate), or else a posed wedding portrait taken of the bride (holding her wedding bouquet) and the groom (with his arm around the bride), taken at the photographer's, while a small couch is placed at the foot of the bed for the child to sleep on (in the small, two-room apartments there is no separate nursery), while along the wall opposite there stand two identical, ungainly wardrobes; the much smaller but more numerous rooms of the prefab (→*panel*) apartments built under socialism (→*szocializmus*) put an end to this arrangement, for in them the beds must be pushed up against the wall, one behind the other, if they are to fit at all, while the child sleeps in a tiny chamber that opens from the hall (→*előszoba*), and instead of holy pictures, there are generally wall hangings (→*falvédő*) above the beds; only the wedding pictures are the same.

Halottak Napja *'the Day of the Dead'* (lit.); →**Mindenszentek**

három per három *III./3.*; a special devision of the secret police of the socialist state (the III./3.) involved with state security, specifically, with those who voiced opinions in any way contrary to the official dogma, and especially with spying on and harassing organizations initiated by them; though it was nothing like the East German Stasi, and especially nothing like the Romanian Securitate, just as in its heyday Hungarian socialism (→*szocializmus*) was not as unbearable as the regime in the GDR or Romania, it embittered the lives of many none the less, and its very existence put fear in the hearts of the people, who were very much conscious of the fact. →ÁVÓ

Háry János (pron. *haw-ry*); a mustachioed hussar (→*huszár*) of the Napoleonic wars who supposedly captured the emperor himself, and the Hungarian version of the "bragging soldier"; Zoltán Kodály wrote an opera based on the tall stories about him.

hat-három *six to three* (lit.); the greatest victory in the history of Hungarian football (→*futball*), when on November 25, 1953 the Golden Team (→*Aranycsapat*) beat the English select team 6 to 3 on home ground in Wembley, where they had never been beaten before; its self-confidence having been destroyed by the war and dictatorship, the nation (→*nemzet*) was in such great need of this victory, that those who were just young boys at the time know the names of the players of the Hungarian team, whom they consider national heroes, by heart; besides, during those years, sports were the only legalized form of giving vent to the need for national identity; according to state propaganda, this victory, too, proved the superiority of socialism (→*szocializmus*). →**Puskás**

hatvanas évek *the sixties*; this decade is not the least bit nostalgic for Hungarians, for it was at its end that the first post-revolutionary (→*forradalom, 1956*) generation came of age, whom, however, the →*Kádár* regime could integrate only by the carefully portioned granting of concessions, such as passports (→*útlevél*), even though the results of the consolidation that followed the "regretable events" (→*sajnálatos események*) were also making themselves felt; for instance, pre-fab (→*panel*) housing was becoming available, people were buying frigidaires and television sets, and instead of food, they were now standing on line for →*Trabant* cars, not to mention their first, cathartic experience of seeing the West first hand; at the same time, the watching and harassment of the intelligentsia (→*értelmiség*) continued, and so the disgruntlement of the youth of the West could break through the Iron Curtain only in the form of their new, defiant music, conceived of behind the Curtain as a message of freedom; still, with all its concessions and promises of economic →*reform*, the decade ended in a general feeling of hopelessness, epitomized in the shameful march into Czechoslovakia, which not only ushered in a new political Ice Age, but also put a quick end to any talk of reforming the Hungarian economy. →**gulyáskommunizmus**

haza, a '*home*(*land*), *the*' (lit.); unless used in a context such as *haza megyek* ("I am going home"), when it means the "family home", the word (when used with the definite article) invariably refers to the homeland ("fatherland"), and has a heightened, noble, and ceremonious ring to it (as a consequence of which, being a political concept, it is used mostly by politicians, while the common folk says *ország*, or "country", instead); it is of 19th century coinage and just like the German *Vaterland*, is charged with emotion (pathos).

Hazádnak rendületlenűl légy híve, oh magyar… '*Oh, Magyar, keep immovably your native country's trust …*' (transl. Watson Kirkconnell); the first words of the poem "*Appeal*" (→*Szózat*), which continues: "*…for it has born you, and at death / will consecrate your dust!*" The sombre ode by →*Vörösmarty*, which provides a survey of the tragic events of Hungarian history, also conjures up the recurring 19th century nightmare of the death of the nation ("*Or there shall come, if come there must, / a death of fortitude; / and round about our graves shall stand / a nation washed in blood. // Around the graves where we shall die / a weeping world will come, / and millions will* *in pity gaze / upon the martyrs' tomb ...*"), and so is one of the first, powerful documents of national pessimism (→*pesszimizmus*); having been set to music, it is the second, unofficial anthem of the nation. →**Himnusz**

házmester '*master of the house*' (lit.), *concierge, super, superintendent*; earlier, on the ground floor of every apartment building there was an apartment (near the main entrance) set aside for the concierge, the all powerful representative of the landlord, then after nationalization (→*államosítás*) of the Council (→*Tanács*); besides seeing to various small tasks around the building, he also collected the rent, kept a record of the tenants, was in charge of peace and order in the house, not to mention its cleanliness, and at night, he opened the gate for those who came in late, for which he received a modest sum (the "*door-money*"); there were many years during the course of post-war history when much depended on his good will, for police investigations always began at his door; he was not a popular figure, but after the disappearance of the institution of the concierge in the sixties (→*hatvanas évek*), the apartment houses (→*bérház*), now owned by the tenants, began to decline at such an alarming pace, that people began to think back on their near tyranny with something like nostalgia; for some unfathomable reason, the strongest type of spritzer (→*fröccs*), which is made with 3 dl. wine and 2 dl. soda water is also called *házmester*. →**gang**

Házsongárdi temető (pron. *hah-zhon-gahrdee*); cemetery; the old cemetery of →*Kolozsvár* which, because of the great number of famous Hungarians (scientists, priests, writers) buried there is considered the Pantheon of Transylvania (→*Erdély*); it is the bounden duty of anyone visiting Kolozsvár from the mother country to pay it a visit. →**Kerepesi úti temető**; **Farkasréti temető**; **Kozma utcai temető**; **Újköztemető**

helyesírás *orthography, spelling*; Hungarian spelling is very simple; with the exception of certain irregularities, everything is written the way it is pronounced, with every sound having an equivalent letter (sometimes with an accent over it) or a certain fixed combination of letters, yet this does not mean that every sound (letter) is always pronounced the same regardless of its placement in a word, or even that every letter is always pronounced (a native speaker, for example, has difficulty pronouncing two consonants placed next to each other, even though, thanks to the logic of Hungarian word formation, he is often confronted with this hurdle); Hungarian spelling also still includes certain letters which are no longer pronounced. →**y**; **magyar nyelv**

Herend (pron. *heh-rend*); the name of the town in the →*Bakony* mountains which has given its name to the internationally known Hungarian porcelain that has been produced there since the mid-19th century; every middle class family in Hungary has a set of Herend tableware stashed away in the buffet (provided there is room for such a big old 19th century piece of furniture in their apartment); the set, which usually consists of 12 or more settings, was generally given to the grandmother (or her grandmother) as a wedding gift, though the antiquated, slightly awkward silverware that accompanied it has long since fallen victim to the ravages of history; this Herend ware, which usually has several pieces broken or missing, is taken out only on special occasions, and with the greatest of care, so that the next generation to inherit it will not have to do with even fewer pieces. Of the several famous Herend patters, the "Victoria" pattern enjoys the most esteem; designed in the 19th century for the Queen of England, its pieces have a whole menagerie of small insects climbing around in between leaves of grass and colorful wild flowers. →**Zsolnay**

Hét vezér, a *Seven Chiefts, the* (lit.); according to the tradition taken from medieval chronicles, seven tribes (whose names have come down to us through place names) formed an alliance for the Conquest (→*Honfoglalás*) with →*Árpád* at its head, whom they (literally) "raised to the shield" which, just like the "compact sealed (literally) with blood" (→*vérszerződés*), has now become a jocular expression.

Himnusz '*hymn*' (lit.); *national anthem*; probably the most solemn of any in the world, the Hungarian national anthem belongs to the literary genre of "prayer" (written on January 22, 1823 by the poet and politician Kölcsey); in it, the Hungarian people turn in supplication to God with these words:"*Bless the Magyar, Lord we pray, / Nor in bounty fail him, / Shield him in the bloody fray / When his foes assail him. / He whom ill-luck long has cursed / This year grant him pleasure, / He has suffered with the worst / Time beyond all measure.*" (trans. George Szirtes); on special occasions this first stanza of the anthem is sung (to music composed by →*Erkel* in 1844) with the audience standing up. →**Szózat**; **magyarok Istene, a**; ***Boldogasszony, anyánk...***

Hogy van? *How are you? (How do you do?)*; the question asked (right after the usual words of greeting) by old acquaintances (not too close) who meet only infrequently; as a rule, it is not taken seriously, but if we feel like, we can go into the details; the usual answer is the cliché „*lassacskán*" (so-so) or the equally nondescript „*megvagyok*" (I'm all right, I'm fine.).

hódoltság '*conquered land*' (lit.), *occupation*; the period of Hungarian history ushered in by the battle of →*Mohács* (1526) and closed with the victorious siege of →*Buda* (1686); lasting for 150 years, it was the time when the middle section of the country, which formed the largest one-third of it, became part of the Turkish (→*török*) empire, while the western and northern regions were annexed to the →*Habsburg* Empire, and Transylvania (→*Erdély*), which paid taxes to the Turk, functioned as a relatively independent principality; the Protestants of the period saw themselves as the defenders of the country in face of two pagan powers (the Catholic and the Muslim empires), while today people hold that it was this period (the never ending wars and the Asian-type trade and administration of the Turks) which put an end to Hungary's European-type (→*Európa*) development; indeed, the country still bears the marks of the *hódoltság* (for instance, the areas that were under Turkish occupation vote differently from the rest of the country even today); the Soviet occupation (the presence of the troops of the new Eastern Empire) was often compared to the Turkish occupation.

Hol volt, hol nem volt … '*once there was, once there wasn't*' (lit.), *once upon a time*; the formula with which Hungarian folk tales begin, and which continues: "*there lived a king who…*"; this antiquated formula, whose meaning has been lost in the mist of time, is Finno-Ugrian in origin, just like the phrase →*mentek, mendegéltek…* ("they went on and on a little"), and many other phrases, too, where the meaning is doubled, and whose parallel motifs can be found in the lore of kindred peoples. →**Óperencia**

Honfoglalás '*the Conquest of the fatherland*' (lit.); also known as "the landtaking of the Magyars", it is the event whose 1100th anniversary was celebrated by the country in 1996, albeit with far less glorious trappings (and especially with far less self-confidence) than the Millennial (→*Millennium*) celebrations of 1896, in whose honor →*Budapest* became a true metropolis with many beautiful new public buildings, among others the railway stations, the underground, and the new Houses of Parliament; the "conquest", or occupation of the Carpathian Basin was a carefully planned military manoeuvre and a masterpiece of logistics, for an entire and numerous people settled in their new homeland with all their beasts and tangibles after traveling hundreds of miles (from the Sea of Azov in the southern part of today's Ukraine) to get out of the way of the Pechenegs, who were on the move as the next wave of the Great Migrations. Its memory lost none of its strength throughout the centuries; in fact, it was with recourse to it that the Hungarian nobility (→*nemesség*) legitimized its power through armed conquest, while the idea that "We have come a long way to build a new nation" is as central to Hungarian culture as it is to American popular lore, and it keeps cropping up in the media as a rather bombastic metaphore. →**honfoglalók**; **Pusztaszer**; **hun–magyar rokonság**; **őshaza**; **Árpád**; **vérszerződés**; **Hét Vezér, a**; **Verecke**

honfoglalók, a '*the* (*Magyar*) *conquerors of the fatherland*' (lit.); the tribes who had come from the *steppes* and who formed an alliance through a blood contract (→*vérszerződés*) in order to proceed with the →*Honfoglalás*, or the settlement of their new homeland in the Carpathian Basin through a series of clever military manoeuvers with chieftain →*Árpád* at their head, had different roots (Finno-Ugric, Avar, Iranian), though according to archeological finds were culturally united; they were about 2 to 3 hundred thousand in number, and must have found about the same number of Slavic and possibly Avar (Turkic) agrarian peoples on their new land; the nomadic, warlike people of the *steppes* brought with them the shamanistic religion and economic culture of wandering tribes (though even the sign of the cross appears on sabretaches found in their tombs); though the "conquerors" must have found it difficult to learn the sedentary lifestyle of the Slavs whom they assimilated (and from whom many words associated with a sedentary lifestyle can be found in the Hungarian language), barely a century later the Kingdom of Hungary came into being as part of the European world order, with St. Stephen (→*Szent István*) as its first Christian king. →**ki a magyar?**

honvéd '*defender of the fatherland*' (lit.), soldier; a word coined during the War of Independence (→*Szabadságharc*) which has become the generic word for a Hungarian soldier); it is also the official name of any (Hungarian) soldier (private) who is not an officer. →**baka**

honvédség '*the defenders of the the fatherland*' (lit.), the official name for the Hungarian military (→*katonaság*), first coined and used for the first independent Hungarian army organized during the War of Independence (→*szabadságharc*); it is the official designation of the military, which is popularly called *sereg*, short for *hadsereg*, or army; when written in capital letters (→*Magyar Honvédség*), it is the official name of today's armed forces. →**baka**; **egyenruha**

horgolás *crocheting*; in times past, when every girl was taught crocheting and embroidery, every proper housewife made her own doilies for her home (called "the poor man's lace"); today, crocheting has become a veritable home industry (a branch of modern folk art, or →*népművészet*), whereby homemakers can make a little extra money on the side by offering their wares on streets and open markets; their pieces, decorated with patters in imitation of those found in 19th century bourgeois homes, continue to hold their own in the homes of the petit bourgeoisie, who like to put them on tables, the headrests of armchairs, atop television sets, and under vases.

Hortobágy (pron. *howr-toh-bodj*); the iconic terrain of the Hungarian →*puszta* situated in the middle of the Great Plain (→*Alföld*), near →*Debrecen* which is a national park today; until the regulation of the river →*Tisza* the entire flatlands were really tide lands and pastures; today it is a desert-like *steppe* where certain types of animals (cattle, goats) brought here by the tribes who settled the land (→*honfoglalók*) are still bred as a kind of "live gene–bank" and also to attract tourists, along with the once famous stud farms. →**délibáb**

hölgy *lady/madam*; the feminine equivalent of →*úr* (sir), and →*úriember* (gentleman), though in the chaos and uncertainty of how to address people (→*megszólítás*) that appeared after the change in the regime (→*rendszerváltás*), it became a veritable "police word" used not as a form of deferential address, but as a way to refer to women who were anything but ladies (such as pickpockets caught in the act or streetwalkers); however, since the other common forms of address, *asszony* ('married woman') or *nő* ('woman', as used on the doors of public places of convenience!), have lately picked up discourteous connotations, so much so that even sport reporters have stopped talking about *női* ('women's') competitions in favor of *hölgy* competitions, the word *hölgy* has become the slightly affected synonym for *woman* instead of what it once was – a sign of social standing. →**úrnő**; **úrhölgy**; **úr**; **néni**

hun-magyar rokonság *Hunno-Magyar family/relationship* (lit.); in its fully developed form, the origin of this "scientific" theory can be traced back to romantic 18th century notions when, alongside the conquering Magyar heroes (→*honfoglaló*) the family trees of proud aristocrats suddenly began sprouting branches leading back to the Hun chieftains as well. Modern science treats this Hunno-Magyar relationship with scepticism, though the idea of Eastern origins was always part of the national consciousness, and early chronicles have recourse to it as the legitimization of the Conquest (→*Honfoglalás*): the people of →*Árpád* occupied their new home, the former land of →*Attila* (→*Hunnia*, the "Promised Land") as their rightful heritage ("*The lord has given back Pannonia to the Hungarians, like the sons of Israel received... the land of Canaan... as their inheritance.*"). Medieval chroniclers also trace the Árpád dynasty (→*Árpád-ház*) to →*Hunor*. →**őshaza**; **sumér-magyar rokonság**; **Csodaszarvas, a**

Hunnia *Land of the Huns*; in present usage the name refers not to the early-medieval empire of the Huns, but to that virtual half of Hungary whose heart (as opposed to the equally virtual →*Pannónia*) prides itself on the heritage of →*Attila*, namely, the Hunno-Magyar relationship (→*hun–magyar rokonság*); emphasizing the (dubious) Asiatic character of the present-day people of the land of Hungary, they are proud to own up to the caricature of the galloping "dog-headed" nomadic horseman which the chauvinists of neighboring peoples like to draw of the barbaric Hungarians as of old; it is also the lyrical synonym for the part of the country which lies east of the Danube.

Hunor és Magyar →**Csodaszarvas, a**

húsleves és rántottcsirke (rántott-hús) uborkasalátával *chicken soup and fried chicken (breaded meat) with pickle salad*; the classical Sunday (→*vasárnap*) lunch whose unmistakeable odor fills the yards and stairwells of apartment houses (→*bérház*) and every nook and cranny of peasant houses as well, all this in brilliant sunshine, to the sound of church bells coming from the radio and signaling the hour of noon; it is traditionally served with onion-fried potatoes (→*törtkrumpli*) in winter, and with parsleyed new potatoes in summer, and is eaten accompanied by a glass of spritzer (→*fröccs*) made with dry white wine.

Húsvét *Easter*; one of the few Church holidays (besides Christmas, or →*Karácsony*) when even non-church goers attend Friday Mass (in Catholic churches, the lifelike statue of the crucified Christ, bedecked with flowers, lies in front of the altar), and they may even join the procession (in which they take the Host around the streets); it is a family holiday which peaks with Saturday night dinner, which always consists of smoked ham (→*sonka*) and hard-boiled eggs, followed by walnut or poppy-seed rolls (→*beigli*). →**locsolás**; **nyuszi**

huszár *hussar*; in every European language a word of Hungarian extraction, a sign that the fighting methods of the light cavalry which were so swiftly adopted all over Europe in the early 18th century were of Hungarian origin; they were spread far and wide by Hungarian soldiers (mercenaries), whose typical frogged jackets and pants were adopted in unison with their characteristic manner of combat, and this is how the colorful and ornate dress of contemporary Hungarian men and soldiers (→*kuruc*) became a standard, prescribed uniform (→*egyenruha*); in Hungary, "hussar" is practically a synonym for "soldier"; boys like to dress up as hussars for their school masquarades, while at country fairs (→*búcsú*) they buy plastic hussar swords and red paper hussar shakos, not to mention gingerbread (→*mézeskalács*) hussars; men sporting ribbons with the national colors (→*nemzetiszín*) who ride in St. Stephen's Day celebrations (→*Szent István*) in the countryside and at harvest (→*szüret*) festivals are also called "hussars" (just like the knights in chess); in the last century, every (non-military) uniform resembled a hussar uniform, even that of porters and gate keepers; as for today, a surprising, quick, clever and daring deed is still called a *huszárcsíny* ('hussar trick') or *huszárvágás* (lit. 'hussar-cut'), and when someone stands his ground in a difficult or dangerous situation, he is praised as being *huszáros* ('like a hussar'). →**magyaros ruha**; **kacagány**; **gyászhuszár**

I

IBUSZ (pron. *eeboos*); the oldest Hungarian travel and ticket office whose initials (the origin of which have been obscured by time) have become synonymous with "travel office" in general. →**útlevél**

ideiglenesen itt állomásozó '*temporarily stationed (here)*' (lit.); the official phrase used to designate the occupying Soviet forces stationed in Hungary; the expression served as the source of many a joke, but none funnier (and sadder) than the official news item from the seventies which informed the populace that in Kecskemét (where there was a large Soviet military base), "the temporarily stationed Soviet officers have just moved into their permanent private residences" (→*öröklakás*).

induló *march, marching song*; today practically a historical concept (except for the military), not so long ago the marching song was the indispensable appurtenance of every holiday; on the First of May (→*május elseje*), for instance, the radio began its morning broadcast with so called mass songs (→*tömegdal*), or pseudo-working class songs, whose rhythm was deemed perfect to get the working masses (→*munkás*) into the mood for the May Day parade. →**Klapka-induló**; **Rákóczi-induló**

író '*writer*' (lit.), *prose writer*; since until recently Hungarian culture was mostly verbal and cerebral, the writer, a term which includes poets, prose writers, essayists, newspaper critics, even professors of literature – in short, everyone having anything to do with literature (the "*irodalmár*"), but most especially poets (→*költő*), enjoyed the sort of fame, popularity and prestige unimaginable in most other cultures. The best writers were influential not only in general, but politically and socially as well, especially since at all times the literate (as well as the non-literate) public expected them to engage in public affairs; consequently, literature was not read (either by the curious public or fearful politicians) only for its own sake, but because it was an ideological 'weapon', as understood by leninists. Indeed, since the early 19th century, literature and politics have been so closely linked that (for want of the real thing) in the 1980s the conventions of the Writers' Association acted as a veritable people's Parliament of sorts, and noted writers, who made many personal appearances, participated in the political preparations for the change in regime (→*rendszerváltás*), not to mention the actual change in government. →**Bánk bán**; ***Talpra magyar …***; **értelmiség**

Isten *God*; →**magyarok istene, a**

Isten áldja (magát) '*God bless you*' (lit.); an antiquated form of bidding farewell with a countryside tone to it, but which none the less continues to hold its own.

Isten, áldd meg a magyart... *'Bless the Magyar, Lord we pray...'* (lit.); the first words of the National Anthem (→*Himnusz*), which continues: "... *Nor in bounty fail him, / shield him in the bloody fray / when his foes assail him...*"; its first stanza closes with the plaintive words "... *This year grant him pleasure, / He has suffered with the worst / Time beyond all measure.*" (trans. G. Szirtes), laden with remorse and self-pity. →**Szózat**

izé (pron. *ee-zay*); a most useful word variously defined as *what's-t('s name), what-d'ye'call-it, thingummy, thinkamabob, thing(ly), whatchamacallit,* and even *gadget.* In short, it's *"that-thing-which-I've-temporarily-forgotten-the-name-of".* Occasionally used az an adjective, to suggest annoying behaviour in constructions that translate like "*Your are such an* izé!" and "*Don't be so* izé!". To be used only in informal situations.

J

Jancsi-kancsó '*Jancsi jug*' (lit.); also known as *Miska-kancsó*, or Miska jug (*Jancsi* is the diminutive of →*János*, *Miska* of *Mihály*); these are richly ornamented masterpieces of Hungarian village potters generally turned on the wheel in the shape of a man, often a hussar (→*huszár*) with a perky turned-up moustache and a pot belly (the Hungarian equivalent of the Toby jug), whose shako is the mouth of the jug, while the painted, convex stripes painted across its body are his short dolman and frogging; sometimes a green serpent is also painted on these jugs (*cf.* Aesculapius) to remind one and sundry that its contents are medicinal.

János *John*; far and wide the most frequent Hungarian first name for a man; there is even a saying that "*God himself is János*".

János vitéz *John the Valiant*; the most popular and best loved literary work for the past hundred and fifty years; the classical long poem by Sándor →*Petőfi* written in the style of an epic folk ballad or tale with an engratiatingly light and jocular touch which has become a veritable national (→*nemzeti*) epic; it tells the story of a poor shepherd boy who, in order to flee his hapless fate, joins up with a regiment of hussars (→*huszár*), and after many incredible adventures (fighting dragons, grappling with giants, not to mention a whole Turkish army), he wins the hand of the beautiful daughter of the king of France in marriage; however, he declines the offer and returns, now as a triumphant hussar, to his humble village and the sweetheart he left behind.

jóember/jóasszony '*good man/woman*' (*lit.*); the from of address used for someone clearly of lower social standing, which contains both a touch of benevolence and condescension.

Jókai Mór (pron. *yaw-kah-yee*); an admirably prolific writer whose brilliant 19th century oeuvre is still read with relish one-hundred years after his death, and not only as a school–classic; a brilliant story teller and a true romantic, he wrote novels which are a veritable encyclopedia of the characteristic figures of 19th century Hungary; his works (including *A Hungarian Nabob* and *Midst the Wild Carpathians*) have also appeared (at the turn of the century) in England and America, where he was known as Maurus Jókai.

jónapot '*good day*' (lit.); since there is no "good afternoon" in Hungarian, this form of greeting (→*köszöntés*) is used throughout the day, except for the morning, when people wish each other "good morning".

jonatán *Jonathan* (*apple*); Hungarians are almost unanimously united in believing that there is no apple as fine as this tasty variety grown in →*Szabolcs* county; it lasts till spring, filling the pantry (→*éléskamra*) or room with its mouth-watering scent when stored atop a wardrobe before it is eaten.

józan, paraszti ész '*sober, peasant mentality*' (lit.); *common sense*; according to popular concensus, when overcomplicated intellectual speculation and standard official thinking gets us nowhere, this is what we must turn to; it is the synonym of rational, practical thinking.

József Attila (pron. *yoh-zhef*); it is now more than sixty years that the brilliant and inspired but poor and humiliated young man threw himself in front of a speeding train, but he is still possibly the best loved poet (→*költő*) in Hungary today whose poems are available on tape and have been set to music, and whom even young people read, reciting his poems by heart; in the course of his short life he experienced the best and the worst stirrings of the human heart and soul, and had the words to set it all down on paper.

június 16. *June 16th*; the day in 1958 when Imre Nagy, Prime Minister during the revolution (→*forradalom, 1956*), was executed along with his fellow politicians, and also the day when in 1989 their coffins were laid out in state (before their reburial) as part of a huge mass demonstration on Heroes' Square – a great and cathartic moment in the change in regime (→*rendszerváltás*). Almost to the day just one year after the reburial, Soviet troop withdrawals from Hungary ended, while ten years later, the young man who addressed the crowds (as "fellow citizens", which is quite unusual in Hungarian) on June 16th was elected the new Prime Minister of Hungary. →**temetés**,

K

kacagány besides being some sort of ancient Hungarian (→*ősmagyar*) piece of clothing, its nature remains shrouded (in part, at least) in mystery for most people; the word, however, has such a humorous sound to it (*kacagni* = to laugh), that it is often used; actually, in more recent centuries, including the 18th, it was the name of a short military cloak made of the fur of wild animals (leopard, lynx, wolf); it can be seen on contemporary representations of →*kuruc* soldiers thrown over the left shoulder; today it forms part of the ceremonial dress of English drum-majors.

Kádár János (pron. *kah-dahr*); though six years after the revolution (→*forradalom, 1956*) the all-powerful law courts were still hanging revolutionaries caught in '56, a decade later Kádár, who had been made First Secretary of the Party (→*Párt*) with the help of Soviet tanks, became "... *the symbol of the golden mean in Hungary. Unlike →Rákosi, he did not attempt to force major social changes on the masses, and unlike Imre Nagy, he refused to accept the restrictions of Communist Party rule. Though enjoying unlimited power, he avoided violating the interests of groups capable of voicing their discontent. He was content with gradually-rationed changes and allowed people to compensate themselves as best they could for their losses. The much-suffering country ... longed for security and peaceful living conditions. In exchange, it acquiesced to the status quo of the Party ruling in the name of the people, and the apparatus ruling in the name of the Party members.*" (*Samizdat*, 1987); his mind failing, Kádár died almost to the hour when the courts ruled to rehabilitate Imre Nagy, the Prime Minister executed on his orders in 1958.

kadarka (*pron. kah-dahr-kah*); a light (and light-colored) red wine produced not in the traditional wine-growing regions but mainly on the Great Plain (→*Alföld*); it is a so-called "sand" wine (because of the soil in which it grows) and is used mostly to make a spritzer (→*fröccs*), which would not taste as pleasant made with a more full-bodied wine. →**bikavér**; **szürkebarát**; **tokaji**

káder *cadre*; a seemingly incongruous word, it conjures up unpleasant and distasteful memories of people picked out by the Party apparatus to eventually fill some position for which they were deemed suited. In everyday usage, a "good cadre" was someone who (often because of his social standing, such as a "working class cadre") was politically trustworthy, though of little use in his work (because he was usually untrained or unschooled), while the duty of the *káderes* (lit., 'one who deals with cadres', the former equivalent of today's neo-capitalist "human resources manager") was to find good cadres and "push" them into higher and higher positions – naturally, all this in the interest of the class struggle (→*osztályharc*). →**ötvenes évek**

kalács *milk loaf, coffee cake*; various pastries made from "milk dough"; one version weighs 25 dk. and is woven from lengths of dough, and there is a version which is baked in one piece in the oven (swelling up and out over the sides of the pan) and is sweeter than the first variety if (and when) raisins are added to it (not to mention the addition of cocoa!), and its dough is very much like kugelhopf (→*kuglóf*); it is an indispensable part of any holiday breakfast and is consumed in pastry shops (→*cukrászda*) with coffee (→*fekete*).

kaláka *team*; traditionally, in the →*Székelyföld*, the people of the village unite to build each other's houses in groups called *kaláka*; the word is also used metaphorically.

kalap *hat*; in the fifties (→*ötvenes évek*), when its use (by both men and women) was considered conservative and even a "bourgeois hangover" – this despite the fact that it was the village folk who refused to go without them – the hat suffered a death blow when Party etiquette dictated that it be replaced by the proletarian clothcap (→*micisapka*), or else by nothing at all, this in the spirit of proletarian simplicity; later, men and women both began wearing "sporty" knitted hats (a fashion which refuses to die) or "youngish" berets (→*svájcisapka*) in both towns and villages, possibly because they preferred to bear no resemblance to the wearers of the fedoras and homburgs, that in the meantime made their comback on parade platforms; in the eighties the hat made a tentative reappearance, this time as part of Western fashion, though young people consider it eccentric, for it always had some connotation attached to it.

kalapkúra '*hat cure*' (lit.); it is generally held that the best cure against the common cold is to drink hot tea with wine or spiced hot wine (→*forralt bor*); it is called a "*hat cure*" because the recipe calls for drinking the "tea" until one sees the hat placed on top of the dresser expressly for this purpose double.

Kalmopyrin the best known medicine against the common cold since time immemorial and is therefore kept in every medicine cabinet in the home of every Hungarian family.

kalocsai hímzés '*(folk) embroidery from Kalocsa*' (lit.); popular taste holds this type of folk (→*népi*) embroidery, known for its colorful roses on a white background, which carry the distant memory of Renaissance motifs, to be the most beautiful in Hungary, and as a matter of fact, even the table cloths made for the thousands of tourists remain pleasing to the eye. →**matyó**

káposzta *cabbage*; eaten almost always as sour cabbage cooked with meat, i.e., as stuffed cabbage (→*töltöttkáposzta*), though sometimes it is eaten cooked with roux (→*főzelék*), or as a salad (*ká-*

posztasaláta), in which the (usually fresh, though sometimes cooked) cabbage is cut into strips and drowned in vinegar (→*savanyúság*). →**kelkáposzta**

Karácsony *Christmas*; it does not differ much, in either towns or villages, from the way it is celebrated in other European countries; gifts are placed and opened under the decorated Christmas tree on December 24th, Christmas Eve, which is followed by a big family dinner, which traditionally consists of fish soup (→*halászlé*) and fried fish (→*hal*) in remembrance of Lent, followed by walnut or poppy seed rolls (→*beigli*); Christmas Day and the day after (Boxing Day in England) are also considered family holidays (→*töltöttkáposzta*, recently turkey, etc.), and even those who otherwise are not church goers go to Mass at least once, usually for Midnight Mass on the night of the 24th; Christmas looked the same even when they tried to "nationalize" (→*államosítás*) it (along with everything else), and re-Christened it "Pine Tree Holiday". →**betlehem**

Karády Katalin (pron. *kah–rah–dee*); a celebrated singer and movie star whose deep, sexy voice and melancholy lovesongs (irresistable tangos) conjure up the war years better than anything else ("*Don't flee, don't run / From your fate you cannot run* …"); legends of love affairs and conspiracy abounded about her even after she defected (→*disszidens*) and opened a hat shop in New York; her former villa in Buda is the official Prime Ministerial residence.

káromkodás '*malediction*' (lit.), *cursing, foul speech*; Hungarians are proud to point out the hights and depths and widths, not to mention the surrealistic turns with which Hungarians can curse (in contrast, obviously, to peoples who speak "less suggestive" languages); according to public lore, the art of cursing has been perfected by none better than carriage drivers whipping their horses, and military drillmasters of new recrutis; it is sometimes referred to as "hussar prayers" (*huszármiatyánk*). →**kurva**; **franc**; **fene**; **bassza meg**

Kárpátalja '*foothills of the Carpathians*' (lit.), *sub-Carpathia, Ruthenia*; the northeastern, hilly-mountainous crescent of historical Hungary (→*történelmi Magyarország*) stretching from the upper →*Tisza* to the watershed, which after WW I was annexed to the new state of Czechoslovakia, and after WW II to the Soviet Union (→*Szovjetunió*), and today is part of the Ukraine, even though its western regions adjacent to the Great Plain (→*Alföld*) are still inhabited by Hungarians; this is where →*Verecke* lies, which is the spot where the Conquerors (→*honfoglalók*) entered the Carpathian Basin.→**Trianon**; **Erdély**; **Felvidék**; **Délvidék**

kárpótlás '*compensation for damages*' (lit.); after the change in regime (→*rendszerváltás*) there was no restitution in Hungary; instead, those who lost their businesses and tangibles during nationalization (→*államosítás*) received vouchers which they could redeem generally only for a fraction of their worth; later, compensation came to include everyone who suffered damages (personal as well as property) due to the official acts of a Hungarian government; a huge bureau was set up to deal with the hundreds of thousands of applicants, yet the gesture of compensating people for wrongs of history ended up in the embarrassing act of putting value of life, liberty, and property, as a result of which everyone across the board felt angry and dissatisfied.

karszalag *armband*; in every form, shape and size (except for mourning ribbons, which have gone out of style), armbands are a sign of officialdom; though it has been rarely seen in the past couple of decades – except on ticket checkers on the Metro and other forms of public transportation, and before that, on pioneers (→*úttörő*) giving first aid, and therefore wearing armbands with a red cross on them; nothing is more revealing of the heady atmosphere of the years during the change in regime (→*rendszerváltás*) than the reappearance of armbands, especially sporting the national colors (→*nemzetiszín*), which served as a clear indication that their wearer believed he was serving the cause of the country, what's more, of the nation (→*nemzet*) itself. →**Nemzetőrség**

kása *mush, groats, porridge*; it can be cooked from any type of ground cereal, though it is generally made with barley; the meal (grist) is made from husked and ground barley, which is then cooked with milk to make *kása*, or formed into balls and added to soup. It is considered poor man's food (especially in Hungary proper), just like polenta, or corn meal mush, which is called *puliszka* and is still eaten (and liked) in Transylvania (→*Erdély*) **tejbegríz**

Katolikus Egyház *Catholic Church*; on paper, at least, 60% of the population of Hungary are Catholics, while the rest belong to various Protestant (→*protestáns*) denominations. The Catholic Church, however, owes its power and influence not only to this fact, but also to its thousand year old role in the history of the country, in the course of which it veritably became one with the State, even when the latter moved its headquarters to Vienna (→*Bécs*); consequently, after the Communist takeover, it was considered a greater enemy than any of the other religious institutions and was relentlessly persecuted, even though, as opposed to Protestant congregations (and unlike the Polish Church, e.g., it was never considered a national (→*nemzeti*) Church. →**Esztergom**

katonadal *soldier song*; though there are cocky and saucy Hungarian soldier songs, the following examples are more typical: "*Jaj, de sokat áztam-fáztam katona koromban* ..." (lit. 'Oh, how much rain and cold I suffered when I was a soldier ...'), "*Nem lehetek én rózsa, elhervaszt Ferenc Jóska* ..." (lit. 'I cannot become a rose, for Francis Joe makes me wither ...'), "*Diófából nem csinálnak* *koporsót, a bakának nem írnak búcsúztatót...*" (lit. 'From walnut wood they don't make coffins, for a private they don't write eulogies ...'), "*Menetelnek messze idegen határba, Mindegyik csak a szabadulást várja ...*" (lit. 'They march in distant foreign lands, Each waiting for his release ...'), "*Jaj Istenem, hol fogok én meghalni, Hol fog az én piros vérem kifolyni?*" (lit. 'Oh, Lord, where will I die, Where will my red blood flow?'). →**baka**

katonaság *the military*; in the 20th century, Hungary experienced such loss of faith in its military, and found the "People's Army", dressed in pseudo-Soviet uniform, so much against its liking, that only the most humbly gifted individuals would serve in it as officers, while everyone else tried to avoid being enlisted, as a result of which there is hardly a country in Europe that is more demilitarized both in spirit and in fact than Hungary. Still, most of the male population were nevertheless called to do national service and had to suffer the cruel jokes played on them as new recruits, or "bald ones", not to mention the sadistic treatment they received at the hands of their sergeants (→*őrmester*); stories from their lives in uniform have an almost folkloristic cast, but even this could do precious little to improve the prestige of the Hungarian Armed Forces (→*Magyar Honvédség*) in the eyes of the populace. →**egyenruha**; **baka**; **honvédség**

kávé *coffee*; during the past fifty years, instead of asking for coffee people in Hungary have been asking for a →*fekete* (lit. "black"), by which they mean (black) espresso (→*eszpresszó*) coffee, and nothing else, for they shudder at the very thought of drinking a "long" (American-type) coffee; the usual portion, which comes in a small cup, is called a →*dupla* ("double") to distinguish it from the no longer available *szimpla* ("single"), and in every town, there are places people will swear by when it comes to a good cup of coffee, while they are careful to avoid other places, like the plague, and will even warn the uninitiated away from them, saying they "must not" drink coffee there at any price. →**tea**

kávéház '*coffee house*' (lit.), *café*; the places along the boulevard (→*körút*) which the petit and grand bourgeoisie frequented to chat or read their newspapers at leisure by the big marble tables (and to which they fled from their small size apartments); from Vienna to Budapest and from Zagreb to Prague, they became the veritable symbols of Central Europe (→*Közép–Európa*) until they disappeared, and people began thinking of them with a sort of desperate nostalgia; they gave way to the coffee shop (→*eszpresszó*), where the service and pace was quicker, and which was therefore considered more "modern", even before WW II. →**New York**; **cukrászda**

Kedves uram (asszonyom/barátom)! '*my kind sir/woman/friend*' (lit.), *dear* *sir*; the set formula by which someone is addressed in a letter who is not known (or is a distant acquaintance only). →**uram**

kegyelmes úr '*graceous sir*' (lit.), *your grace*, *your excellency*; according to the strict code governing forms of address in vogue before WW II, this form of address was used only for men in very high positions (i.e., civil servants in the highest wage categories such as ministers, and university professors); today it is used only in jest. →**megszólítás; méltóságos úr; nagyságos úr**

Kékes (pron. *kay-kesh*), '*Blue Mountain*' (lit.); the highest peak not only of the Mátra mountains but of the entire country, whose height exceeds 1000 meters; it is the home of the sanatorium of Galyatető, built during the inter-war years to replace the elegant mountain resorts of the Tátra region lost to Slovakia as a result of the Peace Treaty of Versailles (→*Trianon*); for years the sanatorium was a constant subject of film newsreels so the audiences of the malodorous movie houses could finally see for themselves (in case they hadn't noticed before), that socialism (→*szocializmus*) was alive and well, and that the workers (→*dolgozó*) were starting their pre-paid trade union "reward (!) holidays" (*jutalomüdülés*) with faces radiant from happiness, whereas "before the triumph of socialism only the privileged classes...", etcetera, etcetera, etcetera.

kékhagyma '*blue onions*' (lit.), *red onions*; also called *purple oninons* (*lilahagyma*) is the variety used when raw rings are called for; often eaten with cracklings (→*töpörtyű*), cheese and larded bread (→*zsíroskenyér*). →**vöröshagyma**

Kelet Európa *Eastern Europe*; Hungarians (→*magyarok*), who consider their country part of Central Europe (→*Közép Európa*), use this expression to refer to the territories to the east of the country's borders; long centuries of experience have taught them that they are situated in a borderland, for the laws of life are strikingly different on the other side of the line defined by St. Petersburg and Belgrade (but bypassing Transylvania, or →*Erdély*), where the influence of the Renaissance did not reach, where there was no Reformation, and where Church and State were not separated. →**Balkán**; **Európa**; **Közép Európa**

kelkáposzta *savoy cabbage*; a variety of cabbage (→*káposzta*) with loose, crisped leaves, which is one of the most common garden vegetables in Hungary, and which, when cooked, releases a characteristically unsavory odor; in Hungary, it is cooked only with roux (→*főzelék*) and with the addition of potatoes (→*krumpli*); few children relish eating it, despite their grandmothers' (→*nagymama*) reassurance that it is good for them; it is typical eatery (→*étkezde*) fare, where it is served with meat-loaf (→*fasírt*), but even so, it conjures up the world of the poor. →**bérház; gang**

kéményseprő *chimney sweep*; it is good luck to meet one, especially on New Year's Day, but only if we quickly grab one of our buttons, give it a twist, and make a wish; the chimney sweep is so much a part of the rites of New Year's Eve (→*Szilveszter*), that at restaurants and dances people dressed as chimney sweeps appear soon after midnight with a small, rose-colored piglet under their arms, which they take around to the tables so people can pull their cute little tails and wish for something into the bargain; finding a four-leaf clover or a horse-shoe also brings luck, and are also symbols of the New Year. →**fekete macska**

kenyér *bread*; in Hungarian culture bread, like the grain harvest (→*aratás*), enjoys the status of an icon and a fetish in one; bread continues as the main food item of the country, and its price is accordingly an important factor in the standard of living, while its quality is a matter of public concern; the Hungarians, who when staying abroad miss nothing as much as the fresh, spongy, soft yet crips white wheat (→*búza*) bread from home, even insist on its traditional size (2 kg.) and shape (a longish loaf peaking at the two ends yet round and bulging in the middle with several cuts made in it before it is put in the oven); the two ends of fresh bread are considered a special delicacy, and children like to pinch the insides out with their fingers; some people will eat bread with everything, including bread, as it is often jocularly said, and are therefore called *kenyeres*, or (lit.) 'a bread-eater'; a custom, now waning, calls for drawing a cross on the back of a new loaf with a knife (kept only for this purpose) before it is sliced (which is done pressing one end to one's chest for support); people do not like to throw any part of the loaf away, even once it is dry, for this is considered wasteful (and if it is done all the same, it is done with a bad conscience), and people are grateful when someone relieves them of it even if only to feed barnyard animals. →**aratás**; **augusztus 20.**

Kerepesi úti temető (pron. *keh–reh–peshee*), *cemetery*; a 19th century cemetery in →*Pest* which has since been engulfed by the city; since it contains the tombs of almost every great 19th century Hungarian, (including the huge mausoleum of →*Kossuth* and the tomb of →*Ady*), it is considered a national (→*nemzeti*) Pantheon of sorts; as a consequence, later the Communists also laid their important dead (→*Kádár János* and →*Rajk László*) to rest here. →**Házsongárdi temető**; **Farkasréti temető**; **Kozma utcai temető**; **Újköztemető**; **temetés**

keres (pénzt) '*look for money*' (lit.), *to earn* (*money*); a Hungarian does not "win" or "gain" money, nor does he "work" for it, he "looks" or "searches" for it in the form of "bread", like in other languages, "bread" being the synonym for "money" (→*pénz*); it is an old, trite joke that one "looks for" but cannot "find" it; also, it is not considered discourteous to count the money one receives (as they say, "Money is best counted, women are best beaten!"), some people even spit on it in jest, saying, "*apád-anyád idejöjön!*", which (loosely translated) is a call for the rest of the "family" to follow.

kereszténység védőbástyája, a '*the (defending) bastion/shield of Christianity*' (lit.); the expression, which has its origins in the 16th century, is the succinct summation of what Hungarians think of as the main cause for the continual disasters of their history, namely, that due to its unfortunate geographical situation, it has been called upon time and time again throughout the centuries to defend (without outside help!) Catholic Europe from the onslaught of pagan empires (the Tatars, the Turk) as their rearguard, not to mention the fact that the tragic loss of blood in the fights to defend its frontier fortresses (→*végvár*) only added insult to its injuries; fatalists are quick to point out that the revolution of '56 (→*forradalom, 1956*) was simply the latest proof of Hungary's ungrateful role as a buffer zone. →**Mohács**; **Nyugat, a**

késés '*lateness*', '*being late*' (lit.); in Hungary, it is all right to be (a few minutes) late compared to the time agreed on, though it is not a courteous act, unless one is invited to someone's home, in which case it is good manners to give the hostess, who is presumable behind schedule, a bit of extra time; if punctuality is called for, the host or hostess will usually say so; there is also a so-called "academic quarter-hour", which is how long it is proper to wait for a professor or colleague to show up (before the start of a meeting, for instance), and for some unfathomable reason, Saturday night guests usually start showing up at least half an hour later than when the party is supposed to start.

keszeg (*carp-)bream*; a small, unimpressive freshwater fish which lives in big schools in the →*Balaton*, and is sold fried in flour and paprika (head, tail and all) to hungry vacationers; the word is also used to describe very thin and scrawny persons (males). →**hal**; **ponty**

kézcsók '*hand-kiss*', '*kiss on the hand*' (lit.); the actual practice of kissing somebody's (a lady's) hand as a form of greeting (by men) is now very rarely seen, though its verbal form – 'I kiss your hand' – lives on not only among blue-collar workers, service people and stall keepers as a form of address to women, but also as a courteous way of greeting older ladies, and it is de rigeur for children of any sex towards grownups in general. →**kezét csókolom**; **puszi**

kezét csókolom '*I kiss your hand*' (lit.); though it is rarely used today in full (→*kézcsók*), and the practice itself is mainly restricted to operettas (→*operett*), men do say →*kezicsókolom*, a slightly shortened form of the full courteous term; it is used by men (especially of the older generation) when addressing a lady (→*hölgy*) including any woman who is not a close acquaintance or (older) relative. →**köszönés**; **kiszti-hand**; **kézfogás**

kézfogás '*handgrip*' (lit.), *handshake*; an almost obligatory ceremony between men (with the exception of close friends) both at meeting and at parting, while women use it only on strictly business occasions (when men often respond by saying →*kezicsókolom*, 'I kiss your hand'); women who are good friends settle for a →*puszi*, which is also how men often greet women they know well (relatives, good friends).

kezicsókolom *kiss your hand*; the shortened form of →*kezét csókolom*, used for the sake of easier pronounciation.

ki a magyar? '*who is Hungarian?*' (lit.); orphaned in the world by a language no one else speaks, Hungarians have been occupied with the question of their identity ever since the continued existence of a (multi-national) "historical Hungary" (→*történelmi Magyarország*) was first endangered, which after the dissolution of the state (Austria–Hungary), ended in scapegoating (pointing the finger at "aliens"), whereas for centuries the Carpathian Basin was a melting pot comparable only to America (→*Amerika*), as a result of which the question "Who is Hungarian?" cannot be answered on the basis of citizenship alone, nor with recourse to a common ancestry, not even through anthropological (genetic) considerations; being Hungarian means sharing a common cultural heritage and language, as well as a question of voluntary self-identification. "Sometimes, my heart beats faster even at the sight of a postal stamp from *Pest.* It gives me such pleasure to be in your company! What is loud applause and endless acclaim worth compared to what all of you give me? ...*Everywhere else I play for the audience, but in Hungary I play for the nation!* And this is a noble and great thing, to make emotional contact in this manner with a nation such as ours," Franz (Ferenc) Liszt wrote in a letter in *German* to a *Hungarian* aristocrat with a *Croatian* name, since neither of them ever learned to speak Hungarian. →**magyar nemzet**; **magyaros (arc)**; **asszimiláció**; **névmagyarosítás**

Kiegyezés, a *Compromise, the*; the Austro-Hungarian agreement of 1867 which put an end to the illegal situation (according to Hungary) that prevailed after the defeat of the War of Independence (→*Szabadságharc*) and established the Austro-Hungarian (or Dual) Monarchy (→*Osztrák–Magyar Monarchia*), which the rest of the world knows as Austria-Hungary, with the Emperor of Austria, Francis Joseph (→*Ferenc József*) being crowned King of Hungary. →**Ausztria**; **Ferenc József**; **Erzsébet királyné**; **Monarchia**

kifli '*crescent*'; a piece of "baker's ware" (→*péksütemény*) the length of one's hand, it is shaped like a croissant (but is more slender), and water is added to the flour, as well as salt which, when fresh, makes it deliciously crisp; school children eat it for breakfast with light coffee and milk or cocoa, and so do office workers; children like to ask each other for the end, which is the crispest part (a plea that cannot be refused); there is also "*vajaskifli*", whose dought is made soft by the addition of butter, and also the "*sóskifli*", on the back of which there glistens large, roughly ground salt, not to mention other kinds, such as "*paprikáskifli*", the dough made light pink by the addition of →*paprika*. →**zsemle**; **perec**

kifőzde *eaterie*; it is in these family-type side-street eateries (restaurants), open only for lunch, that the humble folk of the big city eat at tables covered with plastic table cloths and plates laden with stewed vegetables (→*főzelék*) with a piece of meat, usually pre-paid by the week or month, consumed with lots of bread (→*kenyér*), which the waitress (→*kisasszony*) bills by the slice, and is washed down with soda water. →**étkezde**; **büfé**; **önkiszolgáló**

kisasszony '*little woman*' (lit.), *young lady*, *Miss*; originally used to address the daughter of the lady (→*úrnő*) or mistress (→*nagyasszony*) of the house; today it is the courteous (and somewhat antiquated) form of address used for every "young" lady (despite her age), including sales ladies, waitresses, and telephone operators (but never teachers!), unless the customer is of the same (youthful) age, in which case they will automatically use the informal form of address (→*tegeződés*). →**asszony**; **megszólítás**

kiskapu '*small gate*' (lit.), *loophole*; two gates open onto the yards of village houses, a wider and taller one for the cart or carriage (the "big gate"), and a narrower and lower one for those on foot (the "small gate"); this is the source of the popular wisdom that next to any "big gate" offered by the law, there has to be a "small gate" as well which can be accessed by clever attorneys or the right acquaintances in case the "big gate" is closed to one; thus, when someone finds a "small gate", or loophole, in the law, thereby evading or escaping an obligation, he is not considered corrupt, but the (enviable) son of good fortune.

Kispest '*little Pest*' (lit.); one of the industrial districts that grew up around →*Pest* at the end of the last century; rural or small-town in character, in the fifties (→*ötvenes évek*) these were annexed to →*Budapest*; today, Kispest is characterized by pre-fab (→*panel*) housing estates (→*lakótelep*) which stand among the small workshops and warehouses that have replaced the former plants and factories. →**Újpest**; **Angyalföld**

kisüsti pálinka '*small cauldron brandy*' (lit.), *brandy*; brandy (→*pálinka*) made at home or in small village distilleries in small quantitites under the supervision of the man whose brandy it is; in the eyes of connoisseurs, it is thus considered far superior to mass-produced brandy, most of which is made with artificial ingredients. →**barackpálinka**; **szilvapálinka**

kisvendéglő '*small restaurant*' (lit.), *restaurant*; inexpensive family-type restaurant serving homely food frequented mostly by people who live in the neighborhood; it differs from the eatery (→*kifőzde*) in that it is usually a bit more spacious and a lot more clean, and is easily distinguished (or so it is commonly believed) from other types of restaurants by the (usually red and white) chequered tablecloths which give it a cosy ambiance.

KISZ *Association of Communist Youth* (lit.); the earlier, disintegrated youth organizations were replaced after the revolution (→*forradalom, 1956*) by the *KISZ*, which was at first militant in nature (its members wore uniforms!), but soon became a bureaucratic organization whose size, thanks to compulsory membership, grew tremendous, which made it blatantly ineffective; since the Party (→*Párt*) leadership regarded it as a vehicle for regenerating itself, in turn, people looked down on its leading members as careerists of the worst sort.

kisztihand '*küsst die Hand*' (German), '*I kiss your hand*' (lit.); the Hungarianized (and by now antiquated) form of the German original of →*kezétcsókolom* and →*kezicsókolom*, which all mean the same and which, though elderly gentlemen still use it, is considered highly affected, though it is used even in a jocular manner in the *expression csókolom a kisztihandját* ("I kiss your kiss-the-hand"). →**kézcsók**

kitelepítés '*de-settlement*' (lit.), *deportation*; one of the most distasteful acts of the new Communist government after it came to power in 1948, which it instituted in the name of "class struggle" and "proletarian dictatorship". Based on the Russian model of exiling people, they forced (deported) "former exploiters" and members of the "former ruling class" – in short, all "class-aliens" (→*osztályidegen*) – to distant corners of the county with nothing but what they could carry (on their backs), to live in nearly sub-human conditions under the watchful eyes of the State Security Authority (→*ÁVO*), and to earn their keep with hard physical labor, while their apartments (provided they still had them), along with their furnishings (provided they had any left after →*államosítás*, or nationalization), were taken from them. This is what was succinctly called the "class struggle". →**ötvenes évek**

Klapka-induló *Klapka March*; a 19th century Hungarian military march with an inspiring rhythm which is about a certain army (→*honvéd*) general by the name of György Klapka who during the War of Independence (→*Szabadságharc*) of 1849 successfully defended the fortress of →*Komárom* even after the main body of the army laid down arms; its famous lines (lit. '*Famous Komárom is taken, / György Klapka is its leader, /*

The cannon thunders, the sword clashes, / This rouses the Magyar to battle') have made it one of the most frequently played marches by military bands (and brass bands of all kinds), even today; it is still the custom to march into (and out of) places (including school-yards) to its inspiring rhythms. →**induló**

kocsma *pub*; any sort of place for a quick drink (alcoholic), from the simple and unclean drinking establishments found in villages to the "stand-up" places (→*talponálló*) found in towns, so called because the customers have a "quick one" standing up (not that there's any place to sit down to begin with); they are meant for people (mostly men) who want a drink (mostly beer nowadays) during the day, and who know better than to expect to be served quality wine; sometimes a *kocsma* comes in the shape of a small rural restaurant (→*kisvendéglő*) also known as a →*kiskocsma* (serving simple dishes as well), not to mention the occasional coffee shops (→*eszpresszó*), where contrary to the sign over the door, the sour smell of the stale beer of cheap pubs gives away the real function of the place. →**csárda**

kocsonya (*pork*) *jelly*; really a thick, jellified consommé made from parts of the pork (→*disznó*) such as the tail, ears, cheeks, and feet unfit for anything else, and which is eaten only once it is cold and solidified enough so that it begins to quiver; it is a typical mid-winter food. →**disznótor**

Kohn bácsi *Uncle Kohn/Cohen*; the staple figure of Jewish jokes, a wise but defenceless little man who manages to pull himself out of the worst situations that history plagues him with no end, and who, with his quick wit and clever remarks, unmasks the hypocritical folly of the world around him. Here's one: Uncle Kohn goes to the Ministry of the Interior (→*Belügy*) and asks for a passport (→*útlevél*). They ask him where he wants to emigrate (→*kivándorló*), whereupon he asks for a globe to look for a place that's most to his liking. He keeps turning the globe round and round until finally he looks up at the passport officer and asks, "Is this the only globe you got?" →**vicc**; **Móricka**; **Arisztid és Tasziló**

kokárda *cockade*; a round badge in the shape of a rose made from a ribbon with the national colors (→*nemzetiszín*) worn by the "revolutionary youth" of 1848 on the lapels of their jackets in imitation of their French contemporaries. Ever since, it is customary to wear one on March 15th (→*március 15.*), though today it sometimes comes in the shape of a simple ribbon. →**Nemzetőrség**

kolbász *sausage*; not identical to the sausage the British eat with such relish, the Hungarian *sausage* comes about as the last act of traditional pig killing (→*disznóölés*), and is made as follows: parts of the pork are finely ground, liberally seasoned with paprika (→*pirospaprika*), garlic, pepper, etc., and used to fill the pig's (thoroughly cleaned) intestines, thereby coming up with a very long sausage "snake" (not everyone twists the intestines from time to time to divide it into "sticks" as they fill it), which is then hung up in the smoke-room; after having been properly smoked (and since pig killing takes place in winter, after having been properly frozen as well), it turns reddish-brown, at which point it is transferred to the pantry (→*éléskamra*), to be consumed bit by bit for breakfast (→*reggeli*) and dinner until the next pig killing. Last year's dry sausage, which practically "jumps out of its skin" is considered a special delicacy.

kolóniál (stílus) '*colonial* (*style*)' (lit.); the name of a certain type of furniture which is rustic in character, has twisted feet and is ornamented with carving, the English-inspired creation of anonymous pre-war cabinet makers, though it came into popular demand only when its much simpler industrial variants appeared in the shops and took pride of place as "elegant" pieces of furniture in the offices of company directors and top Party (→*Párt*) functionaries in the 70s.

Kolozsvár (pron. *kaw–lozh–vahr*); the city (called *Cluj* in Romanian), which is considered the "capital" of Transylvania (→*Erdély*), as well as its cultural center (college, theater, journals and publishers), even by Romanian Hungarians, this despite the fact that due to the tens of thousands of new inhabitants settled there from other parts of Romania during the past couple of decades, Hungarians are now in the minority; the beautiful, romantic equestrian statue of Hungary's King Matthias (→*Mátyás király*), who was born there, stands on the main square in front of the fine gothic church (one of the easternmost examples of this architectural style), and is the repeated object of attacks by Romanian chauvinists. →**Marosvásárhely**

koma *godfather*; *in-law* (lit.); a friendly form of address between men with a folksy and slightly antiquated flavor; older men sometimes call boys *kiskoma* (*kis* = "small"); originally it designated an in-law of some kind (mostly the godfather or godmother of a child, as well as the parents of godchildren), but was later used to address just about anyone.

Komárom (pron. *kom–ah–rom*); a city lying on both sides of the Danube (→*Duna*) once famous for its huge fortress; one side of it is located in Slovakia, the other in Hungary. →**Klapka**

kommunista párt *Communist Party*; originally the name of the small political sect established by POWs in the fall of 1918, after their return from Russia; in its later incarnations it became known as the *Békepárt* ("Peace Party"), *Magyar Dolgozók Pártja* ("Hungarian Workers' Party"), and finally *Magyar Szocialista Munkáspárt* ("Hungarian Socialist Workers' Party"), but whatever it was called, it was always a faithful follower of the Soviet Communist Party; in its present reincarnation, it is simply known as the *Munkáspárt* ("Workers' Party"). →**Párt, a**

kopjafa *'lance+rod'* (lit.), *wooden headpost*; popularly considered an ancient Magyar (nomadic) grave post, though its use became prevalent only during the 17th century in Calvinist (→*református*) cemeteries (as opposed to the traditional cross of the Catholics); the carving at the tip of the square wooden post stuck into the ground (a "crown" or a "bun") indicates whether the grave belongs to a man or a woman, and sometimes also his or her status; in the 20th century it became the symbol of the cemeteries of Hungarians in neighboring countries and just like the "székely gate" (→*székelykapu*), is often used as a monument; in Plot 301 of the New Public Cemetery (→*Újköztemető*) of Budapest, the tomb of those executed after the revolution (→*forradalom, 1956*) is also topped with wooden headposts tied round with tricolor (→*nemzetiszín*) ribbons.

korona *crown*; →**Szent Korona**

koronázási ékszerek *crown jewels*; →**Szent Korona**

Kossuth Lajos (pron. *koh–shoot*); one of the heroes of the 19th century to attain epic status, he was the chief spokesman for the revolution (→*forradalom, 1848*) in the National Assembly, a great orator, then the chief organizer, leader and "soul" of the new state and the War of Independence (→*Szabadságharc*), the "Moses of the Hungarians", as the contemporary press called him; after the defeat of the freedom fights he emigrated and died abroad, having almost turned one-hundred, and having outlived most of his contemporaries, with the exception of his great opponent, →*Görgey*; he was the leading figure of the opposition and called the Compromise (→*Kiegyezés*) betrayal and treason, yet was referred to as "Father Kossuth" even after he was defeated by the pragmatic politicians; even 25 years after the defeat of the War of Independence, the English poet Swinburne called him the "Star of the unsetting sunset", a proof of which was the use of his image and ideas by a number of political movements for their own purposes, first by the radical republicans, then the plebeian revolutionaries, and in the end, even by the Communists (→*kommunista*). He also continues to be the subject of heated debates by historians. His image adorned the 100 forint banknote for fifty years, while his bust stands in the Capitolium and his face appeared on an American stamp; on March 15th (→*március 15.*) wreaths are placed in front of his statue from New York to Transylvania, and there is hardly a Hungarian town without a street (mostly one of the main thoroughfares) or a square named after him; there is also a small town in Georgia which bears his name, having been founded by his followers who emigrated (→*emigráns*) in the middle of the last century, even though its present inhabitants probably know nothing of this, not to mention Iowa, which has a Kossuth County. →**temetés; Széchenyi**

Kossuth Rádió the main chanel of Hungarian public radio which, when life resumed in Budapest in 1945, adopted the name of the Soviet radio station broadcasting to Hungary during the war.

Kossuth-nóta *Kossuth Song*; melancholy, pessimistic folk song (→*népdal*) from the time of the War of Independence (→*Szabadságharc*), which not only foreshadows the defeat of the freedom fights, but practically treats it as a matter of course: "*Lajos Kossuth's message says, / he has lost his last men, / should he send this message, / all of us will have to take arms, / Long live Hungarian liberty! Long live the homeland!*"; it is curious that it was this song, and no other, which became the musical emblem for the revolution (→*forradalom, 1848*), and it is even more curious that it was chosen as the musical signature for →*Kossuth Rádió*.

Kovács úr *Mr. Smith* (lit.); the journalistic name for the average Hungarian, which in real life is also spelled "Kováts" and even"Kovách", the latter being considered more aristocratic because it is older; it's American variant is "Coufax"; the name for the average Hungarian could just as easily be "Nagy" (*big*), or "Kis" (*small*), after all, these are equally common surnames.

kovászos uborka *leavened cucumber*(lit.), *dill* (*kosher*) *pickles*; the recipe calls for a big jar, stuffing it with cucumbers, dill and coriander (sliced horseradish optional), then filling it up with boiling water (with vinegar and salt), and topping it with a slice of bread; it is then put out in the sun to ferment, as a consequence of which the yeast from the bread dissolves into the liquid; in a couple of days – even in the sunny corners of outdoor corridors (→*gang*) – the cucumbers become soft and soury and are eaten with meat, etc., (→*savanyúság*), though some people eat them to quench a thirst. It is typical summer fare.

Kozma utcai temető (pron. *cohs–mah*), *cemetery* ; the largest Jewish cemetery of Budapest located on the outskirts of town in the street from which it has received its name; it is adjacent to the New Public Cemetery (→*Újköztemető*); it is famous for its beautiful art nouveau (*szecessziós*) tombstones and crypts. →**Kerepesi úti temető**; **Házsongárdi temető**; **Farkasréti temető**; **Ujköztemető**

költészet *poetry*; Hungarians hold that their poetry, which is (so to speak) the setting for the great riches and eccentricities of their untranslatable language, is also their greatest national (→*nemzeti*) accomplishment, and it pains them beyond measure that it remains unaccessible to the world. Jorge Luis Borges once wrote he is convinced that there must be poets of Keats's stature among Hungarian poets, but he cannot prove it, since he does not speak Hungarian.

That is the essence of the thing. →**író; költő; értelmiség; magyar nyelv**

költő *poet*; the 19th century cult of genius that surrounded poetry (→*költészet*) raised the figure of the poet to sacred heights, alternately seeing him as people's tribune (*cf.* the statue of →*Petőfi* by the bank of the Danube) and as prophet (*cf.* the statue of →*Ady* on →*Andrássy út*), and though the 20th century has grown more restrained, it has always been expected of a Hungarian poet to turn his life into literature, which is what the public expects of him and what they love him for (the poetry of →*József Attila* being a prime example), and this is why it is so profoundly touched by the poems of `*Radnóti Miklós*. →**író**

körözött '*round-about*' (lit.); a spread made by combining savory sheep's curd with butter, finely chopped scallions and paprika (→*pirospaprika*), with caraway seeds being optional. It is eaten spread thickly on a slice of fresh bread. →**túró**

körút '*circular road*' (lit.), *boulevard*; the inner section of →*Pest* (and other large towns in imitation of it) are defined (on their outer limits) by a wide semi-circular road which because of its length is given various names along the way (in Pest, the names of various →*Habsburg* rulers; also, in Pest both ends of the *Nagykörút* (Grand Boulevard, but there is also a *Kiskörút* or Small Boulevard) run into a bridge crossing over to →*Buda*; the architecturally unified road, built around the turn of the century, is lined with theaters, movie houses, former cafés (→*kávéház*) now functioning as a coffee shop (→*eszpresszó*), as well as restaurants and shops; in common parlance, *körúti* ("of/from the *körút*") has become the synonym for big city vulgarity.

köszönés *greeting*; →**jónapot; kezét csókolom; kézfogás; kezicsókolom; puszi; szervusz; tiszteletem**

Közép Európa *Central Europe*; for Hungarians (→*magyarok*) it is self-evident that geographically, politically as well as culturally, their country is located in Central Europe, and they are offended if it is presumed to belong to some other part of the continent; through the course of history this was far from unequivocal (especially when the Eastern empires forced Hungary into their sphere of influence), not even certain whether there was such a place as Central Europe at all (either culturally or as a separate geographic entity), and whether the terrain situated between the German and Russian (or some other Eastern) empires should not be called "East-Central Europe" or "Inter-Europe" instead; though the Hungarian (and Austrian, Czech and Croatian) middle classes tend to think of their similar cultural backgrounds as a manifestation of their shared Central European culture, it is possible that this is merely due to their formerly having been part of the →*Habsburg* Empire which, on the other hand, was not the center of political Europe, but merely its distant outpost. →**Kelet–Európa**; **Balkán**; **Európa**; **kereszténység védőbástája, a**

közért '*for the public good*' (lit.), *the grocer's*; originally the acronym for the the huge food shop chain organized during the process of nationalization (→*államosítás*) which turned out so well, that it even means something; today it is used to refer to the "small corner grocer's" as opposed to the modern →*ABC*, which is what they now call supermarkets; though the old signs are gone from the now privatized shops, people continue to use the old name.

köztársaság *republic*; the present Hungarian republic, established in 1989, is the third in the country's history; the first was the republic established during the revolution in 1918 (→*forradalom, 1918*) and the second in 1946; it is already of longer standing than either of its predecessors, of which the republic of 1918 was followed just six months later by the Republic of Councils (→*Tanácsköztársaság*), while the second was followed three years later (in 1949) by the dictatorship dubbed the People's Republic; between the two there was a monarchy without a monarch, with Miklós Horthy (the last admiral of the Austro-Hungarian Navy) acting as the head of state, holding the office of *governor*.

Krampusz (pron. *krahm–poos*); the presence of the "devil", or *Krampusz*, in the St. Nicholas' Day (→*Mikulás*) rites held on December 6th reveals that in their original form they represented the fight of Good and Evil for man's soul; just thirty or forty years ago, every child still wanted to play the comic role of the black-faced *Krampusz*, who had a long tail, twirled a chain and stick while jumping up and down to scare people; the word *krampusz* is also jocularly applied to people who are considered ugly-looking.

krémes *creamy* (lit.); a square shaped cake (→*cukrászsütemény*) which consists of a thin layer of crumbly, leafy dough on the bottom and an even thinner layer on top, liberally sprinkled with sugar, with nothing but globs and globs of delicious vanilla cream in between. The minute you touch it with a fork, it slips apart. →**dobos**; **rigójancsi**; **zserbó–szelet**

krumpli *tatties, potatoes*; it is eated cooked or baked, crushed, sliced, diced or in one, with or without its skin, on its own (→*főzelék*) or as a side dish; in winter it is consumed in such large quantities that when fall comes, large trucks go around the towns, and housewives buy by the sackful the "winter resistant" variety; it's official name, *burgonya*, is used only on menu cards. →**tészta**; **paprikáskrumpli**; **törtkrumpli**

krumplistészta '*potato noodles*' (lit.); cooked and crushed potatoes are kneaded together with dough to make it more filling, then the mixture is cooked and browned with onions; it is considered the poorest of poor man's fare, and is frequently eaten in school/ college cafeterias and in the army. →**krumpli**; **tészta**

kucsma *fur hat/kalpack*; the ubiquitous winter headgear of men in villages usually made from brown sheep-skin turned inside out, with the lining also made of fur; though it is cut into a peak shape, it is usually worn with the peak crushed in.

kuglóf *Gugelhupf* (lit.), *sponge cake of Viennese origin, suitably magyarized*; since it it baked in a flute tube pan, its shape is reminiscent of a (cylindrical) pyramid with the top chopped off; it is made with lots of butter added to the dough, which gives it a nice yellowish color; weighing about half a pound, it often has raisins added to it and the top is sprinkled with powedered sugar; sliced into liberal portions, it is eaten with coffee or for breakfast (→*reggeli*), though years ago it was a typical name's day cake; if cocoa is also added to the shortbread, it is like marble cake. →**kalács**

kukorica *maize, corn;* though half of all the grain produced in Hungary is corn, Hungarian housewives do not cook with it and Hungarian husbands and offspring, too, know it only in the form of cooked corn on the cob boiled in salted water, which they eat *before lunch*, and only in the summertime, on the beach or at the public swimming pool, picking at the rows with their teeth. Instead, Hungarians use most of the corn yield for fodder (as they reflect with some pity on the nations where people actually *eat* the corn—pop-corn being a recent import); its status is beautifully illustrated by the fact that the name of the hero of →*János vitéz* (before he went from →*peasant* to →*huszár*) was Kukorica Jancsi.

kunok *the Cumans*; a nomadic people with a Turkic language who fled the Mongolians (who moving westward had earlier also slaughtered the Magyar tribe left behind by →*Árpád* in their ancient homeland, or →*őshaza*), and reaching Hungary in 1239, were given permission to settle; they must have been similar in may ways to the Magyars/ Hungarians who settled in the Carpathian Basin (→*Honfoglalás*) only 200 years before, except that the Cumans, who were given part of the Great Plain (→*Alföld*) called the →*Kunság* ever since, assimilated completely, and lost both their language and sense of being a separate people (though at the turn of the century, some old people could still recite the Lord's Prayer in Cumanian); "Kún" and "Kun" are frequent surnames, though not necessarily a sign of Cuman origin, since most people received it during one of the waves of the "Magyarization" of family names (→*névmagyarosítás*). →**tatárjárás**; **Szent László**

Kunság '*Land of the Cumans*' (lit.); despite its name, this area of the Great Plain (→*Alföld*), a steppe, is not inhabited by Cumans (→*kunok*), because there are no families left whose ancestry can be traced back to the original Cumans; the sense of a separate identity has (instead) taken the form of local patriotism, the practice of which does not call for Cumanian origin; the "Tartar" type (Eastern) face, which is not rare in Hungary, is considered Cuman and very "Hungarian", because this is how the Conquerors (→*honfoglalók*) have survived in the public imagination. →**magyaros arc**

kuplé *music-hall song*; the appearance of inexpensive places of musical entertainment was one of the signs of the growth of →*Pest* into a metropolis at the turn of the century; their songs, characterized by jocular linguistic mistakes, double entendres and merry rhymes which told funny stories with surprising clinchers have remained popular to this day, for they conjure up with full force the age now considered "the peaceful peace", for which every new generation feels a strong sense of nostalgia. →**Budapest**; **századforduló**; **Monarchia**

kúria *mansion*;→**falu**

kuruc (pron. *kooh–rowts*); a soldier in the early 18th century War of Independence led by →*Rákóczi Ferenc*, later prince regent of Hungary, who fought the →*Habsburgs* successfully for years; later the label for every adamantly anti-Austrian and anti-Habsburg individual, sentiment or political matifestation, as a result of which it has continued to be part of Hungary's history to this day (though in a widened, metaphorical sense); for example, a *kuruc* today is probably one who is against Western (and American) influence (→*Nyugat-ellenesség*). Though being partisan is popularly considered a crime of sorts against the nation, being a *kuruc* has always been a pardonable sin, as opposed to being a →*labanc* (i.e. conservative or siding with a foreign power). In the popular imagination the word conjures up a handsome soldier with a mustache wearing a hussar-type red uniform and riding a horse, who outwits the dim-witted Austrian generals with admirable ease; it's atmosphere is cogently revealed by the following *kuruc* song (→*kuruc nóta*): "*In the castle of Vienna the German, he cries, / his poor head, how it aches, / for on the shore of the Leithe, for weeks now / he hears the kuruc sing*". →**német**; **Bécs**; **Lajta**

kuruc nóta '*kuruc song*' (lit.); these cocky, early 18th-century soldiers' songs are still sung by Hungarians of all types and classes (when they are by themselves and the mood is properly mellow), especially those which make fun of the Germans (→*németek*) and the →*labanc*, because their manly defiance (and/or melancholy mood) express their feelings so well: "*When my grey mare, the Murza / crosses the Leithe's water, / when it gallops at Vienna's walls, / the emperor will dress in mourning*". →**kuruc**

kurva *whore*; though the Hungarian language is especially inventive when it comes to cursing (→*káromkodás*) and hurling invectives, the most often used word of abuse which continues to hold its own, is this word of Latin origin which, used as a noun, means "prostitute" (and whose use is hardly considered taboo any longer), while used as an adjective it can easily be affixed (just like *bloody*) to any substantive noun, though it is most frequently heard in front of *anyád* ("your mother") and *élet* ("life"). Note: in case of the former pairing, it is still considered taboo. →**anya**

kutya *dog*; as opposed to its use in the English language, when used figuratively in Hungarian (whether in jest or in full seriousness), the word *kutya* invariably refers to something negative (or has a pejorative connotation), whether someone is called *nagykutya* ('big boss') or *kutyuli* ('little dog'), which is a nausiatingly sweet way of lovers to address each other. →**Bodri**; **vizsla**; **puli**; **kuvasz**

kuvasz (pron. *kooh–vos*), *Canis familiaris variatio pastoralis hungarica*; the large, white-haired dog (→*kutya*) of the cowherds of the →*puszta*, which is indiginous to Hungary and is not known elsewhere in Europe, since it was brought by the Conquerors (→*honfoglalók*) with them from the steppes of the northern Causasians.

külföldre szakadt hazánkfia '*expatriate son of the nation*' (lit.), *expatriate*; typical socialist euphemism and journalistic cliché of the recent past used to refer to Hungarians (usually enjoying some modicum of fame abroad, and gladly welcomed back home) who were living in the West (and in whose case it no longer matters how and why they ended up there); its opposite was the highly pejorative "dissident" (→*disszidens*). →**emigráns**; **kivándorló**; **amerikás származású**

kürtős kalács *pastry horn*; a typical Transylvanian (→*Erdély*) baked good (→*sütemény*), made from sweetened butter dough cut into strips and wound round a thick wooden funnel or short rolling pin, and basted repeatedly with honey as it baked, sprinkled with walnuts or hazel nuts; when it is ready, it is slipped off the funnel (or rolling pin) and is served sliced; no country fair (→*vásár*) is complete without it.

L

labanc (pron. *loh–bonts*); when in the early 18th century the →*kuruc* army of Prince →*Rákóczi* fought a war of independence against the Habsburgs (→*Habsburgok*) for nearly ten years, *labanc* became the term of abuse and derision (both as noun and adjective) for the Hungarian advocates of the House of Habsburg; to this day it carries its old, highly pejorative, derisive connotation, though (as opposed to →*kuruc*), it is no longer used metaphorically.

lacikonyha '*Laci's kitchen*' (lit.); a food tent put up out in the open at country fairs (→*vásár*) in which they sell freshly made meat called '*lacipecsenye*'; the word conjures up images of stifling summer days, crowds, noise, and cold beer; the word comes from the hot day in June which is *László* (i.e. *Laci*) day, when religious festivals (→*búcsú*) are held throughout the country in honor of St. László (→*Szent László*), who was always one of the most popular saints, with *László* still going strong as a much-loved first name for boys.

Lajta (pron. *loy–tah*), *Leithe* (Germ.); the undistinguished little stream which flows into the Danube just below Vienna (→*Bécs*), which for a thousand years formed the western frontier of Hungary.

lakás '*living quarters*' (lit.), *apartment*, *flat*; in both cities and towns, apartments in Hungary tend to be very small; they rarely contain more than two (or three) rooms (generally with a bathroom), but even so, acquiring one needs great sacrifice on the part of a family (not least of all due to the difficulties of obtaining bank loans), and so they represent a great value; consequently, young grownups and newlyweds often live together with their parents, which leads to no end of trouble for everyone concerned. →**lakótelep**; **panel**; **öröklakás**

lakodalmas rock '*wedding rock*' (lit.); the name for Hungarian songs (→*magyar nóta*) played by modern dance bands in rock-and-roll rhythm and in the style of dance music, as a consequence of which they have become popular once again; also the name for the modernized →*sramli* music played by Swabian (German, →*sváb*) village bands. →**esküvő**

lakodalom (lagzi) *wedding*; peasant (→*paraszt*) wedding (→*esküvő*) held in a village with the observance of old folk traditions; it is usually attended by a large number of guests and has been known to last for days.

lakosságcsere '*exchange of the population*' (lit.); the euphemism for ethnic cleansing which in the aftermath of WW II was conducted with the approval of (not to say orders from) the "Big

Three" (Stalin, Truman, and Churchill) at Potsdam; it involved the mass 're-settlement' (→*kitelepítés*) of Hungarian peasants from Czechoslovakia to Hungary, from where, in turn, the Hungarian Germans, or Swabians (→*svábok*) were forced to move to Germany, and their abandoned houses and lands were distributed among "resettled" Hungarians, whose homes and property left behind were grabbed by Slovak volunteers from Hungary.

lakótelep '*living settlement*', '*living colony*' (lit.), *housing estate*; beginning with the sixties (→*hatvanas évek*), for twenty years identical pre-fabricated apartment blocks (produced by "housing factories") were put up in desolate groups throughout the country to accommodate villagers drawn to the towns by industry (not to mention the happy prospect of escaping the new producers' co-operatives, the →*termelőszövetkezet*). These people, the new proletarians of socialism (→*szocializmus*), ended up living in identical, and identically small and confining apartments (→*lakás*) in the new drab and unfriendly "colonies", whose prestige was so low from the very beginning, that by now many have turned, wholly or in part, into slums. →**panel**

Lánc-lánc, eszterlánc ... the first words of a children's song which continues: "... *eszterlánci cérna, / cérna volna, selyem volna, / mégis kifordulna* ..."; sung mostly by little girls who hold hands and go round in a circle; its meaning is shrouded in mystery, which also makes it untranslatable.

Lánchíd *Chain Bridge*; the first bridge over the Danube (→*Duna*) as it flows through Hungary; situated in the heart of the Inner City (→*Belváros*) of →*Pest*, it was inaugurated in 1848, connecting, for the first time, the two parts of the future Hungarian capital; along with so much else, both buildings and institutions, it was the brainchild of →*Széchenyi*; the people of →*Budapest* have a sentimental attachment to it: they think it is very beautiful and are proud of it; after it was blown up (along with the other bridges) by the Germans during the siege of 1945, it was the first to be rebuilt.

lángos '*flame cake*' (lit.); the most popular "fast food" at Hungarian markets and fairs (→*vásár*); a big handful of yeast dough is flattened out by hand and quickly fried in lots of hot oil, whereby it develops air pockets, which make it light and soft; it is eaten hot with lots of roughly ground salt, though aficionados also rub it with garlic and spread fresh sour cream on top; not altogether unlike the TexMex speciality "fried bread".

lecsó *ratatouille*; a vegetable casserole made with fresh tomatoes and peppers (→*paprika*) in a base of rendered fatty bacon (→*szalonna*) and a liberal helping of sliced onion (→*vöröshagyma*); fried in oil and stewed slowly, it is even better with the addition of sliced sausage

(→*kolbász*). Considered an authentic Hungarian dish (→*magyaros étel*), especially when prepared with the addition of a hot green pepper or two, it is made in just about every household during the summer months, called the "*lecsó*-season", when tomatoes and peppers grown in the open fileds are cheap, and is usually consumed as a one-dish meal with several slices of fresh bread (→*kenyér*), though in restaurants it is often served as an accompaniment to baked or roasted meat.

legény *lad*; though it used to mean 'assistant' or 'apprentice' as well as 'a young man of the village', today its meaning is restricted to the latter; it is a rural word, though any young man may be called or addressed with it (especially if he is unmarried!), since it is decidedly a familiar and endearing term; if someone has stood his ground in a tough situation, he is referred to as "a lad on the dam" (*legény a gáton*). →**menyecske**

legénybúcsú '*lad's farewell*' (lit.), *stag party*; a rural tradition which has caught on in the towns, whereby on the day before his wedding (→*esküvő*) the groom's friends organize a party (*görbe este*, or "crooked evening") for him to bid farewell to his life as a "lad" (→*legény*); there is also a *leánybúcsú*, or "girl's farewell".

lekvár *jam*; though it can be made from any kind of fruit, it is generally made from apricots, sour cherries and plums, which are grown in great quantities in Hungary; most housewives still find themselves driven to produce their very own home-made jam (even if they do not have their own orchard); the jam, stored in jars in the pantry (→*éléskamra*), is used throughout the year as filling for cakes and is spread on bread for breakfast (→*reggeli*) or a snack; the preparation of plum jam, or *szilvalekvár* (plum butter), calls for special expertise, for it needs be made over a low fire in a cauldron, and requires almost constant stirring; it takes many hours of cooking time to attain just the right thick consistency; a good thing that home-made plum butter can be bought at the market.

Lencsi baba '*lentil doll*' (lit.), *bean baby, Lencsi doll*; a doll made from discarded or left over rags and stuffed with beans for very young girls; it is like the Raggedy Ann, except it is stocky with short arms and legs and a big, round head (and usually no hair); its great big eyes seem wide open from surprise, and remind people of dark lentils.

lengyel piac '*Polish market*' (lit.), *black market*; also ironically referred to as the *KGST–piac* ("Comecon market"); during the shortage economy of the socialist years (→*szocializmus*), many people made a living by smuggling goods from one socialist country to another, either because they were unavailable to begin with, or because they could be sold at a handsome profit, being cheaper in their country of origin; after a while, just about every large town had its own "market", ignored by the authorities, where these early entrepreneurs (→*vállalkozó*) sold their wares, most of whom were adroit and impoverished Poles (→*lengyelek*), who gave their name to these markets. Today, these places, where the poor go in search of poor quality, counterfeit, smuggled goods they can have cheap from Asian vendors are known as "Chinese markets". →**Teleki tér**; **vám**

lengyelek, a *Poles, the*; though the Poles were the immediate neighbors of Hungary for a thousand years, they never went to war (possibly because of the Carpathians separating the two countries) on the other hand, they gave each other kings, queens and saints, took in each other's people when forced to flee (the last time during WW II, when an entire Polish army found refuge in Hungary); the mutual sympathy (kept alive by the sense of a common fate, and unique in Central Europe) has lasted to this day; every Hungarian youngster visits Poland by the time he or she reaches adolescence (if not before), and knows the short ditty in both languages: "*Magyars and Poles are good friends, they fight and drink together*".

lichthóf *lichthof* (Germ.); *light well;* there is always an extremely narrow yard, hardly bigger from wall to wall than a closet, left by the architect between two tall, adjacent apartment houses (→*bérház*), whose Hungarian name, *világítóudvar* (lit. '*yard to let in light*') is however rarely if ever used; it was conceived so that the parts of an apartment farthest from the street (mostly bathrooms and water closets) should receive a modicum of natural light (at least on the upper floors), and most of all, some fresh air; there is hardly anything as sad as depressing as a maid's room (→*cselédszoba*) looking out on the *lichthóf*.

lila hagyma '*purple onions*' (lit.), *red onions*; →**kékhagyma**

locsolás '*sprinkling*'; the widespread Easter (→*Húsvét*) folk custom practiced in towns and villages alike which, though it has become modernized, is as popular as ever. The gist of it is that on Easter Monday the men sprinkle the women, i.e., originally it must have been a fertility rite, though today women are no longer 'sprinkled' by having a bucketful of water thrown at them, but with (cheap) cologne, usually sprinkled on their head. In small towns and villages, the girls compete to see who has the largest number of sprinklers, for an Easter visit to the home of a girl's parents is an accepted form of courting. The sprinklers, who usually go around in groups dressed in their Sunday best, recite some short rhyme proper for the occasion, which invariably ends with the question, "*May I sprinkle the flower?*", after which they receive painted eggs from the women (small boys also get some money), as well as cakes (→*sütemény*) and drinks (which, as the morning wears on, fills many a street with men in inordinately high spirits); then after a short stay, the sprinklers continue on to the home of the next unwed maiden. Still, it is customary to sprinkle every woman in the house the men and boys visit, regardless of age, even old women. Boys (some of whom carry the custom into old age) begin sprinkling when they are eight or ten, for they regard this Easter rite as a pleasant way to earn some extra pocket money.

lovasnemzet '*nation of horsemen*' (lit.), *equestrian nation*; the most striking element of the romantic image of Hungarians (which stood in close relationship to the image of the →*puszta*, or Great Plains), it is probably of German origin (and possibly was inspired by the popular image of the →*huszár*), but it had no basis in fact at any time in the near or distant past, at least not since the Conquest (→*Honfoglalás*); however, this does not mean that the Hungarians themselves did not enjoy seeing themselves in this light; on the other hand, today it merely brings an indulgent smile to people's faces, along with all the other romantic clichés.

Lukács-fürdő *St. Luke's Bath;* one of the oldest thermal baths in Buda (combining a pool and steam bath) in whose waters even the Romans had submerged themselves, and next to whose springs the Knights Hospitallers built a hospital in the Middle Ages. Today, it is the favorite watering hole of Budapest's intelligentsia (each bath in Budapest having its own "regulars", just like the cafés had theirs many years ago); depending on the day and the time of day, it is visited by lawyers, journalists, actors, book publishers, musicians, etc., etc., for a bit of swimming and sweating, but first and foremost, for the sake of each other's company.

Lúdas Matyi *Matthew the Gooseboy*; the tale in which Matyi, a poor peasant lad who suffers a gross injustice at the hands of the servants (→*hajdú*) of the local squire when the goose he is taking to the market is taken from him, decides to teach his tormentor a lesson; he returns three times in various guises to give the rich squire back the caning he had received at his order, and thus manages to avenge himself; the story, which abounds in humorous and unexpected turns and is known in several literary version, is popular among young and old alike; it has been made into a film as well as a play.

M

maga *you*; the form of address (→*megszólítás*) used between individuals who are not on close terms; it is more confidential, though, than the use of →*ön*, though when used to address someone in a lower social position, it can easily turn condescending; strangely enough, among the aristocracy (→*arisztokrácia*) and the grand bourgeoisie, married couples also used to address each other as *maga*, and so do children when speaking to their parents.

magyar ember evés közben ... the starting words of the axiomatic saying which continues: *nem beszél*, (lit.) 'a Hungarian will not talk while eating', used (mostly by elderly gentlemen) to quiet children who are talking at the table; it is a bit of classical but silly nonsense of unknown origin, just like the commonly held belief that the ideal Hungarian style consists of simple, laconic sentences that are co-ordinates, while subordinate sentences (or clauses) are complex and therefore (?!) alien to the logic of Hungarian. →**sírva vigad a magyar**

Magyar Honvédség (MH) *Hungarian Armed Forces*; the traditional name of the Hungarian armed forces brought back into current use after the change in regime (→*rendszerváltás*) to replace *Néphadsereg*, or 'People's Army', used under socialism (→*szocializmus*); the name includes all of the armed forces, the Army, the Air Force, and the Duna Flotilla as well (since in 1918 the Navy was handed over to the new Kingdom of Yugoslavia). →**honvédség**; **katonaság**

magyar kártya '*Hungarian cards*' (lit.); a suite of playing cards consisting of 32 cards and four "colors" (pumpkins/diamonds, acorns/clubs, red/hearts, green/leaves) in which seven is the lowest card, while the highest is the ace (there being no joker); most its figures and illustrations represent the characters and scenes from the story of William Tell, which has a strong anti-Habsburg (→*Habsburg*) theme. →**ulti**

magyar konyha *Hungarian cuisine*; it is a popular, though inaccurate view that Hungarian food is simply hot (→*csípős*) and fatty (→*zsíros*); it is actually quite various, for the many different assimilated peoples all brought something to it, as a consequence of which we could safely regard it as a new cuisine born of the cross-fertilization of Balkan and German cooking in which the onion (→*hagyma*) and sour cream meets with the hot paprika (→paprika) and fat (→*zsír*), not to mention tomatoes picked fresh off the vine or the conjoining of (sour) cabbage (→*káposzta*) or Serbian →*lecsó* with Italian-type ragout. In its present form, it was developed by inventive restaurateurs at the end of the 19th century, who "retailored" the classical Hungarian dishes, made with local ingredients, to satisfy the tastes of a multi-cultural bourgeoisie. →**gulyás**; **túróscsusza**; **palacsinta**; **pörkölt**; **töltöttkáposzta**; **paprikás**; **tészta**

magyar nemzet, a *Hungarian nation, the*; legally and politically, every citizen of the state is part of the nation (and is thus, in this sense, "Hungarian"), because he is part of a common fate; in a more narrow sense, the Hungarian nation is a community of all those whose mother-tongue and culture is Hungarian, which is not a question of citizenship but consciousness of belonging; i.e., anyone, whether living within or without the country's frontiers is Hungarian if he considers himself Hungarian. →**ki a magyar**; **asszimiláció**; **névmagyarosítás**; **magyar nyelv**; **magyar származású**

magyar nóta '*Hungarian song*' (lit.); tunes written in imitation of folk songs (→*népdal*) and performed in the manner of the →*csárdás*, mostly by Gipsy bands (→*cigányzenekar*), which came into fashion in the early 19th century along with the appearance of a new, heightened sense of national consciousness. These songs, which were still very popular during the first half of the 20th century, were written and performed by an impressive variety of talent, from Gipsy violinists (*cigányprímás*) and inspired dilettante army officers, to village apothecaries, a telling sign of their popularity in all manner of social circles. Though Hungarian songs have suffered a loss of prestige in recent years, public radio still plays them regularly (at noon on Sunday, after the chiming of the church bells, at lunch time!); they are also sung by the elderly and the unschooled village populace, who identify with them, for their "Hungarian" tunes seem so familiar; their lyrics usually describe some banal situation in a highly sentimental manner which, when taken metaphorically, makes them the perfect vehicles for the expression of deep feelings and emotions;"*The fields have turned hoary, / the old betyár grey* ...", this and the like are sung by men among themselves when they are well into their cups, for it makes them think of their own lives, which is surely the main function of these tunes to this day – and, of course, the entertainment of diners in expensive restaurants (and cheap village inns), where the programs of Gipsy bands consist of such "Hungarian" songs. →***Akácos út ...***; ***Csak egy kislány van a világon ...***; **Dankó Pista**; **cigányozás**; **sírva vigad a magyar**

magyar nyelv, a *Hungarian language, the*; "the language of the knowing smile", as the poet Gyula Illyés said; when Hungarians (→*magyarok*) meet in some far distant corner of the world it is their secret means of communication in which they engage with pleasure, for it unites them at all times, seeing how no one else can possibly understand it, or even learn it (and if someone does none the less, Hungarians consider it a miracle), and even a couple of words said in Hungarian will bring the best out of them, for they take it a sign of sympathy; they are extremely proud of their language, which comes from two roots (Finnish and Turkic), not to mention words of Persian and Slav, German and Latin origin, and who knows how many other languages, from which it was kneaded together, and they are proud of its expressive power, too, its intricate sentence structure and tricky conjugation, which makes it eminently suited for expressing the finest of meanings, its formatives and prefixes, the rich storehouse of its synonyms, the impressive variety of its poetry, and not least of all, the fact that the finest nuances, versifications and rhythms of any language can be translated into Hungarian, a fact born out by the first longer, coherent piece of poetry to survive, "*Mary's Lament*", translated from the Latin around 1150 (and which can still be understood today!); and they accept with a great sense of loss the sad fact that their literature, which they consider the greatest cultural accomplishment of the nation, must remain their secret treasure for ever; today it is spoken in eight countries of the Carpathian Basin by approximately 15 million people (not to mention another million and a half to two million in the rest of the world), and though it has dialects as well as words used locally, this does not mean an impediment of any sort to anyone, especially since there is a unified sense of culture and tradition throughout the entire linguistic region, from the easternmost Székelyföld (in Romania) to the western őrvidék (in Austria), where anyone who speaks the language, or at least considers himself Hungarian, is thought of as Magyar. →**költő**

magyar származású '*of Hungarian origin*' (lit.); the expression used by Hungarians for Hungarians (expatriate scientists, musicians, artists, successful businessmen) who made a name for themselves outside the Carpathian Basin (but not as a citizen of the fatherland), possibly current because there is not always knowing whether the celebrity in question wishes to be identified with the land of his ancestors; as a result of the practically continuous exodus of people from Hungary which began in the middle of the last century, there are Hungarians in every country of every continent of the world, whose achievements are proudly acknowledged and nurtured by national lore; Hungarians are fully aware that they must not jump to hasty conclusions about nationhood on the basis of someone's name, after all, even in the mother country more people have names indicating foreign origin than Hungarian family names, while the world at large (not to mention the neighboring countries) are full of families with Hungarian sounding names who have long since lost any sense of their Hungarian identity. →**külföldre szakadt hazánkfia**; **mindenki magyar**; **kivándorló**; **disszidens**; **magyarok**; **ki a magyar**

magyar tenger '*the Hungarian sea*' (lit.); the romantic and nostalgic name given to the →*Balaton* during the last century, when the nascent Reform Movement (→*reform*) began the modernization of the country, and the anglophile aristocrats pushing for the development of transportation began commercial shipping on the lake; later it became a naively inflated/bombastic and banal cliché kept alive for the benefit of tourists.

Magyar Tudományos Akadémia →**Akadémia, az**

magyarok istene, a '*the God of Hungarians*' (lit.); it is hard to put your finger on the exact meaning of this strange, quaint-sounding yet frequently used expression; all we know is that it does not refer to some sort of pagan Hungarian god; the idea that the Hungarians are a "chosen people" just like the Jews (and consequently have their own God, to whom they are related in a special way), at least in the sense that the Lord punishes it more harshly for its sins than other nations, most probably originates with the Bible, which influenced Hungarian culture profoundly; Hungarian Protestantism (→*protestantizmus*), too, which called itself the "Hungarian religion" as opposed to the Latinate internationalism of the Catholic Church (→*katolikus egyház*) attempted to explain the bitter trials and tribulations of Hungarian history with recourse to it; the lofty refrain of the National Song (→*Nemzeti dal*), too, goes: "*By all the gods of Hungary / we hereby swear, / that the yoke of slavery / No more shall we wear*"; it can still be heard today as a jocular warning: "*Majd megtudod, hogy hol lakik a magyarok Istene!*", i.e., if you don't watch yourself, you'll find out where the god of the Hungarians dwells, meaning, "you'll get what's coming to you." →**kereszténység védőbástyája, a**

magyarok, a *Hungarians, the*; though fully conscious of the fact that their country has shrunk in size in the course of 20th century history (*nota bene:* Hungarian poets have always written about a "small homeland"), and also that they are few in number (15 million altogether in eight countries of the Carpathian Basin, though the various national censuses come up with contradictory figures), a fact which (lately) they have been taking into consideration when making major decisions; still (especially among themselves) they often pride themselves on the fact that in the world at large the significance of their country and nation far outweighs their number, an argument for which they bring up as proof not only world renowned scientists, artists, musicians, Nobel Prize winners and sportmen of Hungarian origin (→*magyar származású*), which also proves in their eyes what a gifted people they are (for though they may not always be fully conversant with the scale of values honored elsewhere, they meticulously keep track of everyone in the world who had at least one Hungarian ancestor), and they (the more quixotic souls in search of recognition, anyway) will also remind anyone (in case they haven't heard or have forgotten) that Hungary was the "defending bastion/shield of Christianity" (→*kereszténység védőbástyája*); the popular clichés about them (current especially in German-speaking areas) which speak of them as an "equestrian nation" (→*lovasnemzet*), as well as fiery, passionate and unrestrained, not to mention proud, brings an indulgent smile to their lips (although they do think of themselves as "gallant"); on the other hand, they feel offended by the witticism, current in America, that "if a Hungarian follows you through a revolving door, he'll come out ahead of you" (this despite the fact that they see themselves as resourceful and clever); furthermore, almost every Hungarian harbors a grudge against the "outside world" for not acknowledging their talent (especially their neighbors, who rarely do), not to mention their industry and other fine characteristics, of which they are most proud of their cultural accomplishments, such as their poetry (→*költészet*), which is nearly inaccessible to non-Hungarians because it is dependent on their linguistic and/or other traditions, not to mention their other merits and virtues, which they believe deservedly puts them on a par with the union of European (→*Európa*), i.e., Western European, i.e., "worthy", i.e., "civilized" nations (which is one reason they insist on being considered Central-European with any other classification considered an affront); they believe that they are dogged by ill luck and that their history is tragic and unfairly ill-starred (and that is why they dwell on the past so much, hoping it will give rise to understanding and sympathy from others); they consider their short temperedness (and gullability) a national shortcoming, as well as its adjunct, their quick loss of heart, while their penchant for breaking into opposing camps they see as a national (mortal) sin; their famous pessimism (→*pesszimizmus*) is fired by bitter historical experience (though the high rate of suicide is surely due to much more complex factors), though this does not inevitably lead to a state of melancholy; on the contrary, Hungarians are proud of their sense of humor, which they credit with helping them survive their history (which they see as a never ending struggle against a continual stream of conquerors which began with the waning of their glorious Middle Ages, and also the history of justified self-defense); they also consider themselves hospitable and their country a true melting pot (with barely every other Hungarian having a Hungarian surname), and are at a loss when they meet with antipathy or distrust, especially in the territories taken away from the mother country by the Peace Treaty of Versailles (→*Trianon*) in 1921, and where a third of of all Hungarians still live, whereas in the course of 20th century history, they were repeatedly faced with rejection, which made them more circumspect, but certainly not humbler. →**ki a magyar**; **székely**; **magyar nyelv**; **magyar nemzet**; **öngyilkosság**; **Közép Európa**

Magyarország '*Country/Land of the Magyars*' (lit.), *Hungary*; the jocular aphorism from →*Petőfi* according to which "*Ha a föld Isten kalapja, Magyarország a bokréta rajta*" (lit. 'If the earth be God's hat, Hungary is the nosegay atop it') is still current, this despite the fact that one of the two adjectives Hungarians most often use to describe their country is "small" (the other being "sweet"), neither of which has done the least harm to their feelings for Hungary, just as nothing has shaken the faith of generation after generation of emigrants in the old saying (in Latin!) according to which "*Extra Hungariam non est vita* ...", i.e., 'you can't live outside of Hungary', even though this saying is frequently stuck on the banner of arrogant, blind, and self-righteous Hungarian provincialism, too. →**történelmi Magyarország**

magyaros arc (*typical*) *Hungarian face*; though anthropological research has shown that the body-build, head shape and facial features of today's Hungarians do not differ from that of neighboring peoples (statistically speaking, at any rate), what's more, that scientifically speaking, they can best be characterized as the amalgamation of all of their most salient features, popular wisdom has it that a real Hungarian (*magyaros*, i.e., handsome and confidence-inspiring) physiognomy consists of white skin, dark hair, a ("reddish-brown"), rotund face, high forehead, prominent cheekbones, and a straight nose (under which there is generally imagined a mustache, and its wearer is seen parading around in a mailman's or railman's uniform, or else a hussar's pellise). →**magyaros étel**; **magyaros ruha**; **Kunság**

magyaros ruha *Hungarian costume*; not to be confused with folk costume (→*népviselet*), Hungarian costume is the style of dress which received the defiant name of →*atilla* in the early 19th century, when it was adopted from the (Turkish-inspired) fashion worn by the nobility (→*nemesség*) in the 16th and 17th centuries; thanks to the rise of national self-consciousness, city folk, who till then wore European bourgeois-style dress (called "German dress"), discarded them in favor of a special type of jacket which closes high round the neck, hugs the body down to the waist, where it is narrow, and from where it gently flares out, with a slit in the back, and which foregoes the use of buttons in favor of toggles fastened to passementerie; it reaches down to mid-thigh and is worn with tall, narrow boots (→*csizma*) and narrow pants; it was worn by men and women alike, though the cloth and the color of women's jackets were different, and instead of wearing a white shirt with a big collar folded out over the *atilla*, or else a fringed silk scarf thrown over it, they wore a laced bodice instead); though the men's jackets were generally black to begin with, after the defeat of the War of Independence (→*Szabadságharc*) it became black *de rigeur* as a sign of national mourning and resistance, which later became customary; in the War of Independence the Hungarian army (→*honvédség*) wore a "coffee-brown *atilla*", and the →*atilla* was also worn by the members of various national movements between the two World Wars (again as a sign of anti-German sentiment), not to mention school boys (as a school uniform with a hat, which together was by then called the →*bocskai*), while since the change in regime (→*rendszerváltás*) people fired by high patriotic feelings have started wearing it again for ceremonial occasions, though without boots; yet in the 20th century, wearing Hungarian costume has always been considered somewhat eccentric. →**díszmagyar**

május elseje *First of May*; called "the celebration of the international working class" and "the celebration of labor" for forty years (even though it was an off-work holiday), parades were held in every big city, in Budapest the crowds passed by the statue of Stalin (→*Sztálin–szobor*), and everyone carried red flags and signs, and "mass songs" (→*tömegdal*) came blaring from the loudspeakers installed on branches of trees (instead of being sung by the marchers), not to mention the official slogans approved by the Party (→*Párt*); at first participation by the workers (→*dolgozók*) was compulsory, then merely "advisable", and was followed by fairs (free beer and hotdogs) held in the public parks which, however, bore only a faint resemblance to the May Days (*Majális*) of old; ever since the change in regime (→*rendszerváltás*), the old goings on have been everywhere replaced by a simple Sunday (→*vasárnap*) mood, though in trade–union speech a new PC–expression emerged: "the day of solidarity among employees".

mák *poppy seed* (*cone*); formerly found growing in just about every village vegetable garden, for it serves as the main ingredient of poppy seed noodles (→*mákostészta*), which is one of the best loved sweet dishes to this day, while *mákony*, the thick, heady paste that is cooked from it was used as a sleeping potion before the advent of pharmacies; the word is also used figuratively to signify various means of pulling the wool over people's eyes, stupifying them; strangely enough, *mákvirág* (lit. 'poppy flower'), whose official name is *pipacs* (poppy), is used as the slightly jocular designation for an impostor. →**beigli**

mákostészta '*poppy seed noodles*' (lit.); usually this food (a childhood favorite) is missed most by Hungarians living abroad – and, of course, their stable, bread (→*kenyér*); it is made by cooking long strips of dough (→*tészta*) and sprinkling it liberally with ground poppy seed mixed with sugar; it is usually eaten after bean soup (→*bableves*) as the main course; some people also add apricot or plum jam to it, but jam noodles (→*lekvár*) are also eaten as a separate dish, and so is cottage cheese pasta (→*túróstészta*). →**tarhonya**

mama/papa *mum/dad*, *mommy/daddy*; →**anyu/apu**

manó *goblin*; a wicked little creature (dwarf) who lives in the forest (or at the bottom of lakes and streams), and just like the pox (→*fene*) it "takes you away" or "gobbles you up"; it can usually be heard as part of jocular swearing or invectives as well as exclamations indicative of surprise, as in "*Mi a manó?*" (roughly translated, 'Well, I'll be!')

március 15. *March 15th*; the day of the outbreak of the revolution (→*forradalom, 1848*) when the crowds that had gathered in the light spring rain in front of the National Museum (→*Nemzeti Múzeum*) listened to the recital of →*Petőfi*'s the "*National Song*" (→*Nemzeti dal*), completed only the night before, after which, lead by the "revolutionary youth" wearing cockades (→*kokárda*), they stormed a printing plant, declared the freedom of the press, and toppled the government. We know details of this day, one of the happiest in Hungarian history, from the diary of the 25 year old poet himself, who described it in great detail, and whose only child, Zoltánka, was conceived on that day. Ever since, it is customary to wear cockades made from ribbons with the national colors (→*nemzetiszín*) on every 15th of March, which in the 70s and 80s was considered such a dangerous sign of subversion, that the Workers' Militia (→*Munkásőrség*) was called out to disperse the students silently gathered in front of Petőfi's statue near Elizabeth Bridge by the banks of the Danube.

margarin *margarine*; until recently, it was used only by the poor as a substitute for butter (→*vaj*), and even in middle-class kitchens housewives used it for baking with an uneasy conscience.

Markó, a (pron. *mahr–kow*); a street in the Inner City (→*belváros*) of Pest named after an early 19th century Romantic painter, but everyone thinks of it as the "legal Budapest" (hence the definite article), for each of its (uniformly huge and forbidding) buildings houses a law court of some sort (and one also a prison for those standing trial); the street also houses the building of the High Court of Appeals, while the Ministry of Justice is within five minutes' walking distance.

Maroknyi székely… *A handful of Szeklers…* (lit.); the popular name for the Szekler anthem (→*székely himnusz*) taken from one of its lines which continues: "*… turning to dust, like a rock, / On an ocean turbulent with the struggle of many nations, / The current, oh, goes over our heads a hundred times; / Do not abandon Transylvania, Transylvania, oh, Lord!*" (lit.).

Marosvásárhely (pron. *mah–rosh–vah–shar–hey*), '*Market on the river Maros*' (lit.), *Tîrgu Mures* (Romanian); the largest city of →*Székelyföld* half of whose population is still Hungarian-speaking, as a result of which it is gradually taking over the role of →*Kolozsvár* as the cultural and financial center of the Hungarians of Transylvania (→*Erdély*).

maszek (*private*) *entrepreneur/artisan, privately owned*; the word comes from the fifties (→*ötvenes évek*), when abbreviations came into vogue, and it was put together from "*ma*gán *szek*tor" (i.e., the 'private sector' of the national economy); it was a highly pejorative word for those couple of thousand small tradesmen, craftsmen, small dealers and peasants whose shops or workshops were (accidentally?) not touched by nationalization (→*államosítás*), and who, despite being threatened, would not give up their small shop or hand over their land to the farmers' co-operatives (→*termelőszövetkezet*), chosing independence over all the perfidious encouragements and "incentives", wished to make a living on his own, and would rather pay the punitive taxes and put up with police harassment; thanks to its use by official sources, it still carries a highly disparaging connotation, and means someone who makes a living through dishonest means. →**Váci utca**

matrózblúz '*sailors' blouse*' (lit.); a simple blouse (usually white) cut straight at the sides and closing high on the neck with a wide (usually dark blue) square-shaped collar that covers the shoulders and is accentuated by a narrow white (or blue) ribbon; today it is worn only by (reluctant) school girls as a uniform or else during graduation; before the war it was worn by small boys, too, on special occasions (there was a "sailor hat" to go with it); the fashion comes from the late 19th century, from the time of the German (and Austro-Hungarian) drive to build a fleet. →**érettségi**

Mátyás király *King Mathias*; the king who reigned in the second half of the 15th century and who made Hungary into a big and rich country and brought the Italian Renaissance to Hungary, and whose character and deeds became the stuff of folk tales; his image (especially his characteristic, big nose) is recognized by people even today, and a saying which mentions his name is still in current (jocular) use: "*Meghalt Mátyás, oda az igazság*", i.e., 'Mathias is dead, so much for truth'. →**Mátyás-templom**; **Kolozsvár**; **corvina**; **Visegrád**

Mátyás-templom *Mathias Church*; though the common misconception that this was the coronation church persists, only King Mathias (→*Mátyás király*), Emperor Francis Joseph (→*Ferenc József*) and Charles IV, the last king of Hungary, were actually crowned here; its present shape, reminiscent of a Medieval church, is really a masterpiece of reconstruction and architectural historicism which, along with the imaginary coronations and mock-Gothic (reconstructed) royal sarcophagus (in which only the bones are for real) everyone happily accepts as authentic; the original burial site of the Hungarian kings at →*Székesfehérvár*, not to mention the real medieval coronation church, have long since perished, while the coronation church of the →*Habsburg* kings of Hungary is in Bratislava (→*Pozsony*); in the summer it is crowded with tourists and hardly fit for its original function; on the other hand, the *nouveau riche* like to hold their weddings here; otherwise, it is mostly used for concert recitals. →**Halászbástya**; **Vár, a**

matyó (pron. *mah–tyaw*); a person or persons from the village of Mezőkövesd and its surroundings at the foothills of the northern mountains who speak a dialect called *palóc* and are famous for their beautiful folk costumes; these costumes often display the characteristic *matyó* embroidery with brightly coloured floral patterns on a black base; clothing with *matyó* patterns, especially blouses, are popular with tourists, and are sold as authentic Hungarian folkwear; tourists (and expatriate Hungarians) are especially fond of *matyó* dolls dressed top to toe in embroidered *matyó* outfits. →**kalocsai hímzés**

MÁV *Hungarian State Railways* (lit.); since its foundation, it is the largest employer in the country; it used to be famous for its military-style organization and discipline as well as its reliability and precision (according to old legends, at any rate); in its present state of disorganization and decay, it is not an institution any longer, but a state owned company.

megszólítás *address*, *title*; before WW II the proper way to address people was regulated by a strict code of etiquette, which today brings back another historical era; the rules of address and title, which pertained to civil servants, too, and indicated their rank on the basis of their salaries fixed by categories, were strictly applied; today such words of address seem incredibly feudal, and there are few who could possibly sort them out; even without them (and the use of comrade, or →*elvtárs*, which has also melted into thin air), the use of →*ön*, →*maga* and →*te* alone are complex enough (not to mention →*bácsi* and →*néni*); while as a result of the whirlwind social changes that have taken place since the change in regime (→*rendszerváltás*) →*úr* has more or less become the equivalent of *Mr.*, though the use of →*asszony* and *Mrs.* are not at all the same; it is especially difficult to settle on the proper use of language in writing (letters, titles, forms of address), as if it were attempting, of its own accord, to express the new social status, and most people are puzzled when faced with →*úrhölgy*, →*úrasszony* and →*úrnő*, which have suddenly reemerged from former (linguistic and social) times. →**nagysága**; **őnagysága**; **nagyságos asszony**; **nagyságos úr**; **kegyelmes úr**; **kegyed**; **méltóságos úr**; **úrhölgy**; **úrasszony**; **úrnő**; **koma**; **mama/papa**; **anyu/apu**; **bátyám**; **jóember**

megye *county*; Hungary has now 19 counties, which basically follow the administrative boundaries drawn by St. Stephen (→*Szent István*), who first organized the country into counties. Each county has its own identity and character (those of the →*Hajdúság*, for instance, consider themselves strongwilled and adamant, while the people of →*Sopron* are proud of being industrious), so much so that the largest counties and those that lie furthest from the capital think of themselves as veritable separate countries; after all, for a thousand years the county was the administrative basis for the autonomy of the nobility (→*nemes*) and thus the "nest" of the opposition to the centralized powers that be, and also the upholder of traditions, both good and bad; its political power began to wane in the mid-19th century when after the defeat of the War of Independence (→*Szabadságharc*) imperial bureaucrats took over government management, "modernizing" the up till then bureaucrat-free administration, until today counties as units of public administration have only very limited powers. →**főispán**; **alispán**

melegek '*the warm ones*' (lit.); *gay*; the word, which has come to be regarded as politically correct, has nevertheless been unable to to replace either the official expression "homosexual", nor any of the popular, generally used expressions, a clear indication that the aversion still current in Hungarian society has not appreciably lessened, this despite the fact that blatant rejection has given way to tacit acquiescence to the inevitable.

méltóságos úr '*graceful/dignified sir*' (lit.), *your grace*; a title lower than "your excellency" (→*kegyelmes úr*), but higher than "your honor" (→*nagyságos úr*), all three are obsolete and are used only ironically or in jest. →**megszólítás**

menedzser *manager*; a word from the sphere of the new Hungarian capitalism with a highly positive aura which arrived after the change in regime (→*rendszerváltás*), but does not mean the same thing as in English, since it is used in reference to the opposite of the company directors of the former socialist economy appointed by the ministries and therefore answerable to them (one might call them top aparatchniks), i.e., it is used as the synonym for "entrepreneur" and (for the time being, at least) it has a connotation of success and modernity. →**vállalkozó**

mentek, mendegéltek... '*they went/wandered on and on a little ...*' (lit.); the formula used in Hungarian folk tales to link together the episodes about the adventures of the hero. →**Hol volt, hol nem volt**; **Óperencia**

menyasszonytánc '*bride's dance*' (lit.); at a village wedding (→*lakodalom*) the festivities reach their peak when the best man (→*vőfély*) asks the bride to dance; after turning round with her once or twice, he shouts that "The bride is for sale!", whereupon the wedding guests, who have been standing in line, now come up to the bride one by one, throw money into the plate (or basket) held by the bride's vigilant mother-in-law, they spin her round once or twice, too, then hand her over to the next person waiting; each guest must pay more to dance with the bride than the previous guest, with the price (donation) being announced out loud by the best man heading the "auction"; provided the wedding guests are numerous and well-to-do, the custom gives the blushing bride – who also receives wedding presents from those she dances with – a chance to dance herself into a small fortune; the bride's dance traditionally comes to an end when the bridegroom takes the bride from the arms of her last partner, who is usually her father or father-in-law.

menyecske *'little bride'*, *'little wife'* (lit.), *wifie;* a word used in the countryside to refer to a young married woman; older villagers also use it as a more general form of address when townspeople would say "young lady" or "young woman" (→*fiatalasszony*). →**betyár**

Mennyből az angyal ... *'The angel from Heaven...'*; the starting words of the best known Christmas carol people sing under the Christmas tree which continues: "*... has come down to you, shepherds, shepherds, / So that hurrying to Betlehem, you may see / God's son, who was born in a stable, in a stable, / He will be your saviour, truly, truly ...*" →**betlehem**

mézeskalács *'honey cake'* (lit,); before pastry shops (→*cukrászda*) were opened in the countryside (→*vidék*), sweet pastries were made by the so-called honey cake makers (*mézeskalácsos*), without whom no religious festival (→*búcsú*) or fair (→*vásár*) is complete; to this day, the most popular items sold by the honey cake makers in their tents are the heart shaped honey cake and the mounted hussar (→*huszár*), both of which are dry and hard, since they are not meant to be eaten, though there are also sweets sold for consumption, though never with cream; the red "hearts", given to girls as a message of love by their suitors, is ornamented with designs (sometimes texts) made from white sugar strips and have a mirror in the middle, so whoever looks in it will see herself or himself in it; the braids on the hussar's uniform (→*egyenruha*) are also made out of sugar; what's more, he is often given a face with a moustache (→*bajusz*), printed especially for pasting on the honeycake figure; the "babe in swaddling clothes" honeycake figure, whose message is unequivocal, is also popular, and so are the soft honeycakes made of brownish honey dough and covered with chocolate, which are the Hungarian countryside equivalents of the cookie.

MH →**Magyar Honvédség**

micisapka *cloth cap*; a soft flat hat with a visor made of cloth or leather; it was the typical headgear of workers back in the twenties, which by the fifties (→*ötvenes évek*) was also worn by functionaries (→*funckcionárius*) as a symbol of their (political) sympathy with the proletariat (as opposed to the tie, which they discarded); in the eighties, it reappeared as a Western fashion, and along with the beret (→*svájcisapka*), it was adopted by the intelligentsia (→*értelmiség*). →**kalap**

Mikulás (*Saint*) *Nicholas*; since Santa (Santa Claus) and Rudolph are (for the time being, at least) still not part of Hungarian Christmas lore, it is his close relative, St. Nicholas who comes bearing gifts for children on December 6th, his name's day; just like Santa, he appears dressed in an ankle-length red coat (as it befits a bishop!) with a red cap on his head and soft white beard (made out of cotton wool); he comes on foot, holding a shepherd's crook in one hand and carrying a sack on his back full of gifts (lit. '*... there are all sorts of good things in your bag, / red apples and peanuts, too ...*', the best known *Mikulás* song says); he knocks on the window and asks the children if they were good, in which case they will receive a gift, or bad, in which case the →*Krampusz*, or black devil, who has come along with give them a birch cane (→*virgács*) instead, and who makes all sorts of frightening faces and gestures as the short morality play to welcome the *Mikulás* is performed; in the fifties (→*ötvenes évek*) an all-out effort was made to displace the clerical St. Nicholas in favor of the Soviet "Father Winter" (*Télapó*), who was accompanied not by the black (reactionary) devil figure but a fairy dressed in white and called "Little Snow Flake" (*Hópelyhecske*), and truth to tell, the effort was not in vain, for in kindergartens, where *Mikulás* festivities are most often held today, Father Christmas has replaced the bishop St. Nicholas, and though poor Little Snow Flake has melted away, and the devilish *Krampusz*, too, is a rare sight these days (not so the cane!), Santa and his train are spotted in the shop windows with increasing frequency as the years go by, with only the chocolate Mikulás, who comes wrapped in colorful red foil in a variety of sizes continues to hold his own; children in Hungary put a pair of brightly polished (!) shoes in the window and not their socks on the mantle to be filled with gifts, which invariably include "golden" walnuts as well as apples (or oranges); by the way, the Hungarian St. Nick lives in a small village in Fejér County called Nagykarácsony (lit. *Great Christmas*), and that is where children write to him. →**nyuszi**

Millennium, a *Millennium* (*of 1896*), *the*; in Hungarian usage, when the Millennium is mentioned, everyone knows what is meant by it: the great millennial celebrations of 1896 to commemorate the 1000th anniversary of the Conquest (→*Honfoglalás*) of Hungary; visited by over 10 million people, it is still remembered with nostalgia, which is no wonder considering the nation's 20th century history; it was seen (then and now) as the veritable embodiment of the age, the turn of the century (→*századforduló*), which was self-assured and successful, and an occasion for shaping the nation's identity; the large-scale construction work in →*Budapest*, which has continued to shape the cityscape to this day, the national exhibition held there (dedicated to industry, agriculture, art and folk art) as well as the spectacular mounted county (→*megye*) paraders (including the descendants of the greatest names from the country's history), all dressed in medieval costume or →*díszmagyar*, meant the legitimation of "historical Hungary" (→"*történelmi Magyarország*"), which was being threatened from all directions, as well as the publishing abroad of the country's historical rights. →**Pusztaszer**

mindenki magyar '*everyone's Hungarian*' (lit.); a subject which comes up time and again in conversation, especially when people talk about all the famous individuals who have (or might conceivably have) some connection to Hungary (possibly a family relationship); though such conversations often take a jocular turn, they are never conducted merely in jest, since the repeated waves of emigration which began in the 19th century dispersed so many Hungarians to so many parts of the world, that who knows, a Hungarian grandmother may even be found lurking among the ancestors of some prime minister of some distant country. →**magyar származású**; **magyarok**; **ki a magyar?**

Mindenszentek *All Saints' Day*; also called the Day of the Dead (*Halottak Napja*), in Hungary it has been secularized along with Christmas (→*Karácsony*); several days before it is actually commemorated on November 1st, the pilgrimage to the cemeteries begins, the price of asters shoots sky high, people travel to their home towns to visit the graves of their parents, they chat with relatives they otherwise never see, and in the early twilight, the autumn mist shimmers from the light of thousands of candles placed on the graves; in every cemetery there is a small plot, flower bed or stone cross near the entrance where candles are lit for those who died abroad or have no graves, and the candles, which continue to be placed there in abundance to this day, melt from each other's heat, their wax spreads in flaming little rivulets as the small pine branches from the wreaths give out a soft hissing and cracking sound as they burn; All Saints' Day (Hallowmass, the day after Halloween) is a Catholic holiday which falls on November 1st, with the Day of the Dead falling on the 2nd, but life (or death?) has long since melted the two into one.

mit sütsz kis szűcs ... '*what are you baking little tailor...*' (lit.); this tongue twister is so horrifically hard, it is even difficult to write: *Mit sütsz, kis szűcs? Sós húst sütsz kis szűcs?* (lit. '*What are you baking, little taylor? Are you baking salt meat, little taylor?*'). It has to be repeated again and again, with an accelerating tempo, until your tongue does get all tied up in knots.

Mohács (pron. *mow–hatch*); a small town by the Danube near the southern boundary of (today's) Hungary, and the scene of possibly the most tragic battle in Hungarian history; this is where, after having conquered the Balkans (→*Balkán*), the Great Sultan Suleiman and his troops annihilated the Hungarian army in 1526, and with it the medieval kingdom of Hungary, the middle section of the country came under Turkish occupation (→*Hódoltság*), Transylvania (→*Erdély*) was separated from the mother country, while after the death of the Hungarian king, who fell at Mohács, the smaller northern and western parts of the country became part of the Habsburg Empire (→*Habsburgok*); from then on, the Habsburgs and the Turkish Empire engaged in what seemed an eternal battle for power, and which lasted for 150 years, on Hungarian soil, as a result of which large portions of the Great Plains (→*Alföld*) became depopulated and were cut off from the process of European development; Hungarians regard the battle of Mohács and the annihilating victory of "the Eastern Empire" such a tragic occurrence, that in many respects it's consequences can still be easily seen today. →**kereszténység védőbástyája**

Monarchia '*the Monarchy*' (lit.), *Austria–Hungary*; in the Hungarian vernacular, this is not a form of state or government, but a bygone country, and the popular name for the Austro-Hungarian Monarchy (→*Osztrák–Magyar Monarchia*); it was a state above nations which came about as a result of the Austro-Hungarian Compromise (→*Kiegyezés*) of 1867, and provided the framework for the identity of the Hungarian nation (which existed only within the framework of the empire) in contrast to the other nations (including the Germans) whose identity was shaped in opposition to the Habsburg Empire (and Hungary, which formed a part of it); having forgotten their conflicts with it, Hungarians today think of the Monarchy with nostalgia, as they have come to identify it with the idyllic world of the turn of the century (→*századforduló*). →**Ferenc József**; **Közép Európa**; **Trianon**; **Ausztria**

Móricka '*little Maurice*' (lit.); the best known figure of jokes for over a hundred years, he is a young boy who, with his combination of simple-mindedness and cunning, always manages to say something in the clincher which exposes the hypocricy of adults; with the passing of the years, he has shed his original Jewish (→*zsidó*) character (the name 'Móric' was considered a typically Jewish name). →**vicc**; **Arisztid és Tasziló**; **Kohn bácsi**; **székely góbé**

MSzMP *Hungarian Socialist Workers' Party* (Magyar Szocialista Munkáspárt); the last incarnation of the Communist Party (→*kommunista párt*) created in 1956 and dissolved in 1989. →**Párt, a**

MTA *Hungarian Academy of Sciences* (Magyar Tudományos Akadémia, HAS) →**Akadémia, az**

MTK →**FTC**

Mucsa the synonym for dull witted and stupid countryside thinking and behavior (with someone who acts in a boorish manner being called *mucsai*, i.e., 'from Mucsa'); however, contrary to popular belief, there is no such village on the map.

multik '*multies*' (lit.), *multinational companies*; the diminutive form of the word for multinational companies should not lead anyone to assume a friendly, loving attitude, for the average Hungarian watches their proliferation with a great deal of suspicion – their foreign ways, their commercials and advertisements, translated from Indo-German languages into atrocious Hungarian, and showing alien lifestyles which for him are unattainable. On the other hand, the cities of →*Székesfehérvár* and →*Győr* have the 'multies' to thank for the recent upsurge of their economies.

Munkácsy Mihály (pron. *moon–kahtchy*); for the Hungarian population at large, the embodiment of the painter par excellence; he achieved this status not only because his huge, beautifully painted late 19th century canvases were as popular overseas (one is hanging in the 42nd Street Public Library in New York) as in Paris or Budapest, but also because he led a life of adventure and fabulous abundance. →**Csontváry**

Munkás *worker* (lit.); the aptly named cigarette, whose bitter smell lingers on in the second class carriages of many a train, and the waiting rooms of many a railway station; cheap, foul-smelling and rolled from scratchy black tobacco, it has been replaced by the →*Szimfónia.*

munkás *worker*; though according to socialist ideology "all power is in the hands of the working people" (which included "the peasantry allied to the workers"), in actual fact the Hungarian workers, the majority of whom were peasants (→*paraszt*) driven off their land in the fifties (→*ötvenes évek*) did not even have their own independent unions, and though the Party (→*Párt*), which regained its power after the revolution (→*forradalom, 1956*), and which called itself "the Workers' Party", tried to court their favor (out of fear), their situation was best exemplified by the extremely high mortality rate of middle aged men working in the cities, who literally worked themselves to death. →**proligyerek**; **Munkás**; **dolgozó**

Munkásőrség '*Workers' Guard*' (lit.); *Workers' Militia*; a Party's army created after the defeat of the revolution (→*forradalom, 1956*) made up not so much of workers (→*munkás*) as functionaries (→*funkcionárius*) wearing sinister gray overalls and flat hats with visors (→*micisapka*) which was fortunately disbanded (in 1989) without having been used for anything besides disrupting demonstrations.

must *must*; grape juice before it ferments and becomes wine is a thick, unclear and sweet (slightly alcoholic) drink that young and old imbibe in October and November, even though everyone knows that it brings on diarrhea. →**bor**

N

nagyasszony '*great woman*' (lit.), *grande dame*; the counterpart of *nagyúr* (lit. '*great lord*', *prince*), now obsolete; if used, it refers to a woman who carries a lot of "weight", demands (and gets) respect, and has something of the old world about her; it is, however, rather antiquated, and no one is actually called this face to face. →**kisasszony**; **asszony**; **megszólítás**

nagymama *grandmother*; in Hungarian families, three generations often still live together, generally too close for comfort, in two, or at most three rooms, even in the countryside (→*vidék*), and even if they live in a family house (→*családi ház*). It is the grandmother who is generally in charge of the household; she watches over the grandchildren and is veritably a mother to them because the young couple are working; the village (→*falusi*) grandmother who is old and solitary is also a frequently described character in literary works, for during the past decades hundreds of thousands have moved to the cities to find work in industry, and so most of the people living in towns have close relatives in the villages, whom they visit for pig killing (→*disznóölés*), weddings (→*lakodalom*) and funerals (→*temetés*).

Nagymaros a small town and holiday resort by the Danube across from →*Visegrád*, which is well known throughout Hungary because it was supposed to be the site of the last of the "great Stalinist plans to transform nature", namely, the dam of a Czechoslovak-Hungarian power plant; the construction, which was begun after decades of planning, was luckily curtailed by the popular grass roots movement of the change in regime (→*rendszerváltás*), which made it into the symbol of the all-around failure of socialism (→*szocializmus*); unfortunately, at great cost Slovakia went ahead and built the upper level of the dam (without Hungarian consent), which is just as destructive to the environment, and considers it as the symbol of its new independence, which means that the battle between the two countries over the dam promises to be long and arduous.

nagysága *your greatness* (lit.), *your ladyship* (vulg.); stall keepers (at markets), butchers, beggars (in general, unschooled people, especially women) use this term of address to women socially superior to them as a sign of respect, but in fact it sounds rather vulgar, since it has lost its original 19th century content, having been deprived of the social context in which every social rank and official position had a proper form of address, and to mistake one's title was considered an offense, as a result of which it was customary (safe) to call everyone by a title higher than their own; →*nagyságos asszony* is its respectful (and equally current) counterpart. →**őnagysága**; **megszólítás; köszönés**

nagyságos asszony *your greatness* (lit.), *your ladyship*; pre-war form of address which seems to be coming back into vogue as a sign of respect towards a female "client"; it is used by salespeople especially in expensive shops, as well as by tailors, sometimes also plumbers, etc.; its original 19th century use as a form of address for every "gentlewoman" (→*úriasszony*), i.e., every woman who was not a "worker" (→*munkás*) or peasant (→*paraszt*), made it the lowest title of respect; today it is simply considered courteous (and in expensive shops, practically *de rigeur*). →**nagysága**; **megszólítás; köszönés**

nagyságos úr '*your* (*lordly*) *greatness*' (lit.); *your honor*; while its feminine counterpart →*nagyságos asszony* is still very much alive, *nagyságos úr* as a form of address went out of use after WW II; originally, the title of any official or clerk who belonged to the 6th salary level of civil servants, today it is used only in jest or mockery, just like "your grace" (→*méltóságos úr*), another earnings-dependent title, and "your excellency" (→*kegyelmes úr*). →**megszólítás**; **köszönés**

nagyúr →**nagyasszony**

nemecsek ernő (pron. *nem–eh–tchek*); the tragic hero of *The Paul Street Boys*, an early novel for young people written by Ferenc Molnár, world renowned for his plays (*The Swan*, *The Guardsman*, *Carousel*); when the putty club (→*gitt-egylet*) goes to war to protect a vacant city lot (→*grund*) and the boys assign military ranks, Ernő Nemecsek, a weak little boy who is looked down on by the others becomes the only private in the group; later, when he is unjustly accused of cowardice, his name is written without capital letters into the minutes of the club in order to humiliate him, yet it is thanks to his unflinching loyalty and unselfish heroism that the gang triumphs over the Red Shirts; ever since, someone who feels he is not getting the recognition he deserves (or thinks he isn't) is called *nemecsek*, but the appellation has become pejorative in tone and intent. →***Paul Street Boys, The***

nemes(ség) *nobility*; its privileged status having been legitimized by a royal charter (the so-called "Golden Bull Edict" in reference to the golden seal appended to it) issued by Andrew II in the early 13th century (like the Magna Charta in England), said charter also guaranteed its liberties and set down what the king could and could not do, which meant that the nobility were as powerful as the king, and equal to him; the nobility were "members" of St. Stephen's Crown (→*Szent Korona*), "*membrum sacrae coronae*", and being of equal rank with each other as well – the various ranks were introduced only later by the Habsburgs (→*Habsburgok*) – together they were the nation in the political sense, the body politic; their privileges were revoked by the national Assembly of 1848 (when "all of the Hungarian people were united by common interest under the law"), though the king donated titles of nobility until 1918. Being a noble did not necessarily mean that the individual was wealthy, and by the 19th century a large portion of the populous petty nobility, who were traditionally in the military or took up service in county (→*megye*) administration, had lost all their fortunes (as a consequence of which they became gentrified bourgeois or peasants), now bragging about one's noble background is considered eccentric at best. →**arisztokrácia**

németek, a *Germans, the*; formerly, the Hungarian language made no distiction between Austrians (→*osztrák*) and Germans, calling the German-speaking population who settled in Hungary centuries ago Swabians (→*sváb*) or Saxons (→*szász*); only with the advent of PC usage have they become known as "Germans". Because since its foundation Hungary was always the outer, south-eastern frontier of the German speaking empire (from which came German priests, soldiers, indigent peasants, builders, painters, teachers and government clerks in droves), whereby for a thousand years it was an object of German expansionism as well as of German cultural influence. Accordingly, Hungary's feeling towards its stronger western neighbor was always ambivalent, characterized on the one hand by the need to preserve its political and cultural identity, and on the other, by the willing acceptance of European influences that came in via German culture and thought. →**labanc; kuruc**

nemzet *nation*; the Hungarian nation (→*magyar nemzet*) is not defined by the country's geographical frontiers but by a shared mother tongue (and the homogenous culture it has engendered), as well as a shared national identity. →**magyar nyelv; nemzeti**

nemzeti *national*; in Hungarian usage, this word does not refer to the country, but to things (anything) that basically belongs to the nation as such or has anything to do with it; in short, it is a lofty political concept expressive of communal belonging; for instance, the National Theatre is the theater of the Hungarian populace in the political sense, expressive of their political identity and belonging; the word also comes up as the antonym for "not national", i.e., "alien", but is also used as the sentimental synonym for "Hungarian". →**magyar nemzet**

Nemzeti dal *National Song* (lit.); the poem by →*Petőfi* that every school child knows by heart and everyone calls by its first two words, →*Talpra magyar!* (*'On your feet, Hungarians!'*); composed just before the outbreak of the 1848 revolution (→*forradalom, 1848*), it is a real incendiary, people's tribune-type oration, and is thus considered the epitome of revolutionary poetry; as legend has it, the poet recited it to the crowd assembled in front of the National Museum (at the time one of the largest buildings of Pest), then proceeded with them to a printing shop they took over, where they printed it, whereby it became the first uncensored document of the new (short lived) free press.

nemzetiszín (zászló) '*national-coloured*' (*flag*) (lit.), *tricolor*; since in Hungarian the world "color" or "colors" does not conjure up images of a flag, the word *nemzetiszín* ('national colors') has come to be reserved for the tricolor combination (red, white, and green) found on the Hungarian flag, as well as the flag itself; the tricolor can be seen not only on official occasions or on national holidays, and not only atop public buildings or only on the flag of the nation; it also makes an appearance on other emotion-charged days (when Hungarians put out flags of their own free will, without even being called upon to do so, and sing the →*Himnusz*, or National Anthem), and also when, worn as a cockade (→*kokárda*) or an arm band (→*karszalag*), it is meant to symbolize common joys or dauntless determination: tricolor arm bands in Hungary have always meant that the wearer is especially determined and is convinced that he is fighting for a just cause. Though it had been used for centuries, the use of the tricolor became official by an act of the 1848 revolutionary National Assembly. →**piros-fehér-zöld**

Nemzetőrség *National Guard*; the name given by the French-oriented organizers of the revolution of 1848 (→*forradalom, 1848*) to the enthusiastic army of armed civilians carrying the national colors (→*nemzetiszín*), and wearing national color rosettes (→*kokárda*) or arm bands (→*karszalag*); the armed volunteers during the revolution of 1956 (→*forradalom, 1956*) were given the same name as a pointed reference to its predecessor (the parody of which was the Workers' Guard, or →*Munkásőrség*, set up in 1957 from volunteers in order to defend "the peoples' democracy").

néne '*older sister*' (lit.), *aunt*; the rustic, rather antiquated name and form of address used for an older sister (→*testvér*); it is also the rustic form of →*néni* (aunt), and invariably refers to an old woman. →**megszólítás**

néni '(*little*) *older sister*' (lit.), *aunt*; the form of address used by children when talking to every adult female, whether a relative or a stranger (for example, *tanítónéni* i.e., 'aunt teacher'); grownups (both men and women) can also use it when addressing an older woman, though coming from a young woman it can sound condescending or hurtful (unless the difference in age is striking); it is used both with and without first names, depending on the degree of familiarity. →**bácsi**; **megszólítás**

nép *the people*; the "simple people", i.e., everyone, as opposed to the ruling class or circle and (regardless of its size or whether it is in the "majority"), its leader or leaders; in socialist political jargon, it is (in a more restricted sense) the workers (→*dolgozó*), meaning physical laborers (→*munkás*), or even more bombastically, the "working people" as opposed to the "exploiters"; the older, traditional use of the word restricts it to the peasantry (→*parasztság*), to which 50 to 60 years ago the majority of the populace actually belonged.

népdal *folk song*; the collection, documentation and research into folk music is the greatest achievement of Hungarian musicology, while in the 20th century the folk song became so much a part of Hungarian cultural identity, that among the intelligentsia (→*értelmiség*), who have taken it upon themselves to preserve cultural traditions it is expected that they know as many Hungarian folk songs as possible, which they also like to sing; in the countryside, too, there is an appreciable (amateur) grass roots movement to preserve the custom of singing in groups, while (thanks to Zoltán Kodály) music teaching in schools is based on folk songs as the Hungarian "musical vernacular".

népi *of the people, the people*; the most flexible, positive adjective used by politicians under socialism (→*szocializmus*), used to refer, in general, either to the people (→*nép*) or the workers (→*dolgozó*), by which was meant "physical laborers" and "those not in leading positions", not to mention its use in close conjunction with "democracy", which was always "the people's", and so was the "republic" and the "army"; however, like all empty political slogans, it was quickly discredited and just as quickly received an ironic connotation, whereupon it was replaced by the word *össznépi*, meaning 'of/or belonging to *all* of the people', which fared no better; the previous use of the word, also political in orientation, but one which is still current, narrows the scope still further, and is meant as a reference to the peasantry (→*parasztság*) as a subgroup of "the people". →**népies**; **népművészet**

népies *folksy*; from the late 19th century onwards, the music and decorative arts of the peasantry (→*parasztság*) reshaped the Hungarian applied arts and music (with literature having succumbed much earlier to folk poetry, or →*népköltészet*), for they represented a certain "national" (→*nemzeti*) trend which, however, was fraught with the danger of maudlin romanticism; in the fifties (→*ötvenes évek*), all this was suppressed by socialist realism, which was more political dictate than artistic style, and which not only usurped the "folk" elements for ideological purposes, but also discredited them thereby; they were revived only a quarter of a century later, this time with an appeal to →*Bartók*, by professionals in music and the applied arts, not to mention the "dance houses" (→*táncház*), but this time, with very different meaning. →**népművészet**; **népdal**; **népzene**; **magyar nóta**

népköltészet *folk poetry*; though it was not →*Petőfi* whose poetry was both romantic and republican in inspiration who discovered the poetry of the peasantry (→*parasztság*) for the benefit of literature, it was his work which infused Hungarian High Poetry with new lifeblood, and it was his oeuvre which was imitated time and time again by his epigons, until they managed to degrade it to the level of 20th century mock–Hungarian songs (→*magyar nóta*); on the other hand, in response to it, Hungarian folk songs (→*népdal*) were also discovered and researched, adding to the storehouse of 20th century Hungarian culture, and it was thanks to this effort that authentic folk poetry, too, became part of contemporary culture. →**nép**; **népzene**

népművészet *folk art*; along with the peasant (→*paraszt*) way of life, the everyday culture of the peasantry has gradually also disappeared in Hungary, but its forms, colors and genres, distinguishable by area, have survived thanks to artisans, and are bought as decorative objects, while the original pieces are now in museums or expensive antique shops. →**nép**, **népköltészet**; **népdal**; **népzene**; **néptánc**

Népszabadság '*Liberty of the People*' (lit.); a nationwide political daily; founded in the winter of 1956, it was the new organ of the new (Communist) Party (→*Párt*) which after the revolution (→*forradalom, 1956*) was reincarnated under a new name (→*MSzMP*); it was the descendant of *Szabad Nép* ('*The Free People*', lit.), which stopped publication during the revolution (→*forradalom, 1956*), and functioned as the Hungarian *Pravda* (complete with the motto: *Workers of the world unite!*), which it remained until the change in regime (→*rendszerváltás*); it used to be a political bludgeon and a weather–cock cum political compass in one; today the majority of its shares are owned by Bertelsmann, and it has the largest circulation of any political daily newspaper; while the political right consider it liberal, the rest of the country consider it the most knowledgeable news source in the country.

Népszava '*The People's Voice*' (lit.); the oldest Hungarian daily founded at the turn of the century (→*századforduló*). Originally, it was the organ of the Social Democratic Party.

néptánc *folk dance*; →**táncház**

népviselet *folk costume*; in the fifties (→*ötvenes évek*) the Hungarian peasantry (→*parasztság*) suffered major trials and tribulations which forced it to abandon in its misery its traditional way of life along with traditional costumes (each characteristic of a certain region), not to mention the folk customs belonging to it; the peasants fled from the farmers' cooperatives (→*termelőszövetkezet*) into the cities by the thousands, where they became industrial workers (→*munkás*); the modernization of the villages, which was accelerated in the seventies, merely finished the job; today folk costumes are donned only on special occasions, if at all, in which case they function more like fancy dresses or disguise than authentic folk wear. →**nép**; **matyó**; **kalocsai hímzés**; **cifra szűr**; **népművészet**

népzene *folk music*; when →*Bartók* was collecting the ancient melodies of authentic Hungarian (and Slovak, Romanian and Turkish) folk music, he wrote that peasant music is "a phenomenon of nature"; authentic folk music, whose popularity is revived time and time again, has been embraced of late by young intellectuals (→*értelmiség*), but thanks to music teaching in schools, it is so ingrained in Hungarian culture, that there is hardly a Hungarian around who wouldn't be able to produce a strikingly Hungarian folk music motif, if asked to sing "something". →**nép**, **táncház**; **népdal**; **népművészet**; **népköltészet**; **magyar nóta**

névmagyarosítás '*name Magyarization/ Hungarianization*' (lit.); a Hungarian-sounding family name does not automatically mean that one belongs to the Hungarian nation (→*magyar nemzet*), and the other way around, a German or Slovak name does not necessarily point to foreign origin – *Német* (German), *Tót* (Slovak) and *Rác* (Serb) are especially common family names; for one thing, the fashion for families to chose names that sounded Hungarian for themselves, which began in the middle of the 19th century, picked up momentum with time (a famous example being →*Petőfi*, who had a Serbian family name); for another, even though it is no longer necessary or "advisable" to change one's name (as it was, for instance, before 1945 for →*Jews*,) and though the custom has seen various trends, fashions and exaggerations throughout the years, it refuses to die out. →**ki a magyar?**; **asszimiláció**

névnap *name's day*; usually celebrated with a gift of flowers, especially if the celebrant is a woman; those with very common names such as Katalin and József are generally also celebrated where they work as well, with their colleagues arranging for a veritable party in their honor (especially if they are in a top managerial position); for these parties, which are held instead of birthdays (→*születésnap*), the women bringing scones (→*pogácsa*) of their own making, and the men drinks, and all over the country, the price of flowers skyrockets.

New York the oldest, and in fact only authentic turn-of-the-century (→*századforduló*) café (→*kávéház*) on Budapest's Boulevard (→*körút*) to have survived; it was legendary even in its heyday, and was open day and night (its key having been ceremoniously thrown into the Danube by Ferenc Molnár, the playwright); it was frequented by many illustrious writers and journalists, whose caricatures hang on its walls; its Edwardian pomp, a product of the extravagance of the American insurance company, the contractor of its building, which also gave it its name, is breathtaking. →**Zserbó**

nicht vor dem Kind *'pas devant les enfants'*; this German sentence, which is used today only ironically, is a product of the times when, at the turn of the century (→*századforduló*), nearly every middle class adult (parent) could speak German, but not so their children any longer, and so, if the parents wanted to keep something a secret before the children, they spoke German to each other.

nóta →**magyarnóta**

november 1. →**Mindenszentek**

november 4., 1956 those who experienced it will never forget that chilly early morning when after the first few euphoric days of the revolution (→*forradalom, 1956*), the country woke to Nagy Imre, the Prime Minister announcing on the radio that "*Soviet soldiers are pouring into the country... our troops are engaged in battle with them ...*"; as a result, Hungarians felt that their series of national tragedies was now being continued, and 200 thousand people fled to the West (→*Nyugat*). →**forradalom, 1956**; **disszidens**

nyárikonyha '*summer kitchen*' (lit.); during summertime, when the weather is hot, in the villages cooking is done out in the breezy shack in the back of the yard, which is also used for eating, hence the name, 'summer kitchen'.

nyelvújítás '*language renewal*' (lit.); the modernization and effective recreation of the Hungarian language in the first half of the 19th century was not only the largest cultural movement of the times but also a major concerted effort by the Hungarian intelligentsia (→*értelmiség*); the disappearance of the traces of Latin, which till then had been the language of government and jurisprudence, and concurrently, the liberation of the nature of the Hungarian language (syntax!) brought about such major changes, that today we find texts written before the time of →*Petőfi* difficult to understand.

nyilas(keresztes) mozgalom *Arrow Cross movement*; the exact, though much more petty equivalent of German Nazism, which turned people's heads with its wild anti-Semitism and rabble-rousing rhetoric based on the themes of social welfare and extreme nationalism; still, it could not gain control of the country until towards the very end of WW II (and even then only with Germany's help), but during its six months long reign of terror, it was responsible for such horrible crimes, that it will not soon be forgotten.

Nyírség (pron. *nyeer–sheyg*); the ripply ocean of sand to the left of the river →*Tisza* as it enters Hungary, which forms a flat plain between →*Debrecen* and →*Tokaj* in →*Szabolcs* County; dotted only here and there by sparse woods, it is one of the poorest and most isolated regions of the country.

Nyugat, a '*West, the*' (lit.), *Western Europe*; according to the Hungarian (and Polish, Czech, Croatian, etc.) traditional 16th century view, Western Europe is morally bound to help Hungary (Poland, Bohemia, Croatia, etc.), which has repeatedly bled for it (and instead of it); however, seeing how Western Europe has been remiss in its duty, Hungary's view of Europe (→*Európa*), ambivalent to begin with, has been tainted with resentment, not to mention the suspicion which comes from centuries of conducting battles (with various degrees of success) either in self-defense or in the name of liberty against the (always German speaking, and always expanding) great Western power adjacent to it; accordingly, Hungarians would have always liked to be able to turn to the more distant West over the head of their German (→*német*) neighbors, but have rarely been able to elicit sufficient response and interest, which just added to its store of disappointments (and brought to the fore, in response to the nation's resentment, the shamans who trumpeted forth the Eastern origins of the Hungarian soul); all the same, and despite its latest disappointment in 1956, Hungary still continues to hope for the Western solidarity which it feels it is more than entitled to. →**Európa**; **kereszténység védőbástyája**; **Nyugat-ellenesség**

Nyugat-ellenesség '*anti–Westernism*' (lit.); not to be confused with the propagandistic anti-capitalism characteristic of socialism (→*szocializmus*), it is of such long standing, that it can be traced back to 11th century pagan insurrections. This deep-rooted sentiment, which springs from the need to protect traditional, familiar conditions (lifestyles), pits old (i.e., national, or →*nemzeti*) values against the new and sham (i.e., "not national") values coming from the West (→*Nyugat*); it pairs the justifiable need for self-protection with the rejection of modernization, and having recurred time and again ever since the adoption of Christianity, and even though it lost momentum through time, it has been the cause a good number of national crises; →*Jókai*: "*I regard with fear every movement of your attempts at renewal. You are making the nation lose all that it has, and do not acquire for it what it longs for.*" (1884). →**Európa**

nyuszi *bunny, bunny rabbit*; along with the hand-painted egg and the willow twig, the bunny has the starring role in Hungarian Easter (→*Húsvét*) celebrations, for it is the bunny rabbit who brings children their presents, hidden under the bushes in the gardens of family homes (→*családi ház*); in fact, small children today will often get the "real article" (live bunnies) along with chocolate bunnies. →**Mikulás**

O

Óbuda *Old Buda* (*lit.*); the oldest part of →*Budapest* situated on the right bank of the Danube (→*Duna*), which lies on the ruins of the huge, ancient military camp of Roman legionaires called →*Aquincum*; until the unification of the city in 1873, it was a separate town inhabited mostly by Swabian (→*sváb*) farmers which, because of its village-like atmosphere, was a favorite place of the petit bourgeoisie of Pest for outings; in the seventies, the one-storey houses (with only a couple of "islands" being spared) were pulled down, which not only put a stop to the Sunday pilgrimages from Pest, but allowed for the construction of the drab, uncomfortable pre-fab houses (→*panelház*) that still spoil the cityscape. →**Buda**; **Pest**

október 23. *October 23rd*; the date of the outbreak of the revolution (→*forradalom, 1956*). It was on this day that the morning march of the students of Budapest, who organized a demonstration to show their sympathy with the Polish rebels of Poznan, by evening turned into armed conflict; as the news of the conflict spread, within a couple of days revolutionaries toppled the Communist regime throughout the land; this was followed by the short, euphoric reorganization of the country, which however was curtailed by Soviet troops on November 4 (→*november 4. 1956*), which in turn was followed by bloody reprisals; for over forty years any mention of the most important post-WW II event in the country's history was taboo, and its anniversary was always awaited by an anxious police (→*rendőrség*) and People's Guard (→*Munkásőrség*), who were on full alert. →**temetés**; **Sztálin-szobor**; **november 4.**

október 6. *October 6th*; a day of national mournig. After the defeat of the War of Independence (→*Szabadságharc*), it was on this day in 1849 that, as the overture to bloody retribution, the triumphant Austrians (→*osztrákok*) put to death 13 →*honvéd* generals at →*Arad*; it was on the same day that Count Lajos Batthyány, who had been named Prime Minister by the king, was shot through the head in the yard of an army barracks in Pest. →**Ferenc József**

oláh *Wallach, Wallachian*; today, the politically incorrect term for Romanians (→*románok*), originally *'oláh'* was simply the common Hungarian name for them; historically, it designated all peoples who spoke a Latin tongue, and comes from the same root as *'olasz'*, meaning 'Italian'. It received its initial pejorative connotation only in the 19th century, when Romanians came up with *'Romanian'*, a reference to Antique Rome whose descendants they felt themselves to be; it was formulated to replace *'wlach'*, which they themselves had used till then, and which is the root word for the Hungarian *'oláh'*; "Romanian" having by now come into popular usage in Hungary as well, it has not only replaced *'oláh'*, but has emparted it with a pejorative connotation as well. Still, it is a frequently occuring family name, but as such carries no hurtful overtones. →**tót**; **sváb**

olaj →**zsír**; **vaj**

Óperencia a fairytale country, the symbol of a distant (and happy) land, as well as the sea on the outer limits of fairyland; many Hungarian tales begin with the formulas *"beyond Óperencia* and *beyond the Glass Mountain, on the shore of the Sea of Óperencia"*; according to linguists, it is the distorted form of the Austrian *Ober Enns* ('Upper Enns', a river in Austria), and probably comes from the speech of Hungarian soldiers returning from the Napoleonic wars. Its close English equivalent is *Never-Never Land*. →***Hol volt, hol nem volt ...***; ***mentek, mendegéltek***

operett *operetta*; the composers of 19th century, classical Viennese operetta, which became the musical emblem of Central Europe (→*Közép–Európa*), were by the 20th century in fact all Hungarian (Lehár, Kálmán, Huszka, Ábrahám, Fényes); they produced light melodies for the stage with admirable ease and prolificacy, enough to turn any one of their operettas into three of today's musicals, and which, despite the disparagement of intellectuals and the guardians of high culture, not to mention Bolshevik disapprovement, are still popular from Munich to Moscow; by now, much of the music has become independent of the librettos and is enjoyed for its own sake, though audiences continue to love these sentimental pieces with dance populated by young countesses, guards' officers, good hearted servant girls and stable boys courting them, all this within the framework of an imaginary, once upon a time Austro-Hungarian Monarchy (→*Osztrák–Magyar Monarchia*) performed through the years by popular actors and singers, but always in the spirit of the operettas' own archaic tradition of acting. →**Csárdáskirálynő, A**

orosz (nyelv) *Russian* (*language*); from the early fifties (→*ötvenes évek*), to the late eighties (in most places), Russian was the only foreign language taught in Hungarian schools. It was initially taught by hastily retrained Latin and German language teachers, who in the early nineties were just as hastily turned from Russian to English teachers, and who struggled with little conviction against the antipathy and resistance of students and parents alike, a sentiment which was hardly tempered at all in forty years, for in the eyes of Hungarians (→*magyarok*), the Russian language remained the language of the occupiers (an incontestible fact against which paled all other facts); it was felt to be of no use to them whatsoever in life, so that today only former Russian teachers know the language, and those who had studied in the Soviet Union (→*Szovjetunió*); still, it left some traces behind, such as snatches of texts learnt by rote and subsequently recited amidst loud laughter, as well as a dozen or so loan words which are speedily becoming outdated, and which people learned not from their Russian teachers, but the soldiers.

oroszok, az *Russians, the*; thanks to the hundreds of thousands of Hungarian soldiers (→*baka*) fighting in the Ukraine and Russia (→*Oroszország*) during the two world wars, the Hungarian POWs working in the camps of Siberia (→*szibéria*), the occupation by the "temporary stationed" (→*ideiglenesen itt állomásozó*) Red Army, not to mention the tens of thousands of students who studied in the Soviet Union (→*Szovjetunió*) and who brought Russian wives back with them, Hungarian society was in such close contact with so many strata of the Russian population, that the relationship of the two became what one might call intimate, even if not loving, for (to risk an understatement) the always uneven relationship of the two countries inevitably put its mark on the relationship of individuals as well, even though it was always the practice in Hungary to make a distinction between the Soviet state and its citizens; being familiar with the backward conditions prevailing in the Soviet Union, the average Hungarian always felt a comforting sense of cultural superiority vis a vis the Russians (a state of affairs that even the near worship of the Hungarian intelligentsia, or →*értelmiség*, for Russian art and literature was powerless to change), regarding them with a mixture of standoffish, tentative sympathy and benevolent disdain, though also with a sense of fear whenever he remembered the Soviet machinery of state, something he could hardly forget, even for a moment. →**orosz (nyelv)**

Oroszország *Russia*; by this, common parlance simply meant the Soviet Union, and imbued it with antipathy and anxiety vis à vis the Soviet Union (→*Szovjetunió*)as well as a sense of superiority which developed through the years, perhaps to balance out the former negative sentiments; still, despite the involuntary political ties, Hungarians had little personal knowledge of Russia (unless as POWs or students on scholarships), for the Soviet Union never liked foreigners. →**orosz (nyelv)**; **oroszok, az**

osztályidegen '*a stranger to the (working) class*' (lit.); in the fifties (→*ötvenes évek*) anyone who was neither a city proletarian nor a poor (!) peasant was put in this category (provided he was not a member of the former ruling class, in which case he was considered not just a *stranger*, but a "class enemy"); there were various sub-catogories as well, each bringing with it different disadvantages in one's life, justified by an appeal to the class struggle; until the mid-sixties (→*hatvanas évek*), these classifications were even put in the records of school children. →**kitelepítés**

Osztrák–Magyar Monarchia *Austro-*

Hungarian (Dual) Monarchy; the name for the dual state which came about as a result of the Austro-Hungarian Compromise (→*Kiegyezés*) of 1867, whose ruler in Austria was the emperor and in Hungary the king; the relatively complex and bureaucratic state organization, which apart from military, financial and foreign affairs guaranteed complete independence to the two separate parliaments functioned quite well until the collapse of the Empire in 1918, which was due, apart from the defeat it suffered in WW I, to the call for independence of the half a dozen nations living within its borders in provinces with dramatically different states of development; this drive for independence, in opposition to the allegedly supra-national, archaic principles of the Empire, in which ethnic and national groups saw the source of all their troubles, was responsible for finally sweeping away the Monarchy; still, within its former territories it has become the symbol of "peacetime peace", and is remembered with nostalgia. →**Ausztria**; **Monarchia, a**; **Közép–Európa**; **Habsburgok**

osztrákok, az *Austrians, the*; the term has been used only since the independence of Austria (→*Ausztria*); prior to it, its inhabitans were considered German (→*németek*). Though thanks to a 19th century, demure journalistic cliché they are generally referred to as "our brothers-in-law", the relationship was never quite as friendly as one might be led to believe; though in retrospect Hungarians (→*magyarok*) think of the Monarchy – which in many respects really was a common state – with nostalgia, then as now, they have felt a nagging sense of inferiority when dealing with their richer relations, who in turn made no bones about their superiority, which in turn made the Hungarians want to prove themselves at all cost, for even though the relationship between the two nations has in many instances truly become familial, the sense of competition (in the hearts of the Hungarians, at any rate), continues unabated. →**Bécs**; **labanc**; **kuruc**

ovi *kindergarten*; the diminutive form of *óvoda* used by children; in Hungary, where for all practical purposes just about everybody goes to kindergarten, many close friendships are made there, and later in life, one can always find an old kindergarten "buddy" whose friendship one can capitalize on.

Ö

öcsém '*my* (*younger*) *brother*' (lit.); the quaint-sounding yet still current form of greeting (→*megszólítás*) used by older men (especially in the provinces, or →*vidék*), when talking to younger men, especially relatives, though not necessarily; it's shorter version is →*öcsi*.

öcsi (öcskös) '(*little*) *younger brother*' (lit.); the slightly jocular, at times loving, at times uppish name older children (both boys and girls) use to address or talk about children (boys) younger than themselves. →**Puskás Öcsi**

ön '(*your*)*self*' (lit.); a highly respectful and courteous form of address between people unacquainted with each other, and therefore part of the use of formal language; however, when used between people who are acquainted, it becomes not merely courteous, but also extremely distancing. →**maga**, **tegezés**; **megszólítás**

őnagysága '*her/his greatness*' (lit.), also *his excellence*, *his lordship*, *his eminence*, etc.; one of the elements of the sociologically extremely intricate system of greetings (→*megszólítás*) which has come down to us today only in the vulgar form of →*nagysága*; originally, it was used for men as well as women in the form →*nagyságos úr*, though today nobody is quite clear about who was supposed to use it to whom and under what circumstances; today it is used only for women, and only pejoratively, though →*nagyságos asszony* is still current, even if only in certain limited areas of life.

öngyilkosság *suicide*; it is sad and embarrassing that despite the changes in the country's frontiers and the composition of its populace, ever since there have been written statistics on it, the number of suicides (compared to other countries) have been very high in Hungary, dropping only in times of war and in years of the greatest penury. It is a mysterious phenomenon for which there is no satisfying explanation; we can only assume that there must be highly intricate factors related to cultural anthropology to account for it, which seems to be indicated by the fact that in the villages of the southern Great Plains (→*Alföld*) with predominantly Protestants (→*református*) populations and isolated farms (→*tanya*) and in the big cities (religiously mixed and crowded), the number of suicides is permanently and glaringly high; it is also possible, of course, that compared to other cultural circles, the Hungarian statistics are too objective, conscientious and meticulous; some people try to find an answer in the pessimism (→*pesszimizmus*) for which Hungarians are famous, but this is a very recent development compared to the tradition of suicide.

önkiszolgáló '*self-service* (*restaurant*)';

not to be confused with the McDonald's type fast food chains, these are simple eateries with an ambiance reminiscent of public soup kitchens (aluminum trays, blunt knives, gnarled forks, plastic bowls, chipped glasses), though the fare, especially in the small, family-type restaurants called →*kifőzde* is often both tasteful, real Hungarian (→*magyaros étel*) and inexpensive – typically the cooked vegetables (→*főzelék*) and the bean soup (→*bableves*); the regulars (with a good measure of self-irony) call such places "the House of Lords". →**büfé**

őrmester *sergeant*; because military service in Hungary has been compulsory since the 19th century, the male population has accumulated a wealth of near-folkloric, stereotyped and mythicized stories of the military (→*katonaság*), including (from earlier times), the 'soldier's chest' painted green on the floor, and the framed, decorative 'proof of service'; this storehouse of memories is the inexhaustible source of stories, whose main character is always the dull witted, much-feared sergeant with his fearful stupidity, and the embodiment of rigid military thinking as opposed to the much-loved "sober, peasant mentality" (→*józan, paraszti ész*), or plain common sense. →**baka**

öröklakás '*permanent flat*' (lit.), *privately owned apartment* (*in a block of flats*); today, the majority of Hungarians own the apartments (family houses) in which they live, and for which most of them worked half a lifetime; these apartments are called 'permanent' because their owner, once he manages to acquire it, usually does not plan to part with it (nor could he, seeing how it is his only major possession); in most cases, every apartment of an apartment house is in private ownership, which is why such houses are called →*társasház*, or co-operative houses. →**bérház**

Őrség (pron. *owr–sheyg*); a part of the →*Őrvidék* which, however, has remained part of Hungary and which, with its beautiful hills and dense woods, is considered by many as the most spectacular region of the country.

Őrvidék (pron. *owr–vee–deyk*), '*Guardsmen's Land*' (lit.); the former frontier (border guard area) of Hungary annexed to Austria (→*Ausztria*) by the Peace Treaty of Versailles (→*Trianon*), which is known today as Burgenland. →**Felvidék**; **Erdély**; **Kárpátalja**; **Délvidék**

őshaza '*ancient homeland*' (lit.); the search for the lost, legendary eastern homeland of the Hungarians was, for a long time, an important element in the search for Hungarian identity. In the 13th century, two monks, sent specifically in search of the ancient homeland, thought to have found it on the wooded steppes lying just before the Urals; what's more, they even managed to get themselves understood in Hungarian, despite the fact that the inhabitants of the area were separated from the conquering (Magyar) tribes (→*hon-*

foglalók) of the future at least five or six hundred years before; however, thanks to such searches, Hungarian Oriental studies were born (Sádor Kőrösi Csoma, who edited a Tibetan dictionary for the British in Darjeeling was also looking for the ancient homeland in the Himalayas), but even when various academic disciplines joined forces to pursue the common cause, they were unable to come up with anything more than the fact that 2000 years ago the people who can be identified as Magyars lived somewhere around the rivers issuing out of the Urals and flowing to the west, until the last wave of the great migrations swept them first to the south, where they disappeared. →**ősmagyarok**; **hun–magyar rokonság**

ősmagyarok *ancient Hungarians*; in common parlance the *ancient Hungarians* were the people of the conquering tribes (→*honfoglalók*); they appear in the popular imagination either as short, stocky, with thick braids and Mongolian features, bow-legged from sitting on their horses, or else elegant, hawk-nosed, helmeted, Persian heroes, depending on whom the artist calls to his aid – contemporary Western chroniclers or romanticizing Hungarian historians; the average Hungarians does n't know anything about them beyond the amusing "fact" that "they matured the meat under the saddle", a misconception which may have come from Western chronicles, for the raw meat placed under the saddle was in fact used to heal the sore on the back of the horse. →**magyaros arc; ki a magyar**

ötvenes évek *the fifties*; the fifties actually began earlier with the Communist (→*kommunista*) takeover of 1948 and nationalization (→*államosítás*) of 1949, only to continue with the fleecing of the bourgeoisie and the peasantry (→*parasztság*), with secret police (→*ávós*) terror, dire food shortages, deportations (→*kitelepítés*), preparations for war, which were the kiss of death for the economy, show trials, spy stories, penury, co-tenancies (→*társbérlet*), and blaring loudspeakers spewing out mass songs (→*tömegdal*) ad nauseam on the First of May (→*május elseje*); it was the decade of great lies, when children ate larded bread (→*zsíroskenyér*) sprinkled with sugar for lunch, but also, paradoxically, it was the golden age of Hungarian sports; the decade probably came to an end in 1958 with the execution of Prime Minister Imre Nagy and his group; the painful memory of the era, which culminated in the revolution (→*forradalom, 1956*) will not pale, since until very recently its ghosts were still haunting the stage of Hungarian politics. →**Rajk László**; **Kádár János**; **Rákosi Mátyás**; **termelőszövetkezet**; **Aranycsapat**; **Puskás Öcsi**; **Papp Laci**

Ötvenhat *Fifty-six*; when it could not be called a revolution in public, someone who could stomach neither the shameful and perfidious "counter-revolution" (→*ellenforradalom*) nor the nauseating euphemism "regretful events" (→*sajnálatos események*), used this neutral expression when he talked about the revolution (→*forradalom, 1956*).

P

Pál utcai fiúk, A *Paul Street Boys The*; the early novel for boys written by the brilliant writer of drawing room comedies Ferenc Molnár, which is set in the first years of the 20th century and deals with the children of Budapest who live, study and play in places still intimately familiar to people today; for nearly a century now, it has been one of the best loved books of Hungarian children between the ages of 10 and 12, who (apart from *The Stars of Eger*, or →*Egri csillagok*, which is also compulsory reading), learn about friendship, loyalty, treason, group spirit and solidarity from its pages; it has been turned into a film and a play, and has been republished countless times, including a publication in English. →**nemecsek**; **gittegylet**

palacsinta *crepe*; from market stalls to Sunday (→*vasárnap*) lunches and elegant restaurant dinners, *palacsinta* is by far the most popular dessert in Hungary; though it is easy to prepare, some have turned it into an art, and can make it not only paper-thin (without tearing it!), but can flip it by throwing it into the air; the flat, thin pancake is usually spread with a generous amount of jam (→*lekvár*) or sweetened cottage cheese, then is rolled up and served hot; those who have tasted →*Gundel* pancakes, which are filled with creamed walnut, drenched in hot chocolate sauce, then sprinkled with rum (and set aflame!), will never forget it.

pálinka *brandy*; come fall, in (almost) every house of (almost) every Hungarian village they brew a couple of liters of home-made brandy (→*kisüsti pálinka*), on which they either pay taxes or they do not; it is an indispensable part of a hardy welcome, not to mention the pleasure of drinking it on a cold winter morn, or having it relieve a toothache or a bellyache, but it also makes a great antiseptic; the most common type, mockingly referred to as a "fence breaker", is made from all sorts of fruit fallen from the trees, the other being the *szilvórium* made from plums, which grows in abundance all over the country; in wine producing areas the most common type is made from the skins of pressed grapes; there is a saying according to which "the peasant drinks *pálinka* in the morning, the genteman at noon, the fool at night." →**szilvapálinka**; **barackpálinka**

palóc (pron. *pow–lowts*); a group of people living on the slopes of the northern hills of Hungary, who speak a special dialect. Though their name is Slav, they are considered the descendants of the Turkic Khabars, who came to the area along with the Conquering tribes (→*honfoglalók*); they were poor (until vineyards appeared at the foot of the Mátra Mountains), but had colorful folk costumes elaborately embroidered with stylized flowers which, known as →*matyó* costumes, are considered to be one of the most beautiful in the country. On the other hand, the tradition of "jack-knifing" (→*bicska*) in their villages is horrifying.

palotás '*palace dance*' (lit.); an old Hungarian dance with three-quarter or four-eighths rhythms, something like the polonaise, which during the reawakening of national consciousness during the 19th century people tried to revive; today it is part of history, except for graduation balls (→*szalagavató*), when in every high school (→*gimnázium*) throughout the country, the festivities begin with the graduating students (→*érettségi*) doing this dance (which a dance teacher spends weeks teaching them) to the only *palotás* melody still familiar to everyone (from an opera by →*Erkel*), all of which is done in Hungarian costumes (→*magyaros ruha*) rented for the occasion.

panel '*prefab element*' (lit.), *prefab housing, housing estate apartment*; in order to alleviate the catastrophic housing shortage, for twenty years beginning with the mid-sixties (→*hatvanas évek*), all over Hungary there appeared on the outskirts of Hungarian cities and towns so-called housing estates made up of eight to ten storey high apartment buildings put together from prefabricated panels (produced by "*housing factories*"); though most of these houses are badly made and designed and have not stood the test of time, their original inhabitants were glad to have a roof over their heads; most are now privately owned (→*öröklakás*), since those who lived in them were able to acquire them cheaply from the councils (→*Tanács*), while others became the ghettoes of the new proletariat of a socialism under decline, "the people of the panel".

Pannonhalma (pron. *pah–non–hahl–mah*); the bishop St. Martin of Tours was born at the foot of the local hill, while the groundwork for the monastery of the Benedictines was begun here by St. Stephen's (→*Szent István*) father, which in all probability makes this the oldest school in Hungary, even if during the course of its history, there were times when it lay in ruins. It is a renowned boys' school to this day, one which (wonder of wonders) continued to function even during the decades of socialism (→*szocializmus*), when having one's child attend a school maintained by any of the churches, was tantamount to a gesture against the regime. →**Sárospatak**; **Piaristák**; **Fasori gimnázium**

Pannonia the name of the former Roman province whose capital was →*Acquincum* and which included the territory of today's Transdanubia (→*Dunántúl*). Its name is commonly used as the cultural and spiritual opposite of →*Hunnia*, and is thus the symbol of a Westernized, civilized Hungary; another use limits it in scope to the (clichéd) poetic synonym of Transdanubia.

Papp Laci (pron. *pohp–loh–tsee*); the short Gypsy boy who became an Olympic boxing champion in London (1948), then went on to win two more Olympic and three European gold medals, which in the fifties (→*ötvenes évek*), when sports were the nation's sole consolation, made him into a veritable folk hero and the symbol of perseverance, self-discipline and the fight to the last. His fame, which has never been eclipsed, is matched only by the soccer player →*Puskás Öcsi*.

paprika *green/white/red pepper*; →**pirospaprika**; **magyaros étel**

paprikajancsi '*Johnny Paprika*' (lit.), *popinjay*; originally the comic figure of puppet shows at country fairs (→*vásár*) and the Hungarian equivalent of the German Hanswurst, he is actually descended from the devil in mystery and morality plays. Today, a *paprikajancsi* is a person who thinks way too much of himself, and acts it, too.

paprikás *paprika stew*; despite its name, the only difference between stew (→*pörkölt*) and *paprikás* is not the addition of →*pirospaprika*, which goes into both, but the addition of sour cream, slowly stirred in towards the end of the cooking process. *paprikás* is therefore less rustic and never hot (→*csípős*). Also, it is often made with chicken (for example, the ever-popular *paprikás csirke*), which is never used to make plain stew.

paprikáskrumpli '*paprika potatoes*' (lit.); *potato stew*; the simplest (and also the tastiest) Hungarian "poorman's food" which, if included on the menu of a restaurant (in the section with roasts) goes under the pseudonym of "pan-fried potatoes" (*serpenyős burgonya*). It is prepared the same way as →*pörkölt*, except potatoes are substituted for the meat.

paraszt *peasant*; when coming from the lips of a non-peasant and is used as an adjective, the word can be deprecatory and belittling in the extreme (the equivalent of *boor*), or even a strong invective (*stinking/filthy peasant*), while coming from a peasant, i.e., a farmer or landowner (→*gazda*), it can have the effect, even, of boasting. Its meaning has always been changeable; in general it means *farmer* (*földműves*, i.e., '*one who works the land*') or smallholder, but in either case, it is associated with "robustness"; "*it was hanging by a peasant hair*" (lit.), they say when some danger is averted, even if the likelihood of it happening was not very great, obviously because *peasant hair* must be strong. →**józan, paraszti ész**

parasztbútor *peasant/folk furniture*; the name for painted furniture with Renaissance or rococo motifs painted to imitate reliefs or carving, strewn with lots of stylized lilies, lilies of the valley, roses, carnations, and sometimes tulips, depending on local custom, sometimes with a bird or two appearing among the wreaths. The village cabinet makers made benches, tables, chests (and later wardrobes), as well as headboards for beds in this style, but today their works can be found only in public and private collections; the last original pieces are from the years just before WW II. →**népművészet**

párizsi '*Parisian* (*cold cuts*)' (lit.); the most common (and least expensive) cold cut found in Hungarian shops. Made from cheap meat, it is a lightly seasoned mashed meat stuffed into thick (plastic) "intestines" and sold cut into thin rings. It is associated with being poor; bologna is its American near-equivalent.

Párt, a *Party, the*; since time immemorial, there has only been one Party (→*kommunista párt*) in Hungary, which is why it's name begins with a capital letter, despite the fact that it has undergone several transformations, its last incarnation being the Hungarian Socialist Workers Party (→*MSzMP*), formed in 1989. It was not really a party but, like all Bolshevik "formations", an organ used to exercise absolute power over the society it ruled, its rule being (self)justified by the inevitability preached by "scientific" Marxism; its power, in fact, was dependent on the Soviet Union (→*Szovjetunió*), which was no secret to anyone, except that this did not make it any less absolute or real, and it had to be taken as a fact of life. The party of →*Kádár János* was only different from its predecessors and the other similar Eastern (→*Kelet-Európa*) and Central European (→*Közép-Európa*) parties in that it never forgot the traumatic events of the revolution (→*forradalom, 1956*), from which it drew the practical lesson that it's best to appease the people with concessions (which he proceeded to do as long as the economy held out), and the people were accordingly grateful (*re.* Kádár's relative popularity), especially when they considered the lives of their neighbors. →**párttitkár, a**; **párttag**; **szocializmus**; **elvtárs**; **proligyerek**, **funkcionárius**; **gulyás-kommunizmus**

párttag *Party member*; at the time, when the regime collapsed, the Party (→*Párt*) had 800 thousand members, most of whom had joined because they were incapable (or were afraid) of saying no to the local Party secretary's (→*párttitkár*) repeated urgings, and/or because advancement was rarely possible without the support of the Party; others joined because they were determined careerists or eventually hoped to gain political power; still others were hoping to help realize the (desired) reforms (→*reform*) that were always being planned but were never implemented; only a minority joined from a sincere, blind faith in socialism (→*szocializmus*), at least during the past two or three decades. Almost uncannily, people always knew why someone joined, just as they knew "when not to talk" in front of somebody because he was an informer.

párttitkár (*local*) *Party secretary*; the world of socialism (→*szocializmus*) was designed to insure that there should be two people on every rung of the ladder of power and leadership in the almost exclusively state-owned economy in all its shapes, forms and sizes, just as in public administration, not to mention health care and the military: the state appointed, "responsible leader" (today we would call him "manager") on the one hand, and the ubiquitous leader of the "ground organization" (party cell) on the other (made up of the Party members, and an obligatory organ of every workplace), who (in theory) was elected by the Party members (→*párttag*) themselves, and was called the Party secretary. He could officially assess (i.e., check and keep an eye on) the activities of the head of the company (which was not possible the other way around), and the relationship of the two which, however, was not a clearcut subordinate to superior relationship, had a definitive influence on the life of every office and company; from the point of view of the employees, a "good" Party secretary was one who – whether he was "independent", i.e., he had no other responsibilities besides "Party work", and that's why he received his salary, or whether he was one of the workers (→*dolgozó*) – did not interfere in company decisions and left his colleagues in peace (i.e., he did not report them, he did not even complain about them at Party headquarters), and pursued his duties only *pro forma*; without these "good" Party secretaries the soft dictatorship would have been a lot less benign, not to mention the state of the Hungarian economy; on the other hand, an ambitious and zealous Party secretary (who wanted the approval of his superiors, not to mention a career), could make the lives of people a living hell. →**Párt, a**

Pécs (pron. *peytch*); surrounded by the hills of the Mecsek Mountains where an old Pannonian (→*Pannonia*) settlement once stood, it is the largest town of southern Transdanubia (→*Dunántúl*), and has managed to retain its 19th century, small-town atmosphere. It is both the financial and cultural center of the region, a fact which makes its local patriots justifiably proud; adjacent to the local bishopric, King Louis the Great also founded the first Hungarian college here in 1371. →**Zsolnay**

péksütemény '*bakers' cake*' (lit.); the name for croissants (→*kifli*) and rolls (→*zsömle*) regardless of how they are made (buttery, crisp, sweet, salty), consumed mostly for breakfast (→*reggeli*) along with café au lait and cocoa, or else as a mid-morning snack in schools; of course, bakers make other types of "baked goods" (→*sütemény*), too, such as milk loaf (→*kalács*) and "cheese (→*túró*) pockets" (→*bukta*).

pénz *money*; →**keres**

perec *pretzel*; a usually hard or semi-hard, brittle biscuit made from a slender roll of dough the length of two spans shaped into a knot and liberally sprinkled with salt-water, then baked to a crisp, though there is also a "giant" variety, which is twice as big; when fresh, it veritably melts in the mouth;

thirty to forty years ago, when this was the favorite of children, it was sold at playgrounds by "pretzel men" who dispensed it from long rods; today, pretzels are sold almost exclusively in movie theaters, though American-style popcorn is quickly crowding out the competition. →**kifli**; **zsömle**

Pest (pron. *pesht*); the name of the city does not come from *pestis*, the Hungarian name for the plague (pestilence), but in all probability, from an ancient Slav word meaning "oven" or "furnace"; after all, before the Conquest (→*Honfoglalás*) the area was settled by Slavs. Today, the name is used locally to signify the entire capital city, though it is actually only one part of it, namely, the flat expanse of land lying on the left bank of the Danube, whose unified cityscape is due to the turn of the century (→*századforduló*) building frenzy to celebrate the 1000th anniversary (→*Millennium*) of the Hungarian conqest (→*Honfoglalás*). In 1873, at the time of the unification of the three towns that became the city of →*Budapest*, Pest championed the unification, for as opposed to →*Buda*, which was then the capital of the country, Pest was liberal and Protestant, and above all, "modern". Today, it is the seat of government (the Parliament, too, is located here), with many offices, banks, and elegant shops, not to mention theaters and industrial buildings; on the other hand, though the majority of the population of Budapest lives and works here, with few exceptions, the desirable living areas are all located in Buda. Even though the Inner City (→*Belváros*) Parish Church at the foot of Elizabeth (→*Erzsébet*) Bridge was built from the stones of a Roman Age military camp, Pest is a young city, for after the recapture of →*Buda* in 1686 from the Turk, it had to be built from scratch, and even in 1708, when the so-called Péterffy Palace (today's *Százéves* Restaurant), the oldest surviving building in the city was built on the former Main Square (on the corner of Galamb and Piarista streets), it had only 1,700 inhabitants. →**Óbuda**; **Aquincum**; **Vár, a**; **Vörösmarty tér**

Pest-Buda (pron. *pesht–boo–dah*), the name of the twin cities before their unification, from the times when →*Buda* was still the capital of Hungary. →**Budapest**; **Pest**

pesszimizmus *pessimism*; it is a typical psychological trait of Hungarians (which often paralyzes them) that they generally expect the worst, an expectation liberally backed by the bitter fate the nation (→*nemzet*) had suffered at the hands of history, which resulted in an understandable loss of self-confidence (and the development of a strong inferiority complex); indeed, the best-known poem written after the defeat of the War of Independence (→*Szabadságharc*) includes these lines: "*We are dying and perishing, our Nation falling apart like an untied shief*" and in the *Appeal* (→*Szózat*), too, one of the most important poems in all of Hungarian literature, there appears the vision of the approaching death of the nation, which had worried the Hungarians since the beginning of the 19th century, when they suddenly found themselves in the minority in their own country, and this state of affairs only went from bad to worse when as a consequence of the Peace Treaty of Versailles (→*Trianon*) the country also lost a large part of its territory; this pessimism was (to some extent) relieved only by the euphoria of independence regained with the change in regime (→*rendszerváltás*). →***Székely himnusz***; **sírva vigad a magyar**

Petőfi Sándor (pron. *peh–towfee*); the 19th century poet who possibly made the greatest impact on the national and literary consciousness; he not only recreated Hungarian poetry (→*költészet*) in both its form and language, but in his oeuvre, romanticism, patriotism and revolutionary fervor are admirably and perfectly mixed, not to mention the awesome unity of his life and art; the young man, who was a newlywed and the driving force behind the uprising (→*forradalom, 1848*) which broke out in Pest on March 15th (→*március 15.*), died a hero's death a year and a half later in Transylvania (→*Erdély*) at the age of 26, in one of the last battles of the War of Independence (→*Szabadságharc*). To this day, his name stands as the synonym for the quintessential Hungarian poet. →***Talpra magyar …***; **János vitéz**; **nyelvújítás**

Piarista Gimnázium *Pious Fathers' Secondary School*; the school of the Piarists in Budapest famous for its high standards which, wonder of wonders, functioned even under socialism (→*szocializmus*). →**Pannonhalma**; **Sárospatak**; **Fasori gimnázium**

piros-fehér-zöld *red-white-green* according to one explanation, the three colors, red, white, and green, are symbols of "strength", "fidelity" and "hope"; in fact the Hungarian flag was designed at the beginning of the 19th century, at the time the tricolor was in vogue in Europe, by adopting the red-white (heraldic red and silver) stripes of the coat-of-arms of the →*Árpád-ház* dynasty. By way of a footnote, there are two words in Hungarian for the color red, and while the upper stripe of the national flag is invariably called "*piros*" (pron. *pee-rosh*, the origin of the Hungarian girls' name "Piroska"), the color of the former Soviet (Chinese, etc.) flag is referred to as "*vörös*" (pron. *vow-rosh*), which is also the color of blood; paprika, on the other hand, is "*piros*", though we mustn't come to any far-reaching conclusions as a result. →**nemzetiszín (zászló)**

pirospaprika *red pepper, paprika*; though there is green (and white, but also called "green") and red pepper of various thicknesses, by →*paprika* (as a spice and not a vegetable) Hungarians mean the tiny bright-red variety, both rounded and pointed, in both its dried and crushed states; this hot (→*csípős*) variety is the most characteristic spice of Hungarian foods (→*magyaros étel*), though milder *paprika* is also grown.

pite *pie*; one of the most frequently prepared home-made cakes which is similar to apple pie, except it is smaller and cut into squares, and made of grated apple usually mixed with jam (→*lekvár*).

pogácsa *scones*; the most popular Hungarian home-made pastry (→*sütemény*), it is almost never absent from the table of a good hostess. It comes in salty and sweet varieties, and also baked with cracklings (→*töpörtyű*) and cheese, and in various sizes, from bite-size to the size of a small fist, and is prepared according to recipes handed down from mother to daughter. One of its main charms is that it will retain its freshness for days, which is one reason every mother likes to put it in the lunch box of her children when they go off on an outing. Even in folk tales, when a young man sets out into the world to try his luck, he does so with "scones baked in ashes" put in his sack by his mother.

ponty *carp*; this fatty and bony fish (→*hal*), which is bred in artificial ponds and which can grow to ten or twenty kilos in weight, is the most often used ingredient of the few fish dishes that can be found in authentic Hungarian cuisine (→*magyar konyha*). →**halászlé**

Pozsony (pron. *pow–zhonj*); a city on the shores of the Danube (→*Duna*) near Vienna (→*Bécs*) formerly inhabited by a mixed population consisting mainly of Germans (→*németek*) Hungarians and Slovaks (→*szlovák*), which the Peace Treaty of Versailles (→*Trianon*) annexed to Czechoslovakia and which, as the capital of Slovakia, is known today as Bratislava. For a thousand years it served as the western gate of Hungary, then after the battle of →*Mohács* it became the city where the kings of Hungary were crowned, and where the Estates' Assembly convened until the revolution (→*forradalom, 1848*), after which →*Pest–Buda* took over its role in national affairs.

pörkölt (pron. *powr–kowlt*), *stew*; the most easy to prepare, ubiquitous Hungarian meat speciality which can be made from veal, beef or pork, even pork's feet; the meat, cut into cubes and liberally salted, is browned, then stewed in lard and onions (→*hagyma*), and is seasoned with paprika (→*paprika*); it is served with *galuska* (small dumplings), boiled potatoes or →*tarhonya* (egg barley). →**paprikás**

presszó *espresso*; →**eszpresszó**

privatizáció *privatization*; →**ÁPV Rt.**

proligyerek '*proletarian/prole kid*' (lit.); since Marxist ideology saw the embodiment of the future in industry, which in turn it identified with the proletariat, the word soon became an omnipresent prefix of sorts, an adjective with a positive charge that could be affixed to just about anything, while *proli*, the shortened form of *proletár* ('proletarian'), received a certain archaic, near-obsolete cast; when they wished to show off and legitimize themselves, certain Party (→*Párt*) functionaries (→*funkcionárius*) liked to refer to themselves as *proligyerek*, conjuring up thereby the bogus, romantic image of the mythical worker (→*munkás*) who is persevering, ingenious and honest, scorns capitalist superiority and defends his principles in face of it, and is proud of his class. Having lost its aura, today the word is used to designate young people living on the outskirts who are out of work and loaf around aimlessly all day.

protestantizmus *Protestantism*; →**református**

pufajka *padded* (*quilt*) *jacket* (lit.); this shoddy, short winter jacket made by stuffing cotton between two cheap pieces of cloth and holding it together by quilting came to Hungary as the uniform (→*egyenruha*) of the Red Army (the word, too, comes from the Russian), and was frequently worn by people working out in the open. It has come down in history because during the revolution (→*forradalom, 1956*), the occupying forces gave the secret police (→*ávós*) and functionaries (→*funkcionárius*) organized to restore "order" *pufajka* jackets to wear as their uniform.

puli →**vizsla; kuvasz**

Puskás Öcsi *Puskás, the Kid*; the left winger of the Golden Team (→*Aranycsapat*), Ferenc Puskás in civilian life, was the greatest among the "boys with the golden legs" not only because of his phenomenal talent, but also because he was known as a devil-may-care prole kid (→*proligyerek*) from →*Kispest*, legendary for his disdain for the powers that be. His unabashed, playful cynicism was like a breath of fresh air in the age of lies and hypocrisy; the saying, "no money, no game" his answer to the reproaches of a Party leader, has become part of Hungarian folklore. He defected (→*disszidens*) in '56 (→*ötvenhat*) and made a career for himself in Spain, and was officially labeled a "traitor" (→*áruló*) back home. Even in his old age, *Öcsi bácsi* ('*Uncle Kid*') continues to draw nostalgic crowds, for in Hungary, he is considered the embodiment not only of the ideal football (soccer) player, but also of the country's glorious achievement in the field of sports. →**ötvenes évek**; **futball**; **Papp Laci**; **hat-három**; **öcsi**

puszi *smack* (*on the face*); originally used only by children (and possibly onomatopoeic) to mean a loud, smacking kiss (→*csók*) on the face, men never indulged in this kind of greeting, unless (possibly) with female relatives they already knew well as children, in which case it was a sign of affection. Today, it is the general form of greeting between female friends of all ages; what's more, having been a current form of greeting among men in the sixties and seventies, those who were young then will still sometimes kiss close friends (also the husbands of female friends, and conversely, the wives of male friends) in this manner – possibly the effect of the "Beatles culture" as it filtered in through the Iron Curtain. →**kézfogás**

puszta, a (pron. *poos–tah*); (*the*) *barren wilderness*; used without the definite article, *puszta* is generally used to mean 'empty', 'bereft'; with the definite article, it refers to the flatlands of the Great Plain (→*Alföld*) inhabited only by cowherds and sheepherds, and also the horseherds (→*csikós*), and carries a romantic connotation; it also means the fields at some remove from a village (originally, the fields belonging to villages, destroyed during the wars of the Turkish →*hódoltság*), where people live on (temporary) farms (→*tanya*) while they do fieldwork; in this sense it often forms part of place names as well. →**betyár**

Pusztaszer (pron. *poos–tah–ser*); on the flattest part of the Great Plain (→*Alföld*), smack in the middle of the flattest prairie between the →*Duna* and the →*Tisza* (north of →*Szeged*), where in the Middle Ages the monastery and market town of Szer stood, before the Turks (→*törökök*) destroyed it, in place of today's barren wilderness (→*puszta*) with only some scattered farmsteads (→*tanya*), where when the 9th century Conquest (→*Honfoglalás*) was compeleted, in the middle of the country (specifically, of the Carpathian Basin) the allied tribes who settled down with Prince →*Árpád* at their head, held a meeting at which they divided the country amongst themselves and passed certain laws, thereby veritably founding the Hungarian state; on the millecentenary (1100th anniversary) of this meeting, the huge restored round oil and canvas panorama entitled *The Arrival of the Conquering Magyars*, originally made for the Millennium (→*Millennium*) and representing the legendary story of the Conquest in a romantic, heroic style, was set up at this symbolic spot, which is also a national memorial park. →**honfoglalók**

R

Rába (pron. *rah–bah*); a tributary of the Danube (→*Duna*) at whose mouth stands the city of →*Győr*; it gave its name to the many types of tractors and trucks the city's huge Wagon and Machine Plant produced before and after WW II.

rác *Serbian*; though today it bears the same equivocal status as →*tót* (Slovak), →*oláh* (Romanian) and →*sváb* (Swabian, German), none of which had a pejorative ring to begin with, *rác* comes from the word *Thracian*, and is the only one of the group which has survived, mostly only as a family name, or as part of the .sobriquet *vadrác* or '*wild Serb*'.

Radnóti Miklós (pron. *rod–naw–tee*); one of the outstanding 20th century Hungarian poets whose life was perhaps the most tragic of all, for when he could not march on along with the other Jewish forced laborers being driven towards Vienna, the Arrow Cross (→*nyilas(keresztes) mozgalom*) shot him dead by the side of a road in early 1945, when he was still a young man; his last poems, as touching as they are great, were discovered in a mass grave: "...*Shot through the nape. I whispered to myself, / That's how you too will end. No more now, peace. / Patience will flower in death. And I could hear / A voice above me say: der springt noch auf. / Earth and dried blood mingling in my ear.*" (trans. G. Szirtes)

Rajk László (pron. *rowyk*); the most famous victim of the Hungarian show trials conducted in the fifties (→*ötvenes évek*) in imitation of the Stalinist model. Having been the iron-fisted Minister of the Interior who helped usher in Hungary's Communist dictatorship, with several others he was (falsely) accused of spying for Yugoslavia (which at the time was considered the greatest enemy of communism), and was sentenced to death; after the fall of →*Rákosi* he was rehabilitated, and it was with the emotion-charged reburial of him and some of those who shared his fate that the events leading up to the revolution (→*forradalom, 1956*), which broke out on the October 23rd (→*október 23.*), took their start. →**temetés**

Rákóczi Ferenc (pron. raw–kow–tsee); just about every village, town and city in Hungary has a street named after the extremely wealthy aristocrat who became the leader of the →*kuruc* insurrectionist forces in the first decade of the 18th century, who fought against the Habsburgs (→*Habsburgok*), trying to take over the country after the ousting of the Turks (→*törökök*); the struggle, which ended in a compromise, made Rákóczi, then Prince of Transylvania, into one of the great symbolic figures of national independence; he died in Turkey after decades of exile. →**temetés**; **emigráció**

Rákóczi tér *Rákóczi Square*; the traditional center of Budapest's red light district which with its narrow streets, old and decrepit apartment houses and market place, situated in its heart, has something distinctly archaic about it; besides the Gypsies who moved there during the past few decades, it is now also home to many recently arriving Arabs and Chinese.

Rákóczi-induló *Rákóczi March*; a Hungarian military march with the most sprightly rhythm of all, adapted from a melody composed in →*kuruc* times probably by a Gypsy musician (→*cigányzene*) which was also used by Liszt and Berlioz (!); Radio (Budapest) Kossuth (→*Kossuth Rádió*) begins its early-morning broadcast with it; it also signals the beginning of every military review and parade (unless the Klapka March, or →*Klapka-induló* is played instead); it also signals the end of every ball.

Rákosi Mátyás (pron. *raw–koh–shee*); according to a contemporary accolade, he was "Stalin's best Hungarian disciple", and his name stands for a terrible and oppressive era in Hungarian history, specifically, the fifties (→*ötvenes évek*); his grotesque, squat figure and bald pate was the butt of countless jokes, though that is not what led to his downfall; his hateful memory lives on, for he caused the kind of damage and suffering which can never be remedied. →**Rajk**; **ÁVÓ**

rántotthús/csirke *pork/chicken in breadcrumbs*; pork (especially pork chops and spare ribs or daisy ham) is most often prepared by dipping the meat slices first in flour, then egg, and finally in breadcrumbs, then fried in lots of oil or lard (→*zsír*); it is served with potatoes (→*krumpli*) or rice and cucumber salad redolent with the smell of garlic and liberally sprinkled with sour cream; fried chicken is another great favorite, especially if made with young chicken raised on a real farm. →**vasárnap**; **esküvő**

Rátót (pron. *rawh–towt*); jocular and satirical songs and stories abound about the "lads of Rátót", or '*rátóti legények*' who, regardless of what they attempt, always ruin it by trying too hard; there is also a village by this name on the map. →**legény**

Recsk (pron. *rechk*); an isolated village among the hills of northern Hungary where in the first half of the fifties (→*ötvenes évek*) the secret police (→*ÁVO*) set up a prison camp for condemned political prisoners (as well as those who were not even condemned); it was the largest "island" of the Hungarian Gulag Archipelago which the men who were kept there compared to the Nazi death camps.

reform *reform*; a key concept in Hungarian politics whose content has changed many times since the early 19th century. At its first appearance, for the generation of →*Széchenyi* it meant the modernization (i.e., re-creation) of the country, then during the revolution (→*forradalom, 1848*), the prevention thereof; from the sixties (*hatvanas évek*), it was used to refer to the repeated, circumspect attempts at putting the planned socialist economy, which from the first moment of nationalization (→*államosítás*) was out of gear, in some sort of working order (attempts which always faltered on the solid rock of resistance put up by functionaries afraid of the rational changes that might lessen their power), until most recently the word was meant to convey the safe transferral of the political structures of socialism (→*szocializmus*) to the era that would follow the approaching and inevitable change in regime (→*rendszerváltás*).

református '*reformed*' (lit.), *member of a Protestant Church, Protestant*; the term Hungarians generally used for Calvinists, who make up approximately 30% of the population, especially in the eastern half of the country, in the areas of the former Turkish occupation (→*Hódoltság*), including →*Debrecen*, the "Calvinist Rome"; this religion has preserved its "Hungarian" character, an obvious example being the black capes worn by the priests which still bear the marks of 18th century Hungarian costume (→*magyaros viselet*), this in contrast to the latinate (though also, through the influence of the →*Habsburg* emperors, also Germanic) internationality of the Catholic Church (→*Katolikus Egyház*); still, religious conflict has not been an issue among the Hungarians for a long time, if for no other reason, than because sociologically speaking, the congregations have become indistinguishable from each other, as a result of which there are more and more Ecumenical churches, especially in Transylvania (→*Erdély*); while the Hungarians educated in Jesuit schools were culturally bound to triumphant baroque and Catholic Vienna (→*Bécs*) and Rome, the 40 thousand young men (most of them Transylvanian) who in the 17th and 18th centuries studied at the universities of Protestant Holland (Utrecht, Franeken) and England, brought the tradition of a Western type of bourgeois culture and mentality with them back to Hungary.

reggeli '*morning meal*' (lit.), *breakfast*; Hungarian breakfast does not differ appreciably from breakfast anywhere else in Europe, unless we take into consideration that it is not unusual to start it with a small glass of brandy (→*pálinka*), especially in the villages, and elsewhere, where the people engage in heavy physical work. →**kalács**; **aludt tej**; **péksütemény**; **szalonna**; **kolbász**

rendőr *policeman*; in Hungary, people do not like the police (which may very well have historical reasons, since the police force did not always limit its activities to fighting crime); accordingly, there are countless jokes (→*vicc*) in circulation the clincher of which is the stupidity of the police, and there are hardly any exciting crime stories on film with likeable cops. →**csendőr**

rendszerváltás '(*the*) *change in regime*' (lit.); though it reflects events and processes taking place in world politics, and the results can be interpreted as the triumph of rational consideration, the change in regime would not have been possible without the ten year long preparation for it by the intelligentsia (→*értelmiség*) and the opposition (who later split up into various camps), not to mention the political and personal daring with which they defied the dictatorship of the weakened ancien regime (whose economy, too, was in its death-throes), a dictatorship which, though "soft", was also unpredictable; nor could it have happened without the people rehearsing it hundreds of times over and over again in both thought and writing (through discussions in various circles, not to mention the journals, both legal and illegal, published in numbers however small); without this background, the Hungarian people surely would not have been so well prepared psychologically for the change that they knew, as if by instinct, what they should do when it finally happened, as a result of which the return to Parliamentary democracy occurred with complete national concensus, a fact that even the political infighting which broke out almost immediately after the change in regime could not alter, and indeed, was of minor significance compared to the overriding importance of the former; the Hungarian change in regime was not determined by the small oppositional elite who forced the changes by recourse to public law and hard negotiation, but the little man of the →*Kádár* era, the embodiment of popular political culture. It was his attitude and perspective that had changed during the second half of the eighties, and it was the pressure, and subsequently the vote from this *homo kadarikus*, who kept his distance from the elite and entertained a healthy scepticism in face of politics, which brought about the monumental change called the *rendszerváltás* or →*rendszerváltoztatás*. →**Nagymaros**; **Kádár János**; **vállalkozó**

rendszerváltoztatás '*(the) changing of the regime*' (lit.); closely synonymous with →*rendszerváltás*, except that it is in the active voice, while the other expression in the passive, which certainly has some clear implications.

Repül a nehéz kő ... "*There flies the heavy stone ...*" (lit.); a quote from János Arany's →*Toldi*, which continues: "*... who knows where it will stop, who it will strike?*" The passage from the long epic poem which contains these lines (and in which the powerful Miklós Toldi throws a millstone and inadvertently kills somebody) is compulsory reading in elementary school and must be learned by heart, but people refer to it metaphorically, especially the beginning, to suggest (with a mysterious smile) that there's no knowing how far the investigation of some otherwise petty abuse of power at a low level of competence might lead.

rétes '*layers*' (lit.), *strudel*; this "genteel" desert which probably came to Hungary from Austria (→*Ausztria*) is something every Hungarian housewife is most proud of, for it is tasty only if the dough is stretched wafer thin (which means that it often tears and gets holes in it, and then the entire procedure has to be started from scratch) so that it can be baked very quickly; naturally, the stuffing, which is traditionally made from apples, poppy seeds (→*mák*), sour cherries, or cabbage (→*káposzta*), is also a very important part of any good strudel.

rigójancsi '*Johnny Blackbird*' (lit.); a square shaped "confectioner's cake" (→*cukrászsütemény*) full of chocolate cream and covered with chocolate, which bears the name of a famous, handsome Gypsy *prímás* (violinist) who lived at the turn of the century (→*századforduló*); the tie between this cake (→*torta*) and the violinist is probably the colour brown. →**dobos**; **krémes**; **zserbó–szelet**

Riska (pron. *rish–kah*); one of the diminutive forms of *Mariska* (Mária) which is, however, used only for cows.

rokonság '*relations*' (lit.), *relatives, the family*; as the nuclear family becomes smaller, relations are becoming less important. →**sógor**; **koma**

roma *Romany*; the name of Gypsies for themselves which is just becoming politically correct (along with the slow development of the sense of pride of Gypsies), i.e., it is becoming both official and compulsory, making *cigány*, Hungarian for *Gypsy* taboo; earlier, the word was considered slang when not used by the Gypsies (→*cigányság*) themselves, especially since an appreciable portion of Hungarian slang words come from Gypsy or Yiddish.

románok, a *Romanians, the*; Romanian-Hungarian relations have been strained ever since the late 18th century, when the Romanians became the majority in Transylvania (→*Erdély*), especially in its southern counties; relations have been strained not only politically but personally as well, having been poisoned on both sides by a near mythological picture of the wicked "Other One", combined with prejudice; when after WW I the Peace Treaty of Versailles (→*Trianon*) annexed Transylvania to Romania, the old animosity went from bad to worse, for its Hungarian population, a million and a half souls at the time, felt their identity threatened in face of government directed romanization, which during the socialist years took on unprecedented proportions (for instance, the closing of Hungarian schools), and which culminated in the eighties with Ceausescu's program to destroy the villages of Transylvania (the infamous "bulldozing"), thus creating a wave of frightened refugees; furthermore, Hungarians felt out of place in Romania, which they considered part of the Balkans (→*Balkán, a*) and which was Greek Orthodox in religion, while for its part, jealously watching over its newly acquired territories, triumphant Romanian nationalism felt the existence of Hungarians within its borders a constant threat, and considered Hungarians traitors by virtue of their nationality.

Still, in Transylvania itself, Romanians and Hungarians lived side by side in relative peace (a fact proven by the large numer of inter-marriages despite the religious differences), which after the change in regime resulted in the political party of the Romanian Hungarians being even invited into a coalition government. →**oláh**; **székely**

rozs *rye*; fresh, snow-white bread made from wheat is a veritable fetish for Hungarians, so much so that until very recently, brown rye bread was generally frowned upon; Hungarians even felt sorry for the Russians and the Germans who, for lack of white bread, had no choice but eat bread baked from rye. Brown and black bread found their way into shops only with the new vogue for "healthy" diets. →**búza**; **zab**

Rózsa Sándor (pron. *row–zhah*); a historical figure and the romantic embodiment of the highwayman (*betyár*), he was in fact the leader of a group of robbers despoiling the farms (→*tanya*) around →*Szeged* in the southern Great Plain (→*Alföld*), an area which at his time, in the mid-19th century was still uncultivated and sparsely populated, and given over to animal husbandry. Though he was responsible for the death of many people, the popular imagination turned him into a Hungarian Robin Hood, whose figure pops up again and again in Hungarian literature as the archetypal *betyár*. In 1849, during the War of Independence (→*szabadságharc*), he was also infected by the new national sentiments, and organized an independent cavalry of *betyárs*; however, they were of not much use to the Hungarian army, and speedily disbanded. →**Sobri Jóska**

Rózsadomb '*Rose Hill*'/'*Hill of Roses*' (lit.); one of the hills surrounding the inner areas of →*Buda* which stretches down almost to the shore of the Danube (→*Duna*). Ever since the end of the 19th century, when the vineyards of Rózsadomb were uprooted to make way for *haute bourgeois* villas with panoramic views, this area has been considered the most prestigeous residential district of the capital, despite the serious damages it sustained during WW II. The majority of the houses, which were turned into co-tenancies (→*társbérlet*), are just regaining their former beauty and elegance.

S

sajnálatos események '*regretable events*' (lit.); the painfully hypocritical political (and journalistic) euphemism for the revolution (→*forradalom, 1956*), which was invented by way of concession to replace the confrontational term, "counter-revolution", and to serve as the linguistic equivalent of the limited compromise offered by the authorities to the vanquished. It carried the message that if you weren't politically active but accepted the inevitable, you would be left in peace. In 1957 →*Kádár* summarized this (by way of his program, one might say), in a famous sentence, "He who is not against us is with us." →**ötvenhat**

saláta '*salad*' (lit.), *lettuce*; in Hungary, the only vegetable eaten as a salad (when the ubiquitous pickles, or →*savanyúság*, is not served) is made of lettuce, which thus became known as *saláta* (Hungarian for *salad*). A disordered bunch of papers or a book read to shreds is also called *saláta*; salad dressing, however, is new to Hungary, and until recently, lettuce was served drenched in water seasoned with a dash of sugar and vinegar.

sapka '*cap*' (lit.); real tight-fitting caps which hug the head (baseball caps, for instance) were not known in Hungary, except for knitted ski caps sometimes worn by the young; on the other hand, there are other types of caps, such as the →*bocskai sapka*, the →*mic sapka* and the →*svájci sapka* (beret), but wearing these was not simply a matter of heeding the call of fashion. →**kalap**

sárga *yellow*; in Hungary, it is considered a "German" color, the characteristic "imperial" color of Catholic (→*katolikus*) churches, mostly built in the Baroque style; accordingly, it was not worn by a true patriot, especially combined with black, until the Habsburgs (→*Habsburgok*) were no more than a bad memory; in Hungarian, you turn "yellow with envy", or are consumed by it, as in "*He's being consumed by yellow envy*".

Sárospatak (pron. *show–rosh–pow–tahk*); a small town lying at the foot of mountains in northern Hungary, site of a Calvinist (→*református*) school/college for over four-hundred years, whose graduates (clergymen and teachers) took its teachings to the entire eastern part of the country; since the change in regime (→*rendszerváltás*), the school once again belongs to the Church. →**Fasori gimnázium**; **Pannonhalma**; **Piaristák**

savanyúság '(*something*) *sour*' (lit.), *pickled vegetables*; just like German and Slav cuisines, Hungarian cuisine (→*magyar konyha*) also prefers pickled vegetables with meat dishes instead of fresh salad →(*saláta*); just about anything found in a kitchen garden can be used to make pickles (from beets, which are used only for pickling, to small, unripe watermelons), though at the stands and shops at the markets, where only pickled vegetables are sold, pickles with various seasonings (and of greatly varying sizes) and soured →*paprika* of all sorts (sometimes incredibly hot!) continue most in demand. →**kovászos uborka**

sertés *pork*; the "official" name for *pig* or *swine* (→*disznó*) found on restaurant menus.

Siófok (pron. *shee–ow–fok*); a "summer" city on the southern shore of the →*Balaton* which quickly grew from a sleepy hamlet to "the capital of the Balaton"; it makes its living from the hundred-thousand vacationers who visit it yearly, and thus its inhabitants are forced to put up with the fair-ground (→*vásár*) noise, which escalates year by year, not to mention the crowds who take over every square inch of space, come summer; not long ago, this was also the favorite meeting place of East and West German families separated by the Iron Curtain.

sírva vigad a magyar '*the Hungarian makes merry by crying*' (lit.), '*the Hungarian takes his pleasure sadly*'; a piece of silly nonsense of uncertain origin from the storehouse of maudlin and sentimental clichés of Hungarian self-pity. The favorite dramatic scene in pre-war movies showed a handsome young gentleman (→*úriember*), possibly a →*fiatalúr*, or →*nagyságos úr*, who, through no fault of his own (though perhaps he'd been a bit too liberal with what little fortune he had left, which only makes him more endearing) finds himself in a hopeless situation, and decides to squander the pitiful remains of his inheritance on a last supper with champagne and Gipsy music (→*cigányozás*), singing his favorite Hungarian song (→*magyar nóta*) one last time in a devil-may-care fashion ("*My fortune is squandered, I have no more cares*"), or else, with a heavy heart ("*I don't know how I ruined my life*"), then, embracing the Gipsy violinist (*prímás*), who feels for him, he bids a tearful farewell to his ruined life (which does not exclude a happy end); the general public found this exceptionally touching and beautiful, and who knows, there might be something to it, for such (imagined) scenes have caught the imagination of Americans, too, who say that "Hungarians cry into their wine", and envy them for it. →**magyar ember evés közben ...**

snóbli a primitive game of chance played in pubs (→*kocsma*); the players, who stand in a circle, hide some coins in their palm, then on a given sign open it, and the one who can guess how many coins were hidden wins all the coins. →**snúrozás**

snúrozás game played by boys and young men in villages (and the outskirts of towns); a line is drawn in the dust, and the players throw coins from a distance of five or six feet, and the one who can hit the line wins all the coins; at one time (for example, in *The Boys of Paul*

Street, or →*A Pál utcai fiúk*), a similar game was played with glass balls (marbles) or (if the players were very poor), with clay balls. →**snóbli**

Sobri Jóska (pron. *shob-ree yowsh-kah*); a legendary mid-19th century highwayman (→*betyár*) of the →*Bakony* mountains whose figure has been kept alive by folklore. →**Rózsa Sándor**

Sok az eszkimó, kevés a fóka ... "*Too many Eskimos, not enough seals*..."; a line from the last scene of Imre Madách's *The Tragedy of Man* (→*Tragédia*) in which Adam and Eve, having come to the last station in the history of manking, appear as two miserable Eskimos dragging on a wretched life; it is so often quoted to signify that there is not enough of something to go around, that by now it has become hackneyed.

sonka *ham*; smoked ham, which has been stored since pig killing (→*disznóölés*) in winter, is an indispensable part of every Hungarian family's Easter (→*húsvét*) dinner; it is always cooked in one piece and is eaten with the eggs (and potatoes!) cooked along with it, and freshly grated, strong horseradish.

Sopron (pron. *shop–ron*); called Ödenburg in German, it is Hungary's westernmost and perhaps visually the most westernized town, which along with its immediate environs, is veritably wedged into the map of Austria (→*Ausztria*); although in the Peace Treaty of Versailles (→ *Trianon*) the victorious powers annexed it to Austria, as a result of the the only popular referendum held after WW I to decide the fate of the territories taken away from Hungary, it remained within the mother country, even though a significant portion of the population were German-speaking; it was thus accorded the name of "the most faithful city", which is written in Latin (*Civitas Fidelissima*) above the gate of the town's medieval fire tower.

Sopronkőhida (pron. *shop–ron–kow–hee–dah*); the most hardened criminals with the longest sentences are traditionally incarcerated in the old jail of this small township on the western border; in the winter of 1944-45, the Arrow Cross (→*nyilaskeresztes mozgalom*) brought the arrested leaders of the antifascist resistance here, to the country's western border, where the hangings continued until the last moment of the Arrow Cross's defeat. →**Vác**; **Szeged**

sör *beer*; for centuries considered a German drink (which did not stop people from drinking it), it is commonly held to make one dull (as opposed to wine), more and more beer is being consumed in pubs (→*kocsma*) by those who used to prefer spritzer (→*fröccs*), while the social status of wine is on the rise. To clink glasses with beer is considered bad manners.

spájz →**éléskamra**

Sport–szelet '*sport slice*' (lit.); a small bar of nugat chocolate with rum and walnut flavoring and the best loved and least expensive sweet for the past half a century; its easily recognizable grass green paper wraper conjures up the green of a soccer field. →**Tibi**

spriccer →**fröccs**

sramli (pron. *shrom–lee*); folksy German dance music, traditional and friendly, performed in Swabian (→*sváb*) villages by the local brass band with an accordion; thanks to the *petit bourgeoisie* of German origin, it also moved into the cities, then after decades of disfavor, "wedding rock" (→*lakodalmas rock*) has given it a new lease on life.

sumér-magyar nyelvrokonság *Sumero–Hungarian family of languages*; an erroneous 19th century theory which holds its own despite all its detractors, for it is nourished by the romantic vision of some ancient glory; its adherents (amateur linguists) base their arguments on the similarity of certain words in ancient Sumerian and Hungarian. →**finn–ugor rokonság**; **Attila**

süllő (*giant*) *pike–perch*; a fish of prey of the →*Balaton* with dry white meat; baked on the grill, it is the queen of any restaurant menu. →**hal**

sütemény '*baked* (*goods*)' (lit.), *cake/cookie*; Hungarian housewives usually make three kinds of baked goods: strudel (→*rétes*), rolls with various fillings (→*beigli*), and pie (→*pite*) according to recipes handed down from mother to daughter; there are also many kinds of small tea cakes and scones (→*pogácsa*), generally made for guests; on special occasions, such as birthdays (→*születésnap*), cake (→*torta*) with rich cream fillings and toppings is also made at home, though these are usually considered something best left to the care of a good bakery (→*cukrászsütemény*).

svábok *Swabians* (lit.), *Hungarian Germans*; lately a word with the same (low) status as →*oláh* (Gipsy) and →*tót* (Slovak), though unlike them, *sváb* does not occur as a family name, only *német* (German); indeed, according to the rules of Hungarian PC, one should say "(Hungarian) German" instead; on the other hand, they do not call themselves "German" (→*német*), only their language, and even that only lately; they call themselves "Swabians", in which they see nothing hurtful or pejorative (and which comes from the simple fact that in the 18th century, most settlers to Hungary came from Swabia); they are the largest ethnic group in Hungary (excepting →*Gypsies*), despite the fact that after WW II the winning world powers ordered that 200 thousand of them be deported to Germany, partly in retaliation because many joined organizations supported by Nazi Germany (though they were not the only ones deported), and also in order to make their houses available for Hungarians who were fleeing from neighboring countries as a result of ethnic cleansing (also done with the approval of the world powers), especially from Czechoslovakia, as part of the so-called "exchange of populations" (→*lakosságcsere*); most of their settlements date back to just after the Turkish occupation (→*Hódoltság*) ended, when people were brought in (according to the policy of the government) to work the land depopulated during the 150 years of war (especially in the middle and southern parts of the country, which had been part of the Turkish Empire); the Swabian peasant (→*paraszt*) – for the Swabian, too, is Swabian only as long as he stays on his land; people who go up to the city and become bourgeois or part of the protelariat, leave their ethnicity behind along with their village and traditional profession – is considered hardworking, good at his job, meek, clean, order-loving and thrifty, even miserly who, thanks to these traits, is (usually) better off than the Hungarians, for which he is (or was) often an object of envy and found unlikable, especially while their villages were untouched, and they removed themselves from the outside world; the years of socialism (→*szocializmus*) dispersed the Swabian communities, too, however, while as a result of the trauma of resettlement (→*kitelepítés*), most who stayed in Hungary did not pass their language on to their children. →**szászok**; **asszimiláció**

Svájc *Switzerland*; whenever Hungarians think of this country, they invariably do so with infinite envy for having been left out of the 20th century, making it (in their eyes) the land of the good life and security beyond their reach, a symbol of sorts for the West (→*Nyugat*), where only a lucky few were welcome as immigrants (→*disszidens*); at the same time, it is considered a boring and dull country, and its life style, despite all their yearning for it, they deem unbearable.

svájci sapka '*Swiss cap*' (lit.), *beret*; the ubiquitous headgear of the past half a century which women also wore for a time; it was seen on the heads of unskilled laborers, the intelligentsia (→*értelmiség*), as well as white collar workers, until it lost its original significance, which made it the opposite of the "conservative" hat (→*kalap*), and a sign of the contempt for fashion and other formalities disapproved of by the age; now it is worn only as "reinterpreted" by designers, while the classical *svájci sapka* is worn only by old men with small pensions. →**micisapka**

SZ

Szabad Európa Rádió *Radio Free Europe*; for decades "the voice of the enemy", the only unofficial news source to penetrate the Iron Curtain; in the fifties (→*ötvenes évek*), listening to it (provided it was possible, considering the state of the old, junky radios, not to mention the jamming) was a crime on par with "spreading of disquieting rumours" (i.e., scare-mongering), a serious criminal offence, but even later listening to it was banned, even though during the revolution (→*forradalom, 1956*), when it irresponsibly promised U.S. help to the revolutionaries, it lost its credibility to such an extent that until its demise people listened to its news broadcasts with a certain degree of reservation; still, it was difficult to sell a radio in Hungary that did not have short wave on it, and those who were young back then got their first taste of the beat revolution from its program entitled "Teenager Party".

Szabad Nép '*The Free People*' (lit.); →***Népszabadság***

Szabadságharc '*War of Liberation*' (lit.), *War of Independence*; a war in which the subjects of the Hungarian king fought, in the name of the Hungarian constitution, against the Austrian emperor, who rejected it, except that the Hungarian king and the Austrian emperor happened to be one and the same person; though the Hungarian army, organized in haste, poorly armed and in desperate straits, won several battles, it was finally vanguished by the superior numbers of the enemy, bolstered by Russian troops; Hungary's year-long, solitary struggle for its independence won the good will of the world, however, and Hungarian emigrants were received with open arms; the contemporary English poet, Matthew Arnold, wrote: "*Hungarians! Save the world! Renew the stories / Of men who against hope repelled the chain / And make the world's dead spirit leap again!*"; the price to be paid was some fifty thousand killed in action, and more than a hundred death sentences in the course of reprisals. →**forradalom (1848)**; **áruló**; **Kossuth**

Szabó család '*The Szabó family*' (lit.); the soap opera on →*Kossuth Rádió* which has been broadcast for almost thirty years now, and which before the advent of television was mass entertainment and cleverly manipulated propaganda in one; it has lost much of its popularity, though, and is today listened to mostly by housewives, especially of little schooling, beyond middle age, and living in the provinces (→*vidék*), often probably from sheer force of habit, for they can still remember the good old days when half the country religiously followed the story of the lives of the Szabó family, an average Hungarian family in every way (*szabó* is the Hungarian for *tailor*), and could see their own daily problems reflected in an "artistic" manner.

Szabolcs megye (pron. *sow–bolch*), *Szabolcs county*; county on the farthest point from the center of the country, in north-eastern Hungary which bears the name of one of the Conquering (→*honfoglaló*) chieftains, and which is considered the most backward county in Hungary; it is commonly referred to as "dark Szabolcs". →**Nyírség**

szakáll *beard*; today a question of fashion and male vanity, for several months after the revolution (→*forradalom, 1956*) it became the symbol of defiance ("I refuse to shave until the Russians leave!"), and in the sixties (→*hatvanas évek*) the symbol of rebellion against a generation of clean-shaven fathers, but also a provocation of sorts against the (also clean-shaven) Party (→*Párt*), which suspected counter-revolutionary (→*ellenforradalom*) intent in rebellion of all sorts; then after a decade or two, it became the typical fashion of the young (then the not so young) intelligentsia (*értelmiség*); it is sociologically an interesting fact about the first freely elected Parliament after the change in regime (→*rendszerváltás*) that in contrast to the earlier, unanymously clean-shaven house of representatives, there were (at the time) a strikingly large number of representatives with facial hair; furthermore, the "beards" tended to sit on the liberal side, while the "moustaches" (→*bajusz*) on the national conservative side, until those with beards or moustaches once again found themselves in the minority among politicians.

szaktárs *'companion in trade'* (lit.), *colleague*; the traditional (and today almost obsolete) term of address used by the trade unions and trade union members among themselves. →**elvtárs**

szalagavató bál *'ribbon inauguration ball'* (lit.); during the last semester before taking their final exams and graduating (→*érettségi*) high school students wear (rather reluctantly) a blue ribbon on their lapels with the first and last year of their studies; they accept these ribbons at a ceremony attended by their friends and relatives, held in some rentable space near school; the ceremony is followed by a dance at which the first dance is always the →*palotás* followed by a Viennese waltz, for which the boys wear tuxedoes and the girls evening dresses; they practice the dances for months ahead, so they won't bring shame on the head of their homeroom teacher in front of their deeply moved guests.

szalámi *salami*; of the many kinds of smoked and heavily spiced ground meat stuffed into (real or artificial) intestines, only the so-called winter salami (→*téliszalámi*) is called by this name. →**kolbász**

szalámizni *'to salami'* (lit.); *salami tactics; "the piecemeal attack on or elimination of (esp. political) opposition"* (Oxford ED); propably the only word (concept?)

of Hungarian origin in English political lingo, which originates from the late 40's, when →*Rákosi* and the Communists were gearing up towards introducing their totalitarian dictatorship: "*In Budapest, the citizens considered that the Smallholders' Party had been wrecked. 'Rákosi has eaten the last of the salami', was the word.*" (*Time* Latin Amer. ed., 1947); "*Mr. Rákosi describes one stage in it as 'salami tactics', by which slices of the Small-holders' Party were cut away and its strenght worn down, even while the Small-holders' leader was Prime Minister and Mr. Rákosi his deputy.*" (*The Times*, 1952); a prime example of political cynism, now blissfully obsolete.

szalonna *bacon*, the most important "people's food" in Hungary not only because it is inexpensive (being the skin and adjoining layer of fat from the pig which is cooked and/or cured, then and/ or smoked), and because it can be eaten on its own, fried or raw (bacon with onion, bread and dry, sparkling white wine used to be the classical outdoor menu during the harvest or →*aratás*), but it is still eaten daily by millions for breakfast (→*reggeli*) or dinner (→*vacsora*), sometimes with scrambled eggs; furthermore, there is hardly any authentic Hungarian food (→*magyaros étel*) whose recipe (because of the smoked flavor) does not begin with the words, "fry some bacon in a pan"; it comes in a number of sub-categories (meaty, fatty, cooked, cured, paprika, smoked), and is also categorized by region; since pigs are still killed in many Hungarian households, it is also cured and smoked according to traditional family recipes. →**disznóölés**

szalonnasütés '*bacon roast/barbecue*' (lit.); the romantic, evening (!) rite of school outings which grownups gladly indulge in themselves; the boys cut fresh twigs and carve them into sharp spits with their jacknives (→*bicska*), then stick pieces of bacon (→*szalonna*) on it, possibly with onions (→*hagyma*); squatting by the fire, everyone quickly begins to bake their own portion, whereas they should wait until the fire is reduced to glowing embers; naturally, big globs of fat drip from the bacon as it cooks, making a characteristic sputtering sound, and so a thick slice of bread (→*kenyér*) is held under it, since often the bacon slips off the spit just as at long last it is about ready to eat; the bacon, which is slit in several places before cooking, is ready when it shrivels into a half-moon shape and opens up at the slits; the idea of a bacon barbecue, however, is not to fill your belly, but the singing around the camp fire.

számháború '*numbers' war*' (lit.); a favorite game of adolescent boys (especially on school outings); the members of the two competing teams (with equal number of members) tie a piece of paper on their heads with a four-digit number on it, then disperse; when a sign is given, they begin to crawl on all fours from tree to tree, hiding from each other, and trying to read the number on the other's forehead; if a boy's number is called by the "enemy", he "dies".

szamorodni (pron. *somoh–rodnee*); the equally fullbloodied but drier version of →*aszú* wine with a taste much like sherry. →**tokaji**

szászok *Saxons*; a historical term which has by now been relegated to oblivion; it was the name for Germans (→*németek*) who in the Middle Ages settled in Transylvania (→*Erdély*) and Upper Hungary (→*Felvidék*); they lived in towns and enjoyed an appreciable measure of autonomy, as a result of which their descendants kept their language and identity intact; after WW II, their descendants were first deported from Czechoslovakia, then during the Ceausescu regime, from Romania as well. →**svábok**

szatyor *bag*; →**háló**

századforduló *fin de siècle*; in Hungarians' memory the last decades of the seemingly solid and eternal reign of Francis Joseph (→*Ferenc József*), grown into a tamed, sad old man, became the nostalgic age of "the peaceful peacetime years", an idea which, in the light of the tragedies engendered by the 20th century, seems quite justified, to say the least, something that belongs to a time before the Fall, a world of perfect harmony in retrospect, whereas in fact, those who would put an end to the fanciful operetta (→*operett*) being played out on the stage of the Monarchy (→*Monarchia*) were already waiting in the wings.

Széchenyi István (pron: *sey–chey–nyee*); his most adamant political foe, the radical Kossuth, called him "the greatest Hungarian"; in the mystery play of 19th century Hungarian history he is cast into the role of the "reformer" whose creations are innumerable; from the introduction of modern horse breeding to the regulation of the river Tisza, from the foundation of the Hungarian Academy of Sciences (→*Akadémia, Magyar Tudományos*) for which he donated his total income of a year, to the construction of the Chain Bridge (→*Lánchíd*), an impressive list of accomplishments are connected with his name: "*They cut off my wings, I walk on my feet; they cut off my feet, I walk on my hands; they tear out my arms, I crawl on my belly. Anything, as long as I can serve.*" (from his *Diary*); a wealthy aristocrat, he gave impetus to the drive for modernization which began in the first half of the last century, and came to a head in a revolution (→*forradalomban, 1848*), in which he saw the ruination of his work of patient construction; having become divided within himself, he finally committed suicide. Even just a decade or so ago, the Hungarian intelligentsia (→*értelmiség*) was still pretty much divided into Széchenyi and Kossuth believers, for their names became part of the political lingo, a shorthand for different strategies of development; what's more, during the crucial decade before the change in regime (→*rendszerváltás*), the dilemmas faced by the nation reminded many of the Kossuth-Széchenyi debate.

Szeged (pron: *seh–ghed*); the largest city of the Great Plain (→*Alföld*) in southern Hungary which is situated adjacent to the Yugoslav border on the shore of the river →*Tisza*, which has wrought havoc with it more than once; its name conjures up another, that of the Nobel Prize physicist Albert Szent-györgyi, the discoverer of vitamin C, who was a professor at the local university until he emigrated to the US after WW II; the large square in front of the city's huge cathedral, is the scene of well publicized summer theater productions, especially operas, but the town also has an infamous old jail where hardened criminals are incarcerated.

székely *Sekler*; the ethnic group living in Eastern Transylvania (→*Erdély*), who are part of the Hungarian nation yet have an identity of their own, for though their language may be identical with Hungarian, enthnographically they differ in may ways; since their origin remains shrouded in mystery, it has engendered many legends (according to which they are the last descendants of the people of →*Attila*); during the Middle Ages and afterwards, they acted as the defenders of the country's frontiers, living in self-governing military organizations, which partly explains their enthnographical differences; they are generally considered tenacious and hard-working, not to mention clever jacks-of-all-trades (whose speech is accordingly cunning), as a result of which the *góbé*, or Sekler man, is the hero of many a joke who in the end gains the upper hand; the touching and beautiful Sekler folk songs are musically more archaic than their Hungarian (Magyar) counterparts, while their often enigmatic folk ballads are distinctly medieval in subject and character, and are much loved in Hungary, too; what's more, in a certain sense, they are regarded as more "authentically" Hungarian than the Hungarians (living in the mother-land), and their language, too, is seen as older and more beautiful, than the language spoken in Hungary proper. →**Székelyföld**; **székely himnusz**; **Erdély**; **Csaba**; **csángók**

székely himnusz *Sekler anthem* (lit.); just like the Hungarian Anthem (→*Himnusz*), the words of the song of lament composed after Transylvania (→*Erdély*) was annexed to Romania are a prayer to God: "*Do not turn Your back on Transylvania*"; for decades, it was under serious interdiction in both Romania and Hungary, and was sung in secret with teary eyes. →***Maroknyi székely...***; **székely**

Székelyföld '*Sekler Land*' (lit.); the cold basin lying within the south-eastern lobe of the Carpathians which is historically the territory of the self-governing Seklers (→*székely*), and which the Peace Treaty of Versailles (→*Trianon*) annexed, lock stock and barrel, to Romania along with the whole of Transylvania (→*Erdély*); it is the home to one and a half million Seklers, who are geographically linked to the Hungarians of the mother country through a chain of linguistic islands; Hungarians like to imagine Székelyföld as some sort of romantic folklore village museum where the people, living in a gothic, wild and "balladic" land, have preserved the original virtues of the Hungarian language (→*magyar nyelv*) in its most pristine state. Its largest town is →*Marosvásárhely*. →**székely himnusz**

székelykapu '*Sekler gate*' (lit.); the gate of Sekler peasant yards is a huge wooden structure (not unlike a traditional English lich-gate) beautifully carved with a hatchet. It consists of two parts, a smaller one for pedestrians, and a larger one for carts. Its top is often a dovecot with shingles. It usually has the name of the owner/maker and the date carved into it, as well as a stylized sun and moon, which stands for the Seklers, and is also on the coat of arms of Transylvania (→*Erdély*). In the 20th century, it has become the symbol of nationhood, often found standing on its own as a memorial.

Székesfehérvár (pron: *sey–kesh–feheyr–vahr*); '*seat-white-fort*' (lit.); as its name indicates, this town was the seat of the kings of the House of Árpád (→*Árpád-ház*), and in the Middle Ages, the spiritual center of Hungary; its cathedral, founded by King St. Stephen (→*Szent István*) and completely destroyed in the 16th century, is where the kings were crowned and buried; in the 17th century, a lovely baroque town was built over the medieval ruins, which is today one of the richest and fastest growing communities in the country. →**multik**

Szent Gellért *Saint Gerald*; Venetian monk (son of a patrician family) who came to Hungary as one of the missionaries invited by the leader of the Magyar tribes and became the tutor of Prince Imre, the son of King St. Stephen (→*Szent István*). His statue as a martyred saint stands on Gellérthegy, the hill in Buda named after him (in the 18th century), because according to legend, this is the spot from where the rebelling pagan Magyars threw him into the Danube in a barrel studded inside with nails.

Szent István *Saint Stephen*; the first Christian king of Hungary and the great-grandson of Chieftain →*Árpád* who headed the Conquest (→*honfoglalás*); he was crowned at →Székesfehérvár on Christmas Day in 1000 A.D. with a crown sent by the Pope; during his long rein, and with the help of the Church and the German knights who came to Hungary with his German wife, he created the Catholic Hungarian state, triumphed over his pagan rivals, had his people Christened (at swordpoint, if need be), and in face of the very real threat from powerful Byzantium, tied his nation to Western Christianity; traditional representations show him as a bishop with piercing eyes and a long beard wearing the Holy Crown (→*Szent Korona*) on his head and holding the apostolic (i.e., missionary) cross in his hand; in more recent times he has been turned into a man with slanted eyes, high cheek bones and a long, drooping moustache, i.e., he sports a typically Cumanian (→*kún*) countenance with a simple hoop crown on his head and the coronation insignia in his hand, this in the spirit of the general secularization; *nota bene*, on the new 10,000 forint note he looks a lot like the reliquary head of St. Ladislas (→*Szent László*); he is celebrated on August 20th (→*augusztus 20.*), which is the major Church as well as lay holiday in Hungary celebrated by everyone regardless of religious conviction or belonging; his name, *István* (the Hungarian form of the Greek *Stephanos*, i.e., "the crowned one"), is still one of the most popular men's name in Hungary. →**Szent Jobb**

Szent Jobb *the Holy Right* (*hand*); when half a century after his death King Stephen was canonized as a saint and the king, (the future) St. Ladislas (→*Szent László*) had his tomb opened in the cathedral of →*Székesfehérvár*, which was a place of pilgrimage by then because it was the scene of miracles, they found that the king's right hand had been preserved. The mummified hand, clenched into a fist and circled round with a string of pearls and the most precious relic of the Hungarian Church, was placed into its neo-gothic reliquary only at the end of the 19th century, and is now in St. Stephen's Basilica in Budapest. On St. Stephen's Day (→*Szent István*), it is carried around the city in a procession which, before WW II, was still done with something like medieval pomp and circumstance.

Szent Korona *the Holy Crown*; for centuries considered the crown of St. Stephen (→*Szent István*), when scientists were finally able to study the gorgeous Byzantine goldsmith's work and determined that it is comprised of two parts, with the hoop having been made at least half a century after the death of St. Stephen, while the upper trusses may have originally been part of the reliquary for the king's head, and also that of the coronation regalia, only the robes of royalty (a chasuble, or vestment) adorned with his image, are from his age, while the golden orb is from the time of the House of Anjou, while the mountain crystal globe sitting atop the scepter, decorated with a carved lion, is an emblem of sovereignty which predates the Conquest (→*Honfoglalás*); still, during the time of the Árpád dynasty (→*Árpád–ház*) it played the starring role in the struggles for the throne because it had become so indelibly linked with the realm, that it was needed to legitimize any new sovereign, as a result of which it was stolen time and again, it was buried (that is why the cross on top is askew), it was hidden, and it was taken abroad (the last time by the guardians of the crown themselves in 1944); it is a mystic object, the embodiment of the nation and also (mystically) the "proprietor" of the country, and also the object of religious awe otherwise due to holy relics only, to which millions of Hungarian citizens made their "pilgrimage" when in 1977 it was returned from Fort Knox where it was held "prisoner of war" since 1945.

Szent László *Saint Ladislas*; a king of the House of Árpád (→*Árpád–ház*) who ruled in the late 11th century, whose figure, traditionally represented as a knight in a suit of armor holding a battle axe, has been surrounded by legend from the earliest times; his victorious battles against the pagan Cumans (→*kunok*) are the standard themes of the legends, while the lore surrounding him was a favorite subject of medieval church frescoes, some of which have survived in the churches of small, hidden villages in the →*Székelyföld* built during the reign of the Árpád dynasty and dedicated to St. Ladislas; to this day, László is still one of the most popular names for men in Hungary. →**Szent István**; **Szent Gellért**

Szép vagy, gyönyörű vagy, Magyarország ... "*You are beautiful, you are enchanting, Hungary...*" (lit.); a song from an operetta (→*operett*) whose primary motif →*Bartók* used in his "*Concerto*", written in the U.S., to convey the feeling of homesickness; in the 30s, it was the hit tune of melancholy Hungarian "merry making" (→*sírva vigad a magyar*): "*When the music sounds, I see your radiant, beautiful face...*"; under socialism, its maudlin lyrics were considered irredentist, but it was banned after 1941, too, because its composer and lyricist "qualified as Jewish".

SZER *Radio Free Europe*; →**Szabad Európa Rádió**

szerb →**rác**

szerelem *love*; the Hungarian language has a separate world for loving a friend or fellow man (which is also used when someone loves a certain type of food), and another for the passion a man and a woman feel for each other; this latter is denoted by the word '*szerelem*', and which →*Petőfi* calls "a dark pit", or "*sötét verem*" (possibly because it rhymes).

szerenád *serenade*; in small towns at the time of the turn of the century (→*századforduló*), giving a serenade was an unavoidable part of courting a woman; the serenade was conducted according to strict rules, mostly with one or more Gypsy (→*cigány*) musicians; the custom has not died out, just changed somewhat, and is a regular custom in the capital city, too, observed on the evening of the day of the graduation parade (→*ballagás*), when the graduating (→*érettségi*) classes look up their teachers (both men and women), and serenade them under their window (which the teacher, if she is a woman, listents to from her window), then they are invited in for cake; if for some reason the situation is not suited to a serenade, it is given inside. →***Akácos út***

szeretetcsomag '*package of love*' (lit.), *charity package*; the poetic name for the first aid packages (mostly American) sent to Hungary after the war; they all had the same content, and the one gallon aluminum boxes with lids that contained powdered milk and bear the inscription: "*Gift of the American People*", can still be found in many pantries (→*éléskamra*); after the revolution (→*forradalom, 1956*), similar packages, containing coffee and cocoa, guaranteed a brisk business for the black market (→*feketepiac*).

szervusz/szerbusz *servus*; the form of greeting (→*köszönés*) which comes from the Latin original of *alázatos szolgája* (*servus humillissimus = your humble servant*), used only by people for the informal form of address (→*tegezés*), which is becoming more and more widespread. It is generally used by children and young people when greeting each other, especially in its playful forms of *szevasz* and *szia*.

Szibéria *Siberia*; a frightening, painfully familiar region for Hungarians, hundreds of thousands of whom ended up there as POWs in both World Wars, not to mention those who were taken there for *malenki robot* (Russian for 'a little work'), never to return from the forced labor camps of the Gulag.

szilvapálinka '*plum pálinka*' (lit.), *plum brandy*; from the foot of the Tátra mountains to Greece, and from the Alps to →*Székelyföld*, there is no hard liquor that is more ubiquitous and better loved; Hungarians call it *szilvórium*, a lovely, mock–Latin word, made up in reference to its assumed healing powers; it is often not up to par, and as a result, the kosher variety, stamped by the Orthodox rabbinate of Budapest and made under strict hygienic conditions, is held in great esteem. →**pálinka**; **kisüsti**; **barackpálinka**

Szilveszter 'Sylvester' (lit.) *New Year's Eve*; the last day of the year, which is Sylvester name day, is an occasion for lots of merriment and partying, in Hungary as elsewhere, much of which takes place on the street and is very noisy (paper trumpets, petards, etc.); dinner traditionally consists of roast piglet and lentils (so that there should be as much money in the New Year as lentils on one's plate), and at midnight the National Anthem (→*Himnusz*) is played, after which the President of the Republic makes a speech on television. →**kéményseprő**

Szimfónia *Symphony* (lit.); a cheap brand of cigarette filled with black tobacco. →**Munkás**

szittya *Scythian*; the romantic conception of history made the Scythians, who once lived on the steppes around the Black Sea, the relatives of the Magyars and the Huns; accordingly, they became the symbol of whatever is ancient, as a consequence of which whatever is considered genuine and deep-rooted Hungarian (including people) were called Schythian, even before WW II, though concurrently it was also the synonym for backwardness and old-fashioned orthodoxy. →**hun-magyar rokonság**

szlovák *Slovak*; when Slovakia was cut off from historical Hungary (→*történelmi Magyarország*) and the Treaty of Versailles (→*Trianon*) made it part of Czechoslovakia, the Slovaks forcefully cut themselves off from the cultural community in which they had lived with the Hungarians for a millennium; however, the effects of a thousand years of historical symbiosis, not to mention a common fate, did not disappear, but left deep traces in both peoples which are nourished to this day by a common, indissoluble, intellectual and cultural tradition, and the day will surely come when both sides will realize that they share both virtues and faults; Hungarians do not consider Slovaks "strangers", just as they do not consider Croatians "alien", which, of course, does not prevent either side from holding a grudge against the other for offences suffered as a result of the two nations (→*nemzet*) competing against each other, a state of affairs which will cease only when everyone involved accepts their Central-European (→*közép–európa*) identity. →**tót**

szocialista *socialist*; there was hardly an idea or concept to which propaganda did not affix this word as the most positive adjective known to *newspeak* (for instance, there was "socialist" democracy, patriotism, public health, contracts, etc., etc.), until it all turned inside out, and in everyday speech the word came to signify the lack of something.

szocializmus *socialism*; as a historical concept it refers to the decades between 1948 and 1989, even though this period itself can be sub-divided into many others; as an economic, political and ideological term it signified the unlimited power of the state, exercised by the Party (→*Párt*), over the people (according to an old joke, it was "*the triumph of ideology over pure reason*"), i.e., the conditions forced on the country by Soviet occupation and the cruel reprisals after the →*revolution* in 1956; a small minority was at first enthusiastically welcoming the "dictatorship of the proletariat" (i.e. communist takeover) as nothing short of a social revolution; while the great majority, the so called "masses", who were to be redeemed, socially as well as culturally, by the Party (→*Párt*), knew perfectly well that the negligible (relative) well being they enjoyed from the late sixties (→*hatvanas évek*) onwards, did not come about because of socialism, but in spite of it, and furthermore, that the Soviet Union (→*Szovjetunió*) was not helping it along, but threatening it; by the time the change in regime (→*rendszerváltás*) finally came, even its former adherents had turned against it. →**párttitkár**; **április 4**; **államosítás**; **kommunisták**

Szomorú vasárnap *Gloomy Sunday*; this melancholy song, written in the thirties, became the greatest hit of the century, and whenever the radio plays golden oldies anywhere in the world, it is sure to be on the program, after all, it was recorded by the likes of Billie Holiday and Elvis Costello, not to mention

Louis Armstrong; it is such a pithy and powerful summation of ennui that at one time the BBC would play it only without the words, because it caused a veritable suicide epidemic among the lonely; its composer, Rezső Seres, who spent his entire life as a humble bar pianist (and supposedly could not even read music), died in Budapest in the sixties (→*hatvanas évek*) by his own hand, and penniless.

szotyola (pron. *soh–tyoh–lah*); *sunflower seeds*; the hundreds of small and dried black seeds of the sunflower are eminently suited for chasing away boredom; some have raised eating it to an art and can put a handful into their mouths at one time, pushing the seeds between the teeth with the tongue, proceeding to bite them in two one by one, then spitting out the husk, which gradually grows into a big pile as the conversation proceeds); it is even cheaper than pumpkin (→*tökmag*) seeds, and at football games is sold by the bulk, being ladled straight into the customer's pocket.

Szovjetunió *Soviet Union*; everyday speech made no distinction between the all too familiar Russia (→*Oroszország*) and its successor, about which (just like about its predecessor) Hungarians had highly ambivalent feelings, to say the least; on the one hand, they learned to respect (and fear) its strength, on the other, they looked down on it, feeling superior to it both as a nation and as a nation of individuals, and in order to give expression to these feelings, they came up with countless jokes at its expense; it felt good to get the better of it by small, daily triumphs of whatever sort, and in the meanwhile to forget that with a single swipe of its paw, even if inadvertently, it could crush them at any time. →**Szibéria**

Szózat *Appeal*; title of the best known poem (1836) by the 19th century romantic poet →*Vörösmarty Mihály*, the first line of which, which every Hungarian knows by heart, goes: "*Oh, Magyar, keep immovably / your native country's trust …*" (→*Hazádnak rendületlenűl légy híve, ó magyar …*) the poem, the classical expression of patriotism, was set to music and became the second (unofficial) national anthem; for the past century and a half, it is sung along with the National Anthem (→*Himnusz*) in schools and churches, while festivities held on national holidays begin with Kölcsey's prayer (the National Anthem) and traditionally close with Vörösmarty's "*Appeal*"; the poem, pathetic in a noble way, deeply moving and tragic in tone, contains four lines which are especially stirring when sung by emigrants (→*emigráns*): "*No other spot in all the world / can touch your heart as home - /let fortune bless or fortune curse, / from hence you shall not roam!*" (trans. W. Kirkconnell)

Sződd a selymet, elvtárs … "*Weave the silk, Comrade*" (lit.); a typical example of the numerous mass songs (→*tömegdal*) of the fifties (→*ötvenes évek*), and one (a rare exception!) which people still remember as it became near folkloristic thanks to the strikingly absurd ring of its words; its first line continued: "... *a silken flag!*", with which, in the militant spirit of the age, one was undoubtedly supposed to join the "peace-war" in the trenches of "industrial production". →**béketábor**

Sztálin-szobor *Stalin statue*; the bronze colossus as high as three men, stood on the edge of Budapest's City Park for a mere four years, but it did so in the place of a church which was blown up to make room for it, not to mention the trees that were felled in the public park, in the middle of a huge concrete desert today used as a car park, built because there was no place in Budapest that could be a worthy partner of the Red Square in Moscow where parades were held on the First of May (→*május elseje*); the tall pedestal of the statue, made of red granite, was surrounded by a parapet from where the leaders of the Party (→*párt*) and the government could watch the "enthusiastic" marchers; on October 23rd (→*október 23.*), 1956, the ecstatic crowd toppled the statue, which was the symbol of the regime, and out of revenge, hacked it into small pieces to take home, with only the boots remaining on the pedestal for another year, as a sort of grotesque memento; during the regime of →*Kádár János* the huge rebuilt pedestal continued to serve as a grandstand for parades, which is nothing if not symbolic; it was taken apart only after the change in regime (→*rendszerváltás*) along with the statue of Lenin which stood nearby, but which was put up much later.

Sztálinváros →**Dunaújváros**

SzTK the abbreviation for the Trade Union Social Insurance Center, the onetime Hungarian equivalent of the National Health Service (whose full name probably noone knows any more), which continues to be referred to by this old acronym; everyone is dissatisfied with the system, patients and doctors alike, whereas considering its dire lack of funds, it is working surprisingly well; still, for most people it is the equivalent of endless waiting on line to see a doctor, not to mention the gratuities (→*hálapénz*), which keeps the machinery of government health care oiled and which, or so some will insist, helps manipulate it to the advantage of the patient.

születésnap *birthday*; in Hungary, grownups consider their birthday a private affair best celebrated only within the family; for a more public affair they prefer to have their name day (→*névnap*) celebrated (where they work, by having a drink or two); it is a strange custom (of unknown origin) that the celebrant has his or her ear pulled to the accompaniment of a short rhyme: "*May God give you long life, may your ear reach to your ankle!*"

szűr *mantle*; one of the most typical pieces of Hungarian folk costume (→*népviselet*), it was made of heavy white or black felt, usually worn thrown over the shoulder, since it usually had no sleeves, just a big, square collar with a large appliqué rosette in each corner; the version heavily decorated on the front, collar and bottom with Oriental-type flowers is called the *cifra* (ornate) *szűr*, but even the most humble version had colorful square cloth appliqué around the pockets.

szüret '(*wine and fruit*) *harvest*' (lit.); when people refer to the '*szüret*', they mean the harvesting of the grape from the vine (and its squashing); it is traditionally a happy time accompanied by feasting and drinking, and when it is done in a private vineyard, relatives come from far and wide to lend a hand; in traditional wine producing regions, it is followed by parades and balls. →**must**

szürkebarát '*grey friar*' (lit.), *pinot gris*; one of the noblest semi-sweet white wines (→*bor*) especially suited to go with a good chat; originally produced on the northern shore of the →*Balaton*, on the shouthern slope of the old volcano called Badacsony, it is still best when grown and produced there.

T

tabló →**érettségi tabló**

tájszólás *dialect*; though people speak Hungarian as their mother tongue in eight neighboring countries now, Hungarian has remained remarkably unified, and has no dialiects that vary greatly one from the other, which, however, does not mean that the various linguistic islands do not have their own characteristic vocabulary or pronunciation. Opinions differ on where the most "beautiful" variant of the Hungarian language (→*magyar nyelv*) is spoken, for example, according to some, in the →*Székelyföld*, while the language spoken in the capital has a kind of negative prestige (which may very well come from the traditional and mutual mistrust of the periphery and the center); the majority of people speaking citified Hungarian feel that "peasant" Hungarian (i.e., spoken in dialect) is more interesting and "strong", though it also sounds more rustic (which carries the connotation of 'uneducated'), as a result of which anyone speaking in public will rarely resort to a dialect. →**Budapest**; **csángók**

talponálló '*standup place*' (lit.), *wine cellar*; the euphemistic name for cellars or basements entered from the street (though sometimes they are storefront places) where the male population of cities go for a quick drink (and a chat); though they vary in quality, along with the wine and spirits served in them, they share a common denominator, namely, that you can't sit down in them, hence their name, and each has its regulars. →**bor**; **kocsma**

Talpra magyar! "*On your feet, Hungarians!*" (lit.); the first, stirring words of *The National Song* (→*Nemzeti dal*) which continues: "*... the nation calls! / The time is now, or never! / Shall we be slaves or free? / That is the question, take your choice!*" On an extant printed copy stands the following in the poet's (→*Petőfi*'s) own hand: "*The very first printed copy after the freedom of the press attained on the 15th of March 1848, and thus the first breath of Hungarian freedom*" →**március 15.**

táltos *shaman*; the name for the priest, magician, and medicine man of the pagan Magyars, who was chosen by the gods; if a child came into the world with six fingers, it was a sure sign that he was destined to become a shaman (for instance, uncannily, the later-day poet →*Ady Endre*); horses with special abilites (magic steeds) were also called '*táltos*', and can be found in many Hungarian folk tales.

Tanács '*(local) Soviet*' (lit.), *Council*; since elected local governments took their place after the change in regime (→*rendszerváltás*), it is now a historical concept; though in theory even under socialism (→*szocializmus*) the "councils" were elected by the people, they were in fact organs of the government, i.e. the rule of the omniperesent Party (→*Párt, a*), and from the point of view of the population, who were in every way subject to it, they were the congregations of heartless bureaucrats who were paid to reject all petitions, if at all possible (unless, of course, they could be bribed), and where they worked, i.e., the city councils, the houses of endless lines where one stood for long hours before being admitted to the presence of a council clerk. →**házmester**

Tanácsköztársaság '*Republic of Councils*'; →**forradalom, 1918**; **köztársaság**

táncház '*dance house*' (lit.); in Transylvania (→*Erdély*) the young people in a village would rent someone's house to hold dances; the custom was transplanted to Hungary in the seventies, when groups of young people went to Transylvania, hoping to follow in the footsteps of →*Bartók*, and also as a sort of national (→*nemzeti*) protest against the Romanian communist government which forbid and hindered relations between the Hungarians of Transylvania and the mother country, and which aggressively destroyed folk tradition; among these young people were musicians and ethnographers, attracted by the traditional peasant music and culture which, due to the isolation of the villages, survived into the modern age; in the eighties, when it veritably became one of the ways of protesting against the regime, organizing weekend "dance houses", which offered an alternative communal experience, became popular throughout the country, not least of all because authentic Transylvanian and *csángó* (→*csángók*) peasant music was played on authentic musical instruments (including rustic violins and violoncellos) to accompany young (mostly female) singers who learned the songs from old peasant women, not to mention the dancers, who danced the dances of the various Hungarian regions, as well as southern Slav, Greek and Romanian syncopated rhythms, with the enthusiasm reserved elsewhere for rock-and-roll.

tangóharmonika '*tango accordion*' (lit.), *piano accordion*; these shiny instruments with buttons and keys, like the ones on a piano, that could be hung round the shoulder, came to Hungary from Germany in the thirties, and their characteristic sound is indelibly linked with the music of the pre-war years; they were so omnipresent for so long, that perhaps only the electric guitars favored by the young people of the sixties (→*hatvanas évek*) could compete with it in popularity; the simple village accordion, jokingly referred to as the "Slovak (→*tót*) organ", never became part of Hungarian folk music, and is used, even today, only by German(→*sváb*) peasant bands.

tanító (*elementary school*) *teacher*; someone with only three years of teachers' college training teaching the first four years of elementary school (as opposed to someone with a college degree teaching in the Hungarian equivalent of junior high and high school, and called *tanár* instead of *tanító*), usually a woman (and therefore called →*néni*, regardless of her age); always poorly paid public servants, many are recalled by their former pupils with affection.

tanya '*quarters*' (lit.), *homestead*, *shelter*; originally, a *tanya* was a simple shelter used by peasants while working the land out in the fields (→*puszta*), so they wouldn't have to return to the village every night; it was especially frequent on the sparsely populated wide expanse of land between the villages (→*falu*) of the Great Plain (→*Alföld*) where, just like a farmhouse on the prairie, it also served as a permanent dwelling (especially for the "old folk", who went to tend the animals), with the farms that were close to each other sometimes forming small settlements; with the transformation of agriculture, some of the deserted farmsteads became the summer homes of people from the nearby towns and cities.

tarhonya *egg barley*; a hard dough is kneaded from flour, egg, a little water and salt, then is rolled until it falls apart into barley-size pieces; these are put out in the sun to dry, and are eaten cooked in water (sometimes having been turned in some hot lard first). It was first eaten by wandering nomads of the plains, for it does not spoil. Today, it is usually eaten as an accompaniment to stews (→*pörkölt*).

társasház '*communal house*' (lit.), *condominium*; →**öröklakás**

társbérlet '*co-tenancy*' (lit.); during WW II so many apartment houses were destroyed in Hungary, there were so many refugees from Transylvania (→*Erdély*) and Upper Hungary (→*Felvidék*), and such huge masses of people fled the farmers' cooperatives (→*termelőszövetkezet*) and moved to the cities, that families were even moved into the recently nationalized (→*államosítás*) shops, and in the end, the dire housing shortage was solved by the local councils (→*Tanács*) according to the Soviet model, whereby several families were moved into the nationalized apartments with as few as two rooms (with a shared kitchen and bathroom), not to mention the villas of the elegant districts, for this means of providing accommodations was also a weapon in the "class struggle", and was put in the service of "social justice", just like deportation (→*kitelepítés*), which was in part also justified by the lack of housing; it took thirty years until people, forcibly made to live together, were able to rid themselves of the inconvenience of such a forced proximity, or the apartment, which had turned from a middle class abode to a slum, either by subdividing apartments, by engaging in highly complex apartment exchanges, or by leaving this world. →**albérlet**; **bérház**; **gang**

tatárjárás *Tartar invasion*; in the middle of the 13th century, when the Mongolian (or Tartar) empire was at the height of its powers and invaded Europe, the Mongolians also overran and occuppied Hungary for two years, wreaking such destruction, that people thought "Hungary had ceased to exist"; hence, to this day if someone (including rowdy children) cause what seems to be unreparable damage, people call it a *Tartar devastation* (*tatárjárás*, or *tatárdúlás*). →**kunok**

te *you*; the second person singular pronoun used as a form of address by people who are on familiar terms with each other; the intricacies of its use (which changes according to one's age, as well as the relationship of one's age to the person being addressed) is governed by unwritten rules which are only distantly related to the rules regulating the use of first names in English; within a family (regardless of age or sex) the use of *te* has become universal, just like its use with children, or among children; what's more, today young people have taken to using the familiar form of address with each other as a matter of course; older people use it among themselves only when one of them proposes it, with the proposal coming from whoever is the oldest; however if there is a woman in the company, she must make the move, for though an older man may use the friendly, informal form of address when talking to a younger man, he is not at liberty to do so with a woman, though not so very long ago (and at times even today), someone of higher (social or other) rank felt at liberty to use the second person singular when talking to someone of lower rank (regardless of age or sex), but not the other way around, which was considered a provocation; at places of work (and also organizations of various sorts) the use of the second person singular between colleagues has become general during the past couple of decades, even without a real intimate friendly (or democratic) relationship backing it up, while within the Communist Party (and the unions) it was strictly compulsory; today its use is general in all the political parties as the sign of belonging (though not necessarily friendship); however, regardless of how liberal the forms of address may have become, the seemingly democratic custom of the use of the second person singular has done little to change the real relationships that it hides; as a matter of fact, after the change in regime (→*rendszerváltás*), certain older forms of address have been reinstated – in writing, at least – in order to highlight the new relationships. →**ön**; **maga**; **megszólítás**; **tegezés**

tea *tea*; in Hungary, tea is for breakfast, or for the sick (with lots of lemon); in any other situation, requesting it instead of the ever-popular coffee (→kávé) is considered a form of some eccentricity, if not a show of over-refinement, this despite the fact that during the past few years the custom of tea drinking seems to be gaining favor among the populace.

tegezés *'saying "you"'* (lit.); though the rules for the use of the second person singular (*tegezés*) are relatively clearcut, if two people meet and are not sure whether they are (have been, or should be) using the familiar form of address to each other, it can result in no end of comic, but embarrasing situations for, due to the rules of Hungarian grammar, the conjugations implicitely give away the form of address one is using, which means that there is no getting around the problem: without coming to some decision, it is practically impossible to conduct a conversation. →**te**

tej *milk*; →**aludt tej**

tejbegríz '*semolina in milk*' (lit.); *pap* (*in milk*); topped with jam or sprinkled with cocoa, is indelibly linked with the early childhood of every Hungarian; its status is very much like rice pudding: at first everyone likes it, then they become sated with it, though some love it even as grownups; corn meal mush (→*kása*) is its rustic equivalent.

Télapó '*Father Winter*' (lit.); →**Mikulás**

telek *plot* (*of land*); even before WW II, the city-dwelling Hungarian *petit bourgeois* (and the worker, or →*munkás*, too) saved for years, often penny-pinching, in order to buy, somewhere on the outskirts of town (or at a resort), a piece of land the size of a handkerchief (even though at the time no one owned a car!), where they could grow and tend a fruit tree or two on the weekends, or spend the summer with the children, provided there was a "weekend house" (→*víkendház*) on it, which turned into small communities, and on the outskirts of Budapest, into entire districts; many even hoped to retire to their plots in their old age.

Teleki tér *Teleki Square*; the name for Budapest's flea market, which at one time really was located on Teleki Square, but has since been moved to the outskirts; there are few antiques here, but loads of junk and bric-a-brac of little or no value; on the other hand, during the shortages under socialism (→*szocializmus*), there were lots of things available here (including blue jeans!) that you couldn't find in the state-owned shops. →**lengyel piac**

téliszalámi '*winter salami*' (lit.); of the many types of Hungarian cold cuts and sausages, people have the highest regard for *téliszalámi* (especially the two that bear the names of Mr. Pick and Mr. Herz, whose rival plants in →*Szeged* were nationalized along with everything else), not only because *téliszalámi* costs the most (*téli*, or '*winter*' salami won't spoil, hence the name), but also because, for some reason (people thought it was all being exported), under socialism (→*szocializmus*) it was harder to come by than caviar. →**kolbász**

temetés *funeral*; the dead are usually laid in state (in a closed coffin) either in the cemetery chapel (if there is one), or else in a building of the cemetery set aside for this purpose; this is where friends and relatives can take their farewell from the deceased, and this is where (official) speeches are made, and possibly where the first half of religious rites are held, which continue at the gravesite after someone (such as a close friend) says a farewell speech as the mourners stand around the open grave; the mourners may even sing, but not necessarily a religious song; it can be anything wothy of the deceased, even the National Anthem (→*Himnusz*), if they feel it suits the occasion; at small funerals, the officiating priest may do most of this alone, with two or three members of the church choir helping the mourners when they get stuck with their hymns. As strange as it may seem, during the past one-hundred years of Hungarian history, many a funeral became a political rite with symbolic significance (e.g. →*Vörösmarty's* funeral of 1855 was also the first silent protest in wake of the defeat of the War of Independence, or →*Szabadságharc*), as well as being a part of some major political change; the 1896 funeral of → *Kossuth Lajos*, who died in exile, was the occasion for the defiant show of strength by groups protesting against the joint Austrian-Hungarian monarchy (→*Osztrák-Magyar Monarchia*); in 1903, the return of the ashes of the 18th century Transylvanian (→*Erdély*) rebel prince →*Rákóczi*, and others exiled with him, followed by his burial in Kassa (now Kosice, Slovakia), was the last great pageant of historical Hungary (→*történelmi Magyarország*); the 1919 funeral of →*Ady Endre*, who brought Hungarian poetry into the 20th century, turned into the untimely celebration of the new republic (→*köztársaság*); the revolution of 1956 (→*forradalom, 1956*) was sparked by members of the crowd gathered for the reburial of → *Rajk László*, who had been sentenced to death at an infamous show trial, and others who shared his fate; the 1989 reburial of Imre Nagy, the Prime Minister of the →*revolution (1956)*, and the others sentenced to death along with him was held on the anniversary of the day (→*június 16.*) of their execution, thus becoming a symbolic gesture of the change in regime (→*rendszerváltás*) and offering the first, communal taste of political freedom to the throngs filling Budapest's Heroes' Square on that day. →.→**tor**; **gyász**

templom *temple/church/synagogue*; in the Hungarian language there is only one word for a place of worship, be it ancient Roman, Catholic, or any other; in the usage of nonconformist religions, however, there is *imaház*, or '*house of prayer*', which conveys the same feel as 'Bethel'; it is worthy of note that in Hungarian, the Church (i.e., the institution itself) is called *Egyház*, which happens the be the old Hungarian name for *templom*..

termelőszövetkezet '*production cooperative*' (lit.), *agricultural cooperative*; this institution is known throughout the world as the *kolkhoz*; it was introduced in Hungary in the fifties (→*ötvenes évek*), practically at gun point, causing countless personal tragedies, not to mention the economic catastrophy on par with nationalization (→*államosítás*); desperate peasants (→*paraszt*), who lost their land, fled the villages (→*falu*) by droves, and ended up working in industry (factories); "large-scale socialist agriculture" underwent various reforms (→*reform*) before it finally could be made work, with some cooperatives becoming so strong, that they even survived the change in regime (→*rendszerváltás*). →**kárpótlás**

testvér '*body+blood*' (lit.), *brother/sister*; the umbrella term which includes the idea of older (*bátya*, *nővér*) and younger (*öccs*, *hug*) brother and sister, including the gender distinction, for all of which there is a separate word in Hungarian, is a good example of those words in the Hungarian language (→*magyar nyelv*) which, often quite simple, carry their metaphorical origins in them, which can make abstract speech difficult at times (ex.: *rascal* = *gaz-ember*, '*weed* + *man*' lit.). →**rokonság**

tészta *pasta*; though it is not considered a typical Hungarian food, it has as many variations as Italian pasta (except that there is no spaghetti and macaroni), and each has a specific use; some are added only to soup (and even then, not all types of soup noodle can be added to every soup), other types are consumed on their own; every housewife knows which dish needs which type of pasta (shape, size, thickness), even though today everyone buys it in a shop; it has many adherents, but also the connotation of "poor man's food", just like potatoes (→*krumpli*), not to mention →*krumplistészta*, pasta with crushed potatoes. →**mákostészta**; **túróstészta**; **tarhonya**

Tibi the diminutive form of the name *Tibor*, but best known as the name of a small, thin chocolate bar finished in a bite or two, but whose popularity refuses to wane. →**Sport–szelet**

Tisza (pron. *tee–sah*); a river which originates in the Carpathians, enters Hungary in the north-east, and joins the Danube (→*Duna*) above Belgrade, thus dividing the Great Plain (→*Alföld*) in two; if we are to believe Hungarian poetry (→*költészet*) and folk songs (→*népdal*), it was always closer to the heart of Hungarians than the Danube, which is rarely mentioned, while the narrower and much more circuitous Tisza (which used to flood the plains every year), is personified and called "blonde"; since only Hungarian fishermen and towboats use it, perhaps they think of it as all their own. →**Szeged**

Tiszántúl '*beyond the Tisza*' (lit.); the eastern, larger part of the Great Plain (→*Alföld*) which the (→*Tisza*), meandering among marshes and bogs, effectively cut off from the middle of the country until it was regulated in the 19th century; accordingly, everything that was beyond it ('*beyond the Tisza*') seemed remote and isolated, and life took on a slower pace there than elsewhere, a state of affairs which has never changed, for even today, passage across the river is afforded by only three bridges. →**Debrecen**

tiszteletem '*my respects*' (lit.); as a form of greeting (→*köszönés*), it is just as archaic as the →*bátyám* form of address (→*megszólítás*), and is used with this in mind; its original, complete form, *alázatos tiszteletem* ('*my humble respects*') is used only in mild (and good humored) jest.

Tisztelt Cím! '*Respected Addressee!*' (lit.); *Dear Sir/Madam*; the usual form of address used in letters when the addressee is not known (companies, offices, as well as private individuals), with *cím* ('*address*') being short for *címzett* ('*addresse*'); today, it is being replaced by →*Tisztelt uram!* ('*Dear Sir*'), or its more courteous form, *Igen tisztelt uram*! ('*Most honorable Sir*'); in whatever form it is used, it is invariably followed by an exclamation mark. →**megszólítás**; **uram**

Tisztelt uram! →**uram**

tokaji (pron. *taw–kah–yee*), (*wine of*) *Tokaj*; →**aszu**; **szamorodni**

Toldi (pron. *tawl–dee*); a historical epic in verse and a veritable national (→*nemzeti*) poem about the semi-legendary medieval hero of immense strength, Miklós Toldi, which is considered one of the best creations of Hungarian romanticism; even though it is compulsory reading in schools and long passages must be learned by heart, it continues in popularity; its author, János Arany, was a contemporary and friend of →*Petőfi*, but was a much more stoic figure; the congenial translator of several plays by William Shakespeare, many consider him the greatest representative of 19th century poetry (→*költészet*).

torta *tart*, *torte*; the term is reseved exclusively for cake (→*sütemény*, also called →*cukrászsütemény*) that is round in shape, layered with various sweet creams, often with some decoration on the top and usually made by a professional baker; it is cut and served in wedges, and is never missing from the table at wedding feasts or childrens' birthdays (→*születésnap*), in which case candles are put on it to indicate the age of the celebrant.

tót *Slovak*; pejorative, though only to Slovak (→*szlovák*) ears, for Hungarians do not use it with pejorative intent, an indication being that it is a frequently used family name in Hungary (though often of assimilated Slovaks); it is simply the Hungarian word for 'Slovak' (just as '*német*' is for '*Deutsch*'), while historically it is the name for various Slav peoples; it was during the awakening of national consciousness in the 19th century that the Slovaks demanded that the Hungarians to use their own name for themselves, declaring the Hungarian word for them as offensive; today, – apart from Slovakia proper, – most Slovaks live in Békés County, along the south-eastern border of Hungary, and are the descendants of Slovak farmers who were moved to the region after its population dwindled as a consequence of the Turkish occupation (→*Hódoltság*). →**oláh**; **rác**; **sváb**

tök *pumpkin, vegetable marrow*; in Hungary, the yellowish-white, longish, cylindrical shaped vegetable marrow is favoured because, grated into long strips, it makes for a delicious →*főzelék*, though cut into rings, it is also eaten breaded and fried; the large, round pumpkin with bright-yellow pulp is cut into large pieces and baked, which gives it a lovely, soft consistency; one variety is eaten in winter hot out of the oven, and is sometimes sold even on the street (in small towns) and at the markets; because it is sweet, it is also given to babies. →**tökmag**

tökmag '*pumpkin–seeds*' (lit); the pumpkin (→*tök*) suitable for baking has innumerable flat, leaf-shaped seeds; when browned in the oven, it makes for a delicious and inexpensive snack (like peanuts or pop corn) consumed while people chat; it is taken between the teeth, crushed so it will open, the hull is spit out, and the seed eaten; it is sold at soccer (→*futball*) games; *tökmag* is also the jocular name for children (and grown men) who are retarded in growth. →**szotyola**

töltöttkáposzta *stuffed cabbage*; some variation of meatballs rolled in cabbage leaves and cooked with sour cabbage (→*káposzta*) cut or grated into thin strips is known all over Central Europe; the Hungarian version is cooked with smoked pork and served with sour cream (with red pepper being optional); people swear that it tastes even better when reheated. →**magyar konyha**; **Karácsony**

tömegdal '*song of the masses*' (lit.), *marching song*; a typical fifties (→*ötvenes évek*) invention; based on the humble (mostly German) musical tradition of the working class movement (not to mention Soviet models), marching songs to rouse and inspire the masses were churned out in great quantities; at political (near-religious) observances they were sung by choirs, immortalized by old, scratchy records. →**május elseje**; ***Sződd a selymet, elvtárs …***

töpörtyű *crackling*; not the crisp browned skin of roast pork (as the word would have one assume as used in the English language), but the brown pieces of solidified fat formed when the fat (→*zsír*) is rendered from the thick, fatty bacon under the pig's skin; liberally salted, it is consumed with bread and onions (→*vöröshagyma*); ground up and added to fatty and salted dough, it is made into crackling scones (→*pogácsa*), often the size of one's fist, and the indispensable accompaniment to beer.

törökök, a *Turks, the*; since during the 16th and 17th centuries, for a hundred and fifty years Hungary fought the Ottoman Empire, which threatened its very existence, historically, the Turks are remembered as a greater enemy even than the Germans, a fact proven by the many songs, ballads, and juvenile literature (→*Egri csillagok*); still, no one would think of blaming today's Turks for the past, and there is a traditionally friendly relationship between the two peoples, even though the only personal experience Hungarians have of the Turks comes from visiting the bazaar of Istanbul, where the Turkish merchants are always extremely amiable with them; *Török* is also a frequent Hungarian family name. →**Mohács**; **hódoltság**

történelmi Magyarország '*historical Hungary*' (lit.), *old Hungary*; the prudish, circumspect name for Hungary before the Peace Treaty of Versailles (→*Trianon*) used instead of "Greater Hungary", for fear that a distrustful Serb, Slovak or Romanian with abnormally acute hearing might interpret it as a covert demand for the return of certain territories that once belonged to Hungary. →**Millennium**

törtkrumpli '*broken potato*' (lit.), *hash browns*; the ubiquitous side dish for most Hungarian meat dishes which is made by crushing the boiled potatoes (→*krumpli*) with a fork (but not mashing them into a pulp!), then the lard or oil in which the meat was cooked is mixed into it, sometimes also onions (→*vöröshagyma*), and the whole thing is returned in the pan to the fire for a minute or two while it is reheated and browned. →**rántotthús**

Trabant the cheapest automobile in the Peace Camp (→*Béketábor*), which also made it very popular, as a result of which thousands of it polluted the air in Hungary, too, for several decades; it was small and bumpy, noisy and very uncomfortable, but it insinuated itself into people's hearts, for although it was characterized inside and out by the perfect charmlessness of East German utilitarianism, from the aluminum door handles to its dirty-gray, dirty-brown or dirty-blue color (it never needed a wash, besides, it would have been in vain), it was considered a reliable and faithful vehicle. →**Zsiguli**; **Wartburg**

Tragédia, a *Tragedy, the* (lit.), the popular name for *Az ember tragédiája*, the drama in verse written by Imre Madách, and considered a masterpiece of 19th century Hungarian literature; in the piece, inspired by the writer's philosophy of history, Lucifer, competing with the Lord, for Adam and Eve, the first pair of mortals, guides them through the future history of mankind; in each episode, Adam and Eve appear as characters typical of the age, and each time end up bitterly disappointed in its ideals (i.e., they are disappointed in Creation itself); they flee forward in time (→*Vezess új utakra, Lucifer!*), but despite Lucifer's cynical derision, Adam decides to brave history after all, regardless of how tragic it may be; staging the play, which is a great vehicle for actors, demands great energy and ingenuity (both technically and intellectually), and all directors dream of directing it, if for no other reason, then because it was always surrounded by controversy, and was bawdlerized in the fifties (→*ötvenes évek*) because of its pessimism; for a long time it could not be performed, while today the cost is prohibitive, yet the change in regime (→*rendszerváltás*) has made Madách's view of history and mankind highly relevant once again. →***Sok az eszkimó …***; ***Ember küzdj és …***

Trianon '(*Palace of*) *Trianon*' (lit.), *Versailles Peace Treaty*; the Hungarian name for the peace treaty of 1921 signed in the Petit Trianon, the late 18th century summer palace within the grounds of the Palace of Versailles, and orchestrated by the victorious Allies; inspired by French diplomacy it annexed, by way of a gift as it were, two-thirds of Hungary to its neighbors, and not merely areas where the Slovak, Romanian and Serbian or other populations were in a majority to begin with, but (out of certain geo-political considerations) also territories with predominantly Hungarian populations, as a result of which one-third of the Hungarian-speaking population of historical Hungary (→*történelmi Magyarország*) found itself under an alien government; the dismembering of greater Hungary was such a momentous event in the country's 20th century history that in one way or another, everything else may be said to have sprung from it; until the outbreak of WW II, the nation expanded all its energy and resources in order to rebuild its economy within its greatly constricted frontiers, while it also attempted to have the most blatant injustices of the treaty altered, those which showed total disdain for "the right to self determination" laid down by the victors, as a result of which, hoping to have the Trianon frontiers changed, the country allied itself with Germany, which in turn led to yet another wartime defeat and the solidifying of the borders prescribed by Trianon; during the years of socialism (→*szocializmus*) any mention of Trianon was strictly taboo, along with any talk of the Hungarians living beyond the country's borders, which was labeled nationalistic (and thus undesirable), whereas every Hungarian family had (and still has) relatives who were forcibly made into the citizens of another country; in other words, the humiliation suffered by Hungarians as a result of the repeated forced attempts at assimilation they experienced at the hands of the so-called "successor states", not to mention the fact that spritually the Hungarian nation (→*magyar nemzet*) is greater than the territory of the state of Hungary, is felt by Hungarians directly through their families. After WW II the post-Trianon Hungarian borders became an international political taboo (because of the war and its consequences), and even the average Hungarian has stopped talking about changing them in favor of their gradual disappearance, placing its hopes in European integration as the only solution for the problems of fellow Hungarians who found themselves in a minority in their place of birth, and who still make up about a third of the nation; all the same, since a not insignificant portion of the Hungarians of Hungary, especially the intelligentsia (→*értelmiség*) are from Transylvania (→*Erdély*), Upper Hungary (→*Felvidék*), Ruthenia (→*Kárpátalja*) and the South (→*Délvidék*), and are thus themselves refugees or the sons and daughters of refugees, and the trauma of losing their homeland is their personal experience, the welfare and legal status of the Hungarian minorities has remained an urgent and delicate issue in the domestic as well as foreign policy of Hungary. →**ki a magyar**; **magyarok**

Tsz →**termelőszövetkezet**

túró *curd, cottage cheese, pot cheese, farmer's cheese*; the physical condition milk attains when it is no longer sour cream, but not yet cheese; buttermilk (→*aludt tej*) is skimmed, placed in a gauze sac, and after the whey drips out, the curd, or cottage cheese remains; cottage cheese made from cow's milk is soury in taste, dry and crumbly, while cottage cheese prepared from ewe's milk is fatty and spreadable, while its taste is reminiscent of tart-tasting cheese, and is eaten on its own (with onions) spread on a thick slice of fresh bread (→*kenyér*). →**túróstészta**

túróstészta *cottage cheese noodles*; along with poppy seed noodles (→*mákostészta*), it is the most often served home-made last addition to a meal; it is also known as "*csusza*" (*csusza* = 'something that slips'), because it is best when the pasta (→*tészta*) does not stick together, but "slides"; as opposed to poppy seed noodles, made from long, flat pasta, cottage cheese noodles are made from square-shaped pasta only; the pasta is cooked, then combined with finely crumbled, salty cottage cheese combined with sour cream and bacon bits (→*töpörtyű*) rendered from smoked bacon (→*szalonna*), and finally, the drippings (→*zsír*) are added, and the noodles served; some people like to sprinkle sugar on top instead of the drippings (and often along with the drippings!); sweetened cottage cheese is used to make other desserts as well, which are reminiscent of cheese cake. →**tészta**; **tarhonya**; **bableves**

turul (pron. *too–rool*); a bird of prey (of unknown species) portrayed either as an eagle or falcon, and the mythical animal who impregnated the ancient mother of the Hungarians as described in the myth of origin of the Árpád dynasty (→*Árpád–ház*); just like the Miracle Stag (→*Csodaszarvas*), it was made into a non-Christian national symbol at the time of the →*Millennium*, and was even put on all Conquest (→*honfoglalás*) memorials erected at the time (it is also perched at the entrance to the Royal Palace, or →*Várpalota*, with its huge wings spread above the Danube (→*Duna*), grabbing the likewise legendary sword of →*Attila* in its claws; it also watches over the M1 highway, perched on top of a hill near the town of Tatabánya, not to mention the pylons of Budapest's Liberty Bridge, a spot much favored by suicides;

almost at the moment of its rediscovery, it became the symbol of narrow-minded, isolationist patriotism.

tündér '*vanisher*' (lit.), *fay/fairy*; as its name suggests, a *tündér* is a creature of fairy tales who appears and disappears with surprising alacrity; it can change its shape at will, and is capable of producing magic, and traditionally appears in the guise of a beautiful and helpful young woman, though there are also wicked fairies (and wicked ugly witches, too, such as the water fairies, who if they want someone, will pull him down with them into the deep; in popular speech, a good hearted and pretty woman is often called *tündér*; the popular name *Tünde*, which comes from *tündér*, was coined by the poet →*Vörösmarty*.

U

Újköztemető (pron. *ooy–kowz–teh–meh–tow*), '*New (Public) Cemetery*'; the largest public cemetery located on the eastern outskirts of →*Pest*; its farthest plot, number 301, was the unmarked mass grave of prisoners executed in the nearby jail, among them people sentenced to death after the revolution (→*forradalom, 1956*); a memorial to Imre Nagy and his companions now stands on the spot. →**Kerepesi úti temető**; **Farkasréti temető**; **Házsongárdi temető**; **Kozma utcai temető**

Újvidék (pron. *ooy–vee–deyk*), '*New Region/Settlement*' (lit.); a city with many nationalities and therefore many names (*Novi Sad, Neusatz*) situated on the banks of the Danube (→*Duna*), the largest city of the former →*Délvidék*, and the southern "gate" of historical Hungary (→*történelmi Magyarország*), once defended by huge fortifications and known as the "Gibraltar on the Danube"; since the Peace Treaty of Versailles (→*Trianon*) it is the seat of the province of the →*Vajdaság*, in Serbia.

ulti (pron. *ool–tee*); the most popular card game played (for small stakes) with so-called 'Hungarian cards' (→*magyar kártya*) among friends; there are three players, and the deck consists of 32 cards; though the idea is to accumulate points, whoever has the last trick (*ultimo*) wins.

Unicum sweet and bitter at the same time, and with the consistency of light syrup, it is a so-called "stomach bitter" made with herbs and spices sold in its trademark round bottle with a red cross on the label; drunk both as an aperitif (in which case it is an acquired taste, some say) and as "medicine"; this digestif has been produced by a family for the past two-hundred years according to a secret recipe, and has been advertised on posters which are still known to everyone and are collector's items.

úr '*sir/lord*' (lit.), *master/lord*; during the prevalence of →*elvtárs* (*comrade*), it had a strange ring to it and was used only in addressing doctors (→*doktor úr*) and teachers (*tanár úr*), plus maitre d's (*főúr*, or *Feri úr*, if the customer was a regular); lately, it is quickly acquiring the meaning of '*mister*', both in living speech and in writing. →**megszólítás**; **fiatalúr**; **uram**; **úriember**

uram '*my lord*' (lit.), *sir*; the most frequent form of address (→*megszólítás*) used for men, and the least that courtesy demands; on the other hand, *tisztelt/kedves uram* ('*my respected/dear lord/sir*', lit.), is considered something of an insult, since it is used only in the middle of heated arguments (or in letters, if the addressee is not personally known to one), while *uram bátyám* ('*my lord and older brother*', lit.) belongs to the defunct patriarchal world of countryside (→*vidéki*) gentlemen (→*úriember*); N.B. although PC–language is gradually pushing out this usage, even today and even in middle class and intellectual circles otherwise quite liberated married women would habitually refer to their husbands as *uram*, without thinking of this as another sign of their "feudal oppression". →**úr**; **bátyám**; **asszonyom**

úrasszony '*master–woman*' (lit.), *dame/lady*; a title used in letters; though it is coming into vogue, people already feel that it is far too artificial and affected. →**asszony**; **úrhölgy**; **úrnő**; **megszólítás**

úrhőlgy '*master–lady*' (lit.), *dame/lady*; the elaborate, over-refined form of →*úrasszony*, which is pretty much limited to addressing someone in writing. →**hölgy**; **megszólítás**

úriasszony '*lordly woman*' (lit.), *lady, ladyship*; the name by which a woman of the middle class (or higher) is addressed or mentioned; today the word has a slightly archaic ring to it. →**úr**; **úriember**; **asszony**; **úrnő**

úriember '*lordly man*' (lit.); *gentleman*; a word with a slightly archaic ring to it which in its content (meaning) and usage is the almost exact equivalent of the English "gentleman". →**úr**; **úriasszony**

úrnő '*mistress*' (lit.), *dame/lady*; just like *úr* (*master*), it has an antiquated ring to it and was used mostly only in combination (*várúrnő*, i.e., '*mistress of the castle*'); amid the recent chaos of addressing people after the change in the system (→*rendszerváltás*) it has reappeared as part of the address on letters. →**úrhölgy**

útlevél '*letter for the road*' (lit.), *passport*; for decades, the coveted object of desire for Hungarians, a document with magical powers, especially if validated for the West (→*Nyugat*); it had to be humbly applied for, and in the application (an official form which asked how the petitioner's relatives ended up abroad) one had to state the reason(s) for wanting to travel; even the existence of relatives whom one could visit (and who had to send a formal "letter of invitation" pledging they would put one up), was not sufficient for securing "permission", which usually could be had only every two or three years, for traveling abroad was considered a privilege that could be revoked at any time if for any reason the authorities decided that one's stay abroad could "endanger the interests of the Hungarian Peoples' Republic", and the length of stay granted rarely exceeded thirty days, while staying abroad without "permission", i.e., defecting (→*disszidens*) was a serious crime punishable by the confiscation of one's fortune and the denial of passports to one's relatives, not to mention other "inconveniences"; traveling to one of the other socialist countries was not much easier, while visiting the Soviet Union (→*Szovjetunió*) was, for all practical purposes, out of the question, unless in strictly organized form with the →*IBUSZ* travel agency.

úttörő '*road breaker*' (lit.), *pioneer*; when the boys' scouting clubs (*cserkész*) were banned, elementary school children were made to join the giant politically oriented Young Pioneer organization inspired by the old *cserkész* clubs, but the exact copies of the Soviet Pioneer movement; the idea was to bring up school children in the "fighting Communist spirit"; joining was compulsory, just like the red triangular tie (at least to begin with), and (also, at least to begin with) wearing a Russian-type cap; despite all the official efforts, however, the movement was a dismal failure, and though its forty years of existence, it was (along with all the other youth movements) highly unpopular and intensely disliked. →**KISZ**

uzsonna (*afternoon*) *tea, snack*; once (before WW II) a light afternoon meal (with coffee, tea, sandwiches or cake, →*sütemény*) indulged in by the middle classes; today, only children eat it when they come home from school.

Ü

ügyvéd '*defender of the case*' (lit.), *attorney-at-law, attorney, lawyer*; Hungary has always been the country of attorneys; for one thing, a young man (from a "better" family) who had no direction in life attended law school, for a law school diploma always came in handy, whether in business life, public administration or politics; furthermore, Hungary is a country of litigants, which means that it has attorneys galore (who are solicitors and barristers in one) who are regarded by civilians with a certain sense of suspicion, yet when trouble arises, are sought after, especially provided they are "clever" and can "twist" the paragraph of the law in a way that will insure that judgement will be brought in their clients' favor (for it is generally believed that this is possible, regardless of who has right on his side in a lawsuit).

V

Vác (pron. *vawts*); a baroque town and bishopric situated on the shore of the Danube (→*Duna*) north of →*Budapest*, familiar to everyone because it has one of the largest jails in the country, where many of those sentenced after the revolution (→*forradalom, 1956*) were incarcerated, including Árpád Göncz, later the first President of the new Hungarian Republic. →**Szeged**; **Sopronkőhida**

Váci út '*the road to Vác*' (lit.), *Váci Road*; at the close of the 19th century, the largest plants and factories of →*Pest* were built along the two sides of the road leading to →*Vác*, and adjacent to them →*Angyalföld* (*Angels' Land*), one of the largest working class districts of the capital; it is symbolic of recent changes that the factories have given way to office buildings, or were turned into department stores. →**Csepel**

Váci utca '*the street to Vác*' (lit.); the main street of the old Inner City (→*Belváros*) of →*Pest* stretching between the Central (Food) Market (*Vásárcsarnok*) and →*Vörösmarty tér*, which had been a shopping street since time immemorial and by the turn of the century (→*századforduló*) became the Bond street of Budapest with expensive and elegant fashion shops, a veritable icon; after WW II, its shops, nationalized (→*államosítás*) in accordance with the dictates of socialist (→*szocialista*) policy, it became paltry and dull, thereby adding extra sheen to the old, legendary *Váci utca* as it survived in the mind's eye, and embuing the handful of private (→*maszek*) businesses that managed to survive, and where items could be had that were not available elsewhere, and were of superior quality to the cheap government goods, with an air of nostalgia; though the primitive capitalism which surfaced after the change in regime (→*rendszerváltás*) turned it into a tasteless and gaudy rag-fair, its legend has not yet faded from memory.

vadászat *hunting/shooting*; the Hungarian language makes no distinction between shooting and hunting, or hunting and the hunt, which may very well be an indication that bagging an animal was always the privilege of the landed gentry, while it became under socialism (→*szocializmus*), the pastime of Party (→*Párt*) functionaries (→*funkcionárius*) and other privileged people, as well as the sport of foreigners paying in hard currency; consequently, people are still distrustful of it.

vadkan (*wild*) *boar*; the wild boar became part and parcel of Hungarian historical myth when in the 17th century, Count Miklós Zrínyi, one of the greatest men of his age and the supreme commander of Hungarian forces fighting the Turks (who almost became king of Hungary, and was the most illustrious Hungarian baroque poet into the bargain) died at a hunt, when a wounded boar charged him; however, in their disappointment, the Hungarian nobles who hoped to rid themselves of Habsburg (→*Habsburgok*) domination by putting Zrínyi on the throne, suspected treason (→*áruló*) in the shape of an assassin sent by the Court in Vienna; in this way, the expression *vadkan* (*'wild boar'*) came to signify the self-deception of Hungarians disappointed in their hopes and suspecting treason behind every failure. →**áruló**

vaj *butter*; never used in cooking, it has gradually disappeared from the breakfast (→*reggeli*) table as well in favor of margarine (→*margarin*); nonetheless, gourmands continue to buy fresh, yellow, home-made butter at the local markets from women (formerly called *tejeskofa*, or *'milk-women'*) selling dairy products at small stands.

vajda *voivode*, *duke*; in Serbian and Romanian territories, the *vajda* was the elected head of an ethnic group or province; *vajda* is also the Gypsy (→*cigányok*) name for their tribal head; since in the Middle Ages it was the title of the king's Transylvanian (→*Erdély*) regent, in Hungarian the word has an archaic ring to it; it is also a frequently used Hungarian family name.

Vajdaság *'the Vajda's lands'* (lit.), *Vojvodina*; the southern counties (→*megye*) of former Hungary situated along the Danube (→*Duna*), with Central Europe's richest arable soil, formed the most advanced part of medieval Hungary; it is inhabited by the descendants of a motley group of settlers brought in to repopulate the region after the Turkish occupation (→*Hódoltság*) – Swabians (→*svábok*), Ruthenians, and Slovaks (→*szlovák*), who gradually settled the land over the course of the past two to three hundred years, not to mention the Serbs (→*szerb*) fleeing the Turks; after it was annexed to Yugoslavia by the Peace Treaty of Versailles (→*Trianon*), and as a consequence of the de- and re-settlement of the population after the two world wars, today its population is predominantly Serbian. →**Délvidék**; **Újvidék**

vállalkozó *entrepreneur*; the new word which has made the most triumphant entry in the vocabulary of the recent past; since the *entrepreneur* was the symbol of the brand new bourgeois self-awareness, it began its career as a motto of sorts, but it soon began to take on pejorative connotations, until by now it has a decidedly derogatory ring to it, for people were soon put off by the "get rich quick" mentality of the years of the change in regime (→*rendszerváltás*); the tactful vernacular of criminal news, for instance, calls those detainees whose profession is suspect *entrepreneurs*, as a result of which the word became a synonym for 'mafioso', though it had first appeared in the late sixties as part of the then incredibly daring economic reforms (→*reform*); its original meaning has been replaced by the expression *üzletember* (*'businessman'*), though the aura of the latter is also becoming increasingly tarnished. →**menedzser**

vám *customs/duties*; the average citizen who, especially under socialism, always found something to smuggle into Hungary from one of the neighboring countries (or the other way around), meaning goods that until recently could be sold at a profit through friends or at the "Polish markets" (→*lengyel piac*) on the outskirts of every larger town in Eastern (→*Kelet-Európa*) and Central Europe (*Közép–Európa*); but even if people did not go abroad in order to make a little money, they always had some hidden dollars (or other hard currency with them, not to mention letters, hidden inside the lining of a jacket or bra) when they crossed the frontier, as a result of which they were always afraid or at least uneasy and hated all customs officers; in turn, the customs officers knew this (and also that everyone had something to hide), and acted accordingly; they were arrogant despots, blackmailing marauders or sly profiteers on the lookout for baksheesh; there were many horror stories about them, and people listened to them with glee, for they were about how someone managed to outwit them; in Hungarian, the thick, hard stalk of the tobacco leaf which, if it gets mixed into the cigarette, will make it explode, is called *fináncláb*, i.e., 'customs officer's leg'. →**útlevél**

Vár, a '*Castle/Fortress, the*' (lit.); refers to the royal palace of →*Buda* (which today houses various museums and the National Library), as well as the entire Castle complex, once a small town enclosed by walls, situated on the low but steep hill by the Danube; since the 13th century it has served as the seat of the kings of Hungary; it has seen many castles and palaces, each built atop the ruins of the old; today, some of these ruins, along with statues and artifacts unearthed after the devastating siege of Buda Castle in WW II, are on display in the lower level of the rebuilt baroque wing; the district itself, which is now like a baroque town in character, was rebuilt atop the medieval town, ruined in the siege which ousted the Turk (→*törökök*) in 1686 (to be destroyed once again in 1945); a distinguished place to live and dine, the petit bourgeoisie of Budapest like to visit its restaurants on special occasions, and to walk their children on sunny Sunday (→*vasárnap*) mornings, and to walk up to the terrace in front of the main wing of the palace (now the National Gallery) in order to ascertain once again that the panorama of the city is breathtaking indeed. →**Mátyás–templom**; **Halászbástya**; **Budapest**

vármegye →**megye**

vásár *fair*; though almost every household now owns a car, and though there are now department stores and shopping centers in the countryside (→*vidék*), too, fairs (and wandering merchants who sell their wares at fairs), along with their characteristic tents, buffets (→*laci-*

konyha), and merry-go-rounds continue in popularity, probably because people like their atmosphere; every larger settlement has its own traditional fair days (two or three a year), mostly on holidays celebrating the patron saints of the local churches; these fairs are held concurrently with parish feasts (→*búcsú*), when people come home to visit their relatives; there are several famous national fairs, too (which at one time included animal markets), and which are reported in the media; it is revealing that *vasárnap*, the Hungarian word for Sunday, comes from the two root words *vásár* (*fair/market*), and *nap* (*day*); on the other hand, *vásári* ('*of the fair*', '*from the market*') has come to signify cheap and shoddy stuff lacking in taste. →**augusztus 20**

vasárnap *Sunday*; walking the children, digging in the garden of the "weekend house" (→*vikendház*), washing the car, visits to parents, leisurely breakfasts, soccer (→*futball*) games, a mug of beer with friends, housework that was neglected during the busy weekdays, going to church or on an outing or hike, window shopping in the Inner City (→*Belváros*): Hungarian Sundays are pretty much like Sundays in the rest of Europe, except, perhaps, for the Sunday lunch, which is traditionally chicken soup and fried chicken (→*húsleves és rántottcsirke*) with cucumber salad with garlic and sour cream sauce.

Vasorrú bába '*iron-nosed woman*' (lit.), *witch*; the wicked and ugly old woman (sometimes with magic powers) of Hungarian folk tales, though the term is also used in jest for real people, too; strange as it may seem, well into the 20th century, the carved wooden idols of southern Siberia also had iron noses, used to impale the flesh of the sacrificial animals.

vattacukor '*cotton sugar*' (lit.), *cotton candy*; by constant stirring, the heated sugar is turned into a light, fibrous mass like a cloud, and is sold wrapped around a stick; this sticky, cloyingly sweet candy, which is not easy to eat because one's nose keeps getting stuck in it, is sold mostly at fairs (→*vásár*) and parish feasts (→*búcsú*).

végvár '*frontier castle/fortress*' (lit.); it was the defensive line of castles of various sizes (all of them later destroyed in sieges), that for 150 years (during the course of the 16th and 17th centuries) defended, as they were forced to move farther and farther afield, what was left of the country's territory against the Turk (→*törökök*); the word is still frequently used today as the metaphor of steadfastness of purpose. →**Eger**

Verecke (pron. *veh–rets–keh*); a small village situated among the mountains of the north-eastern Carpathians, which owes its fame to the fact that according to tradition (fortified by scientific findings), it was through the Pass of Verecke that the conquering tribes (→*honfoglalók*) came to the territory of today's Hungary. →**Kárpátalja**

Versailles-i békeszerződés *Peace Treaty of Versailles*; →**Trianon**

vérszerződés '*bondage/contract of blood*' (lit.), *blood pact, covenant*; the leaders of the tribes who formed an alliance for the Conquest (→*Honfoglalás*), electing →*Árpád* as their chieftain, or prince, slashed their arms and allowed their blood to collect in a goblet, then drank from it, sealing their alliance thereby, as can be seen on innumerable 19th century paintings and illustrations; along with just about everything else referring to the mythical Hungarian past, we know this, too, from the chronicles of a 13th century monk known as *Anonymus* ("the Nameless Notary"); today, the term is used to refer to contracts that seem secure, whether in business or in politics.

Vezess új utakra, Lucifer! "*Lead us along new paths, Lucifer!*"; a well-known quote from *The Tragedy of Man* (→*Tragédia*) used however only in banal situations, and in jest; Adam says it at the end of the various scenes of the epic drama.

vicc *joke*; though there have always been jokes dependent on language or paradox, the really popular jokes with strong punch lines have always been political; however, these were born only when the people felt helpless against the government, and wanted to laugh at the witticisms highlighting the lies of whatever self-conceited power was in authority; in the 20th century, it has become a minor art form in its own right which was at its best when life was at its worst. →**Arisztid és Tasziló**; **Kohn bácsi**; **székely góbé**; **Móricka**

vidék '*surroundings*', '*environment*' (lit.), *the countryside/provinces*; the expression is used not only for villages (→*falu*), but for everything (towns and countryside) that is not part of the capital city (though each town in the provinces also has its own 'countryside'); since →*Budapest* has grown so disproportionately large (at the expense of the countryside, many say, for its has syphoned off both men and capital) that other towns could no longer compete with it (especially since some of its prospective rivals such as Kassa, Nagyvárad, →*Kolozsvár*, and →*Újvidék* were taken away by the Peace Treaty of Versailles, or →*Trianon* in Hungarian usage, and annexed to neighboring countries) and everything else became a "backward" province in comparison, the political, economic, intellectual and cultural differences between the capital and the 'countryside' have put their stamp on all of 20th century Hungarian history; for the past one hundred years, at least, there have always been demagogues who have tried to capitalize on the growing resentment of "provincial Hungary" (i.e., "uncorrupted", "patriotic" and "healthy" Hungary, the "heartland") as opposed to the "corrupt and cosmopolitan" capital city which has "cut itself off from the country"; the problem is made more complex by the fact that the capital does lead its own life independently of the rest of the country; furthermore, the degree of centralization which has come about of its own accord gradually and which it embodies is indeed not desirable; what's more, modernization (both in the economic and intellectual-cultural spheres) is much more evident in Budapest, which considers itself on a par with the rest of the European capitals (as a result of which it often acts too proud of itself), not to mention the fact that those who live in the "center", and are therefore in a position to make decisions, have a tendency to forget about the rest of Hungary, just as those living in the county seats tend to ignore the needs of the nearby settlements. →**tájszólás**

víkendház '*weekend house*' (lit.), *summer home*, *vacation home*; the word conjures up images of a small house (possibly built from prefabricated wooden panels) jam-packed next to other small houses of a similar nature on the outskirts of towns or in humble resorts, each standing on a small plot with half a dozen or so fruit trees, and a →*Trabant* (for which there was a five to six year waiting list) parked up front, possibly near some body of water fit for fishing; in the seventies, this became the next realistic aim of every industrious middle class Hungarian after he coughed up the monthly instalments on the family's two and a half room prefab (→*panel*) apartment; the much more expensive summer homes around Lake →*Balaton* are popularly referred to as villas. →**telek**

VIM since time immemorial, Hungarian housewives have used this scouring powder to clean (among other things) sinks and bathtubs; accordingly, its name has become the generic term for scouring powder in general.

virgács *besom*; a bundle of twigs tied together or affixed to a handle and used as a broom, but only to sweep up peasant yards and fallen leaves, though it can still sometimes be seen in the hands of street sweepers; the kind of *virgács*, however, that the →*Krampusz* (Devil) gives children (along with other presents) is to remind them to behave, and is only just big enough to fit in their hands; the twigs are sprayed with gold paint and sometimes have Christmas candy (*szaloncukor*) hanging from them, and the bunch is held together with red crepe paper.

Visegrád (pron. *vee–sheh–grawd*); on top of a tall hill in the Danube Bend (→*Dunakanyar*), where the river makes a hairpin turn towards the south, there stand the ruins of a castle, with the ruins of a large, terraced palace under it, by the shore; this was the summer residence of the medieval kings of Hungary, of which the unearthed remains of the Renaissance palace of King Mathias (→*Mátyás király*) are on display (including the red marble fountain which is also on the new 1000 forint bill); the dam of a huge Czechoslovak-Hungarian power plant would have been built here, between the villages of Visegrád and →*Nagymaros* across the way, had not the anger of the people swept the last great Stalinist plan to "restructure/transform nature" away together with the regime itself.

vizsla *Hungarian setter*; any of a breed of medium-sized hound with a short, smooth, rusty-gold coat and big ears; it is a Hungarian breed, a faithful, sweet and lovable animal. →**puli**; **kuvasz**; **kutya**

Voronyezs *Voronezh*; a city in the Ukraine which conjures up cruel memories for older generations of Hungarians; it was here, at the bend in the river Don, that the Red Army broke through the front lines in the freezing cold January of the year 1943, and this is where 200 thousand soldiers of the Second Hungarian Army bled to death or fell prisoner to be taken to →*Siberia*, provided they did not freeze first.

vőfély *best man*; according to a tradition still practiced in Hungarian villages, a young man is chosen to invite the guests to the wedding (→*lakodalom*) in the name of the bride or groom; he acts as a master of ceremonies (the sign of his office is the flower-decorated 'best man's stick/baton', or *vőfelybot*), but is also a sort of entertainer who entertains the wedding guests with long and funny (sometimes naughty) poems, some traditional, some of his own composition. →**menyasszonytánc**

vöröshagyma *'red onion'* (lit.), *onion*; despite its name, the Hungarian *vöröshagyma* is not the red-skinned variety (which is called *lila hagyma*, or *purple onion*); perhaps there is no true Hungarian dish whose recipe does not begin with the words, "Fry some onion in lard"; because of the climate, Hungarian onions tend to be stronger than further down south, and is rarely eaten raw; when raw rings are called for, red onions (→*kékhagyma*) are used; the best onions, white, juicy and succulent, come from the southern town of Makó and its vicinity.

Vörösmarty Mihály →***Szózat***; **temetés**

Vörösmarty tér *Vörösmarty Square*; if →*Budapest* had one main square, this would be it; however, it has nothing to do with the poet →*Vörösmarty Mihály*, except for the fact that a romantic marble statue of him and some of his famous characters stands in the middle of the square, showing him as the national poet incarnate; in the 18th century it was a market place in front of one of the city gates at the beginning of →*Váci utca* (which has contributed to its present atmosphere), but after the walls were torn down, the expanding city incorporated it; it is surely best known for the →*Gerbeaud* café and confectioner's shop which bears the name of its former owner, and which many consider the best café in Central Europe (→*Közép Európa*); after its nationalization (→*államosítás*), someone had the grotesque idea of renaming it in honor of Vörösmarty, but the people continued to refer to it as the Gerbeaud;

it is on this square that the National Book Week is traditionally held at the end of May, for which publishers put up tents, and authors come to dedicate their books; in short, it becomes the place to see and be seen, and to have authors sign their works. →**Pest**

Vuk (pron. *vook*); one of the best loved characters of Hungarian children's literature, Vuk is an orphaned little fox who learns about life through countless adventures; having been adopted by animation, however, Vuk could not escape falling victim to merchandising.

W

Wartburg this conveyence with a two-stroke engine, strident and grating on the ear like a cement drill, coughing up dark, putrescent exhaust fumes, was a product of East German industry like no other, yet it too had its adherents; it was supposed to use little gasoline and was supposed to be long-lived; this is what its square shape suggested, not to mention its colors, like that of dusty side-roads; it was especially sought after by those with small private (→*maszek*) businesses and agriculturalist village dwellers, for it was cheap, and its trunk relatively ample. →**Trabant**; **Zsiguli**

Y

Y it is commonly believed that if a family name ends with a "*Y*", it is an indication of descent from the nobility (→*nemesség*) or the aristocracy (→*arisztokrácia*); however, this is far from the truth, since the letter "*Y*" is simply the old-fashioned way of writing "*I*", a suffix indicating that someone (or something) is from a certain place (eg. *Budai* = '*from Buda*'), and forms perhaps the most frequent type of Hungarian family name, and is furthermore pronounced as if it were a simple "*I*"; it is true that the manner of spelling of the names of the nobility was fixed a long time ago, which often makes the spelling old-fashioned, but this does not simply mean the use of "*y*"; for instance, the name of the counts →*Széchenyi* (lit. '*from/of Szécsény*', a village in northern Hungary) happens to end with an "*I*", while the "*CS*" sound is written in the old-fashioned way, as "*CH*", not to mention the fact that not all names of the nobility refer to geographical origins or their estates.→**helyesírás**

Z

zab *oat*; unlike elsewhere, in Hungary, no one will eat oats in any shape or form, not even for breakfast porridge (→*kása*), because it has been traditionally used only as fodder for horses, since it is considered especially nourishing for animals. →**búza**; **rozs**

zöldség '*greenery*' (lit.), *vegetables*; until recently, vegetables were eaten only cooked with roux (→*főzelék*), or cut small and added to meat soup; it is revealing that the word *zöldség* is the jocular equivalent of '*nonsense*', and it is equally revealing that (until recently) it was very cheap. →**saláta**

ZS

zsemle (zsömle) *roll*; a round, fist-size "baker's cake" (→*péksütemény*) made out of the same dought as Hungarian croissants (→*kifli*), and its crust is just as crisp; it is used to make sandwiches (and "provender" for outings) by cutting it in half lenghtwise and stuffing it with bologna (→*párizsi*) or winter sausage (→*téliszalámi*). →**perec**

Zserbó →**Gerbeaud**

zserbó–szelet '*gerbeaud–slice*' (lit.); many consider it the best of all cakes (→*cukrászsütemény*), and its price lives up to its reputation; thin layers of dough are spread with walnut cream and apricot jam (→*lekvár*) and piled one on top of the other, then the cake is covered with chocolate; it is made at home, too, but only for special guests. Its name comes from the famous →*Gerbeaud* café and confectioner's on →*Vörösmarty tér* in →*Budapest*, where it was first made.

zsidók, a *Jews, the*; "*I'd gladly resign my claim to the Hungarian Jews if only I were certain that their patriotism would save them from the misery of antisemitism ... But the Jews of Hungary will also be overtaken by their doom, which will be all the more brutal and merciless as time passes, and wilder, too, the stronger they get in the meantime. There is no escaping it.*" These lines were written in 1903 by Herzl, who was born in Budapest at a time when Hungarian Jews enjoyed full acceptance, and the country's chief rabbi was a member of the Upper House, and though his words proved to be prophetic, thanks to the lucky interplay of various historical circumstances, after the Holocaust only Hungary had a significant number of Jews left in Central Europe (→*Közép–Európa*); having speedily assimilated in the 18th and 19th centuries, and having become part of the Hungarian nation politically (legally), sociologically and culturally (independent of their religion), they shared in its fate; after the wave of antisemitic horror passed, the Communists made any mention of the Jews (called "those persecuted by the Nazis") taboo in any context besides religion (for Jews and non-Jews equally), but only so that after the change in regime (→*rendszerváltás*) the unresolved problems should reemerge, the signs of antisemitism, which were thought to have disappeared once and for all, along with a new emphasis on Jewish identity, which was also considered a thing of the past, perhaps because post-war politics did not allow for the social resolution of this trauma. →**Kozma utca**; **ki a magyar**; **asszimiláció**; **névmagyarosítás**

Zsiguli (pron. *zhee–ghooh–lee*); for decades, this car, originally a Fiat design which through the years hardly changed in shape and was made in the Soviet Union (later under the name of "Lada"), was the most popular and affordable family car of the Hungarian middle class (as a consequence of which, the waiting list was several years long); most people learned how to drive in one of these cars, which were also used (in a dark blue version!) by the lower ranking managers of state owned companies and offices (who were not entitled to the much larger, "American" size, equally Soviet made "Volga"); it was outdated to begin with, slow and uneconomical, but it was also strong and dependable, and people liked it, as a result of which they called it "Zsiga", the diminutive form of "Sigismund". →**Trabant; Wartburg**

zsír '*fat*' (lit.), *lard*; in Hungary, the word is always used to mean pork fat (→*disznózsír*); it is made by rendering the thick fatty layer (→*szalonna*) under the pig's skin in a large cauldron, thus releasing the fat, which then cools down and congeals; when made at home, it is stored in enamel-lined buckets, though today it is usually store-bought; it is used mostly for cooking, unlike goose fat, for instance, which is only a by-product of roast goose and the rendering of goose cracklings (→*töpörtyű*), and is eaten with bread (→*zsíroskenyér*) as a special delicacy. →**disznóölés**

zsíroskenyér '*larded bread*' (lit.); fresh bread (→*kenyér*) spread with a layer of home-rendered pork fat (→*disznózsír*), sprinkled with paprika (→*pirospaprika*) and covered with slices of red onion (→*lila hagyma*) is surely the most horrendous of anything Hungarians eat – at least in the eyes of cultures which look down on pigs (→*disznó*), whereas accompanied by a glass of cold, dry white wine (→*bor*), especially a good spritzer (→*fröccs*) it is delicious beyond words; though the poor eat more of it, it is not considered a "poorman's food" and can be found in most inexpensive wineries or pubs(→*borozó*); most Hungarians can still remember its taste from childhood dinners spent round the kitchen table; on the other hand, larded bread sprinkled with sugar, never eaten nowdays was the "poorman's delicacy", and in the fifties (→*ötvenes évek*) it was given to children as a veritable treat to add variety to their diet.

Zsolnay (pron. ***zhowl-nah-yee***) the "other" major porcelain factory besides →*Herend*, bearing the name of its mid-19th century founder; though the "modern" vases and other *objects d'art* made with a special, greenish, irridescent eozin glaze invented by Zsolnay were coveted at the time of *art nouveau* in Paris, today its dinnerware takes second place to Herend porcelain as an elegant present to newlyweds.

Index of entries

bream	**keszeg**
bride's dance	**menyasszonytánc**
brother (little)	**öcsi (öcskös)**
brother, younger	**öcsém**
brother/sister	**testvér**
Buda, city of	**Buda**
Buda, residential district of	**Rózsadomb**
Buda, royal palace of	**Vár, a**
Budapest, city of	**Budapest**
bunny rabbit	**nyuszi**
Burgenland (in Austria)	**őrvidék**
butter	**vaj**
cabbage	**káposzta**
cabbage, savoy	**kelkáposzta**
cabbage, stuffed	**töltöttkáposzta**
cadre	**káder**
café	**kávéház**
café, name of	***New York***
cake/cookie	**sütemény**
Calvinist school/college	**Sárospatak**
canteen	**étkezde**
cap	**sapka**
cap, cloth	**micisapka**
cap, Swiss	**svájci sapka**
card game	**ulti**
carp	**ponty**
castle in the Danube Bend	**Visegrád**
castle/fortress (on the frontier)	**végvár**
cat, black	**fekete macska**
Catholic Church	**Katolikus Egyház**
cemetery	**Farkasréti temető**
cemetery	**Házsongárdi temető**
cemetery	**Kerepesi úti temető**
cemetery	**Kozma utcai temető**
cemetery	**Újköztemető**
Chain Bridge	**Lánchíd**
change in regime, the	**rendszerváltás**
charity package	**szeretetcsomag**
chicken soup and fried chicken	**húsleves és rántottcsirke**
children's literature	***Egri csillagok, Az***
children's literature	***Pál utcai fiúk, A***
children's literature	***Vuk***
children's song	***Bújj-bújj zöld ág, zöld levelecske …***
children's song	***Lánc-lánc, eszter-lánc …***
chimney sweep	**kéményseprő**
chocolate bar	**Sport-szelet**
chocolate bar	**Tibi**
Christmas carol	***Mennyből az angyal …***
Christmas	**Karácsony**
city by the Danube	**Dunaújváros**
city by the Danube	**Esztergom**
city by the Danube	**Mohács**
city by the Danube	**Sztálinváros**
city by the Danube	**Vác**
city in central Transdanubia	**Székesfehérvár**
city in eastern Hungary	**Debrecen**
city in northern Hungary	**Eger**
city in northern Transdanubia	**Győr**
city in Slovakia	**Pozsony**
city in southern Transdanubia	**Pécs**
city in the southern Great Plain	**Arad**
city in the southern Great Plain	**Szeged**
city in the Ukraine	**Voronyezs**
city in Transylvania	**Kolozsvár**
city in Transylvania	**Marosvásárhely**
city in western Transdanubia	**Sopron**
city in Yugoslavia	**Újvidék**
city on both sides of the Danube	**Komárom**

cleaning lady	**bejárónő**
coat of arms	**címer**
cockade	**kokárda**
codices, illuminated	**corvina**
coffee cake/kugelhopf	**kuglóf**
coffee shop	**eszpresszó**
coffee	**fekete**
coffee	**kávé**
cold cut	**párizsi**
colleague	**szaktárs**
colonial (style of furniture)	**kolóniál (stílus)**
common sense	**józan, paraszti ész**
Communist Party chief	**Kádár János**
Communist Party chief	**Rákosi Mátyás**
Communist Party member	**párttag**
Communist Party secretary	**párttitkár**
Communist Party	**kommunista párt**
Communist Party, the	**Párt, a**
Communist Youth, Association of	**KISZ**
compensation for damages	**kárpótlás**
composer	**Bartók Béla**
composer	**Erkel Ferenc**
Compromise, the	**Kiegyezés, a**
comrade (Communist Party)	**elvtárs**
comrade/companion in arms	**bajtárs**
concierge	**házmester**
condominium	**társasház**
confectioner's	**cukrászda**
conquerors of the fatherland, the	**honfoglalók, a**
cooperative, agricultural	**termelőszövetkezet**
co-tenancy	**társbérlet**
cottage cheese noodles	**túróstészta**
cotton candy	**vattacukor**

council (local)	**Tanács**
Councils, Republic of	**Tanácsköztársaság**
counter-revolution	**ellenforradalom**
countryside/provinces	**vidék**
county	**megye**
crackling	**töpörtyű**
creamy (cake)	**krémes**
crepe	**palacsinta**
crescent	**kifli**
crocheting	**horgolás**
crown jewels	**koronázási ékszerek**
crown	**korona**
Crown, the Holy	**Szent Korona**
Cumans, Land of the	**Kunság**
Cumans, the	**kunok**
curd, cottage cheese	**túró**
customs	**vám**
Czech	**cseh**
Czechs, the	**csehek, a**
csángó–Hungarians, the	**csángók, a**
daily paper	***Népszabadság***
daily paper	***Népszava***
dame/lady	**úrasszony**
dame/lady	**úrhölgy**
dame/lady	**úrnő**
dance (of the csárda)	**csárdás**
dance (of the palace)	**palotás**
dance house	**táncház**
Danish	**bukta**
Danube Bend	**Dunakanyar**
Danube, River	**Duna**
Day of the Dead	**Halottak Napja**
Dear Sir/Madam	**Kedves uram (asszonyom/ barátom)!**
Dear Sir/Madam	***Tisztelt Cím!***
deportation	**kitelepítés**
devil	**Krampusz**
dialect	**tájszólás**
digestif	**Unicum**
dill (kosher) pickles	**kovászos uborka**
dining room	**ebédlő**

doctor	**doktor úr**
dog (of the cowherds)	**kuvasz**
dog	**kutya**
downtown (of Pest)	**Belváros, a**
drama (quote)	***Ember küzdj, és bízva bízzál!***
drama (quote)	***Sok az eszkimó, kevés a fóka ...***
drama (quote)	***Vezess új utakra, Lucifer!***
drama	***Az ember tragédiája***
drama	***Bánk Bán***
dress, Hungarian	**atilla**
dumpling	**gombóc**
earn, to	**keres (pénzt)**
Easter	**Húsvét**
eaterie	**kifőzde**
egg barley	**tarhonya**
Egmont Overture	***Egmont-nyitány***
Elizabeth, Queen	**Erzsébet királyné**
embroidery from Kalocsa	**kalocsai hímzés**
emigré	**disszidens**
emigré	**emigráns**
eminence, his	**őnagysága**
English, the	**angolok, az**
entrepreneur	**vállalkozó**
entrepreneur/artisan	**maszek**
equestrian nation	**lovasnemzet**
espresso (coffee)	**dupla**
espresso	**presszó**
ethnic cleansing	**lakosságcsere**
ethnic minority	**etnikai kisebbség**
Europe	**Európa**
Europe, Central	**Közép Európa**
Europe, Eastern	**Kelet Európa**
Europe, West	**Nyugat, a**
expatriate	**külföldre szakadt hazánkfia**
fair	**vásár**
fairy	**tündér**
fairytale country	**Óperencia**
family home	**családi ház**
farmstead	**tanya**

fat	**zsír**
fata morgana	**délibáb**
Father Winter	**Télapó**
Fifties, the	**ötvenes évek**
Fifty–six (1956)	**Ötvenhat**
fin de siècle	**századforduló**
Finno-Ugric family (of languages)	**finn-ugor rokonság**
fish soup	**halászlé**
fish	**hal**
Fishermen's bastion (in Buda)	**Halászbástya**
flame cake	**lángos**
flea market	**Teleki tér**
FM station	**Bartók Rádió**
folk art	**népmüvészet**
folk costume	**népviselet**
folk dance	**néptánc**
folk furniture	**parasztbútor**
folk hero	**Háry János**
folk music	**népzene**
folk poetry	**népköltészet**
folk pottery	**Jancsi-kancsó**
folk song	**népdal**
folk tale	**Lúdas Matyi**
folksy (German) dance music	**sramli**
folksy	**népies**
food tent	**lacikonyha**
football (soccer)	**foci**
football (soccer)	**futball**
football club	**fradi**
football player	**Puskás Öcsi**
football team	**FTC**
football/soccer, table	**gombfoci**
foul speech	**káromkodás**
Francis Joseph, the emperor	**Ferenc József**
French (disease)	**franc(nyavalya)**
French	**francia**
French, the	**franciák, a**
fruit, canned/bottled	**befőtt**
fuck it	**bassza meg**
functionary	**funkcionárius**

funeral **temetés**
gallery/balcony **gang (függőfolyosó)**
game (of chance) **snóbli**
game (played by boys/young men) **snúrozás**
gay **melegek**
Gellért, Mount **Gellért-hegy**
gendarme **csendőr**
gentleman (young) **fiatalúr**
gentleman **úriember**
gentry **dzsentri**
Gerbeaud's (name of confectioner) **Gerbeaud**
Germans (in Hungary) **svábok**
Germans, the **németek, a**
giddyup **gyia!**
Gipsy band **cigányzenekar**
Gipsy music **cigányzene**
Gipsy violinist **Dankó, Pista**
Gipsy, the **cigány**
Gipsying **cigányozás**
goblin **manó**
God bless you **Isten áldja (magát)**
God of the Hungarians **magyarok istene, a**
godfather **koma**
Golden Team, the (football) **Aranycsapat, az**
good day **jónapot**
good man/woman **jóember/jóasszony**
goulash communism **gulyáskommunizmus**
goulash **gulyás**
graduation parade/valediction **ballagás**
graduation photo **érettségi tabló**
graduation **érettségi**
grande dame **nagyasszony**
grandmother **nagymama**
grape juice **must**
gratuity **hálapénz**
greeting **köszönés**
grocer's, the **közért**
Gundel's (name of restaurant) **Gundel**
Habsburgs, the **Habsburgok, a**
hall **előszoba**
ham **sonka**
handshake **kézfogás**
harvest (grain) **aratás**
harvest (wine and fruit) **szüret**
hash browns **törtkrumpli**
hat cure **kalapkúra**
hat **kalap**
hat, fur **kucsma**
head cheese **disznósajt**
headpost **kopjafa**
highwayman **Rózsa Sándor**
highwayman **Sobri Jóska**
highwayman, the **betyár**
Holy Right (hand, the) **Szent Jobb**
home(land), the **haza, a**
homeland of ancient Hungarians **őshaza**
honey cake **mézeskalács**
horse, white **fehér ló**
horse-herd **csikós**
hot (food) **csípős (étel)**
housing estate **lakótelep**
How are you? **Hogy van?**
humbly report, I **alázatosan jelentem!**
Hungarian Academy of Sciences **MTA**
Hungarian Armed Forces **Magyar Honvédség (MH)**
Hungarian cards **magyar kártya**
Hungarian conquest, the **Honfoglalás**
Hungarian costume **magyaros ruha**
Hungarian cuisine **magyar konyha**
Hungarian dress (ornate) **díszmagyar**
Hungarian dress (style) **atilla**

Hungarian face (typical) **magyaros arc**
Hungarian Gulag **Recsk**
Hungarian hat **bocskai-sapka**
Hungarian language, the **magyar nyelv, a**
Hungarian nation, the **magyar nemzet, a**
Hungarian origin, of **magyar származású**
Hungarian sea, the **magyar tenger**
Hungarian setter **vizsla**
Hungarian Socialist Workers' Party **MSzMP**
Hungarian song **magyar nóta**
Hungarian State Railways **MÁV**
Hungarian, everyone is **mindenki magyar**
Hungarian, who is? **ki a magyar?**
Hungarians, ancient **ősmagyarok**
Hungarians, homeland of ancient **őshaza**
Hungarians, the God of **magyarok istene, a**
Hungarians, the **magyarok, a**
Hungarian-style tunic **bocskai**
Hungary **Magyarország**
Hungary, historic **történelmi Magyarország**
Hunno-Magyar family/relationship **hun-magyar rokonság**
Huns, Land of **Hunnia**
hunting/shooting **vadászat**
husbandman **gazda**
hussar **huszár**
hymn ***Boldogasszony anyánk ...***
Independence, War of **Szabadságharc**
inn **csárda**
insurgent (18th century) **kuruc**
intelligentsia, the **értelmiség, az**
Interior, Department of the **belügy, a**
island on the Danube **Csepel**
jacket, padded (quilt) **pufajka**
jacknife **bicska**
jail **Sopronkőhida**
jam **lekvár**
jelly (pork) **kocsonya**
Jews, the **zsidók, a**
John (name) **János**
joke **vicc**
jokes **Arisztid és Tasziló**
jokes **Kohn bácsi**
jokes **Móricka**
jump, a **bekecs**
June 16th **június 16.**
Kádár János (Communist Party chief) **Kádár János**
kettle **bogrács**
kindergarten **ovi**
kiss on the hand **kézcsók**
kiss you, I **csókolom**
kiss your hand, I **kezét csókolom**
kiss your hand, I **kezicsókolom**
kiss **csók**
kiss/smack (on the face) **puszi**
lad **legény**
lady (young) **fiatalasszony**
lady/ladyship **úriasszony**
lady/madam **hölgy**
Land of the Huns **Hunnia**
landtaking of the Magyars, the **Honfoglalás**
language renewal **nyelvújítás**
lard **disznózsír**
larded bread **zsíroskenyér**
larder **éléskamra**
late, to be **késés**
lettuce **saláta**
Liberation Day **Felszabadulás**
lichthof **lichthóf**
loophole **kiskapu**
Lord Lieutenant **főispán**
Lord Lieutenant's Deputy **alispán**

love	**szerelem**
lunch	**ebéd**
madam	**asszonyom**
Magyarization of names	**névmagyarosítás**
Magyar-style costume	**atilla**
maid's room	**cselédszoba**
maize	**kukorica**
man (young)	**fiatalember**
manager	**menedzser**
mansion	**kúria**
mantle	**szűr**
march (military)	**Klapka-induló**
march (military)	**Rákóczi-induló**
March 15th	**március 15.**
marching song (communist)	**tömegdal**
marching song	**induló**
margarine	**margarin**
master/lord	**úr**
Mathias Church	**Mátyás-templom**
Mathias, king	**Mátyás király**
May, First of	**május elseje**
medicine	**Kalmopyrin**
military (Hungarian)	**honvédség**
military cloak	**kacagány**
military, the	**katonaság**
milk loaf	**kalács**
milk	**tej**
Millennium (1896), the	**Millennium, a**
Miracle Stag, the	**Csodaszarvas, .a**
Miss	**kisasszony**
mom/dad	**anyu/apu**
monastery	**Pannonhalma**
money	**pénz**
mother	**anya**
Mothers' Day	**Anyák Napja**
mourning	**gyász**
moustache	**bajusz**
multinational companies	**multik**
mum/mommy	**anyukám**
mush	**kása**
my respects	**tiszteletem**
mythical bird	**turul**
name for dogs	**Bodri**
name's day	**névnap**
nation	**nemzet**
nation, the Hungarian	**magyar nemzet, a**
national anthem (quote)	***Isten, áldd meg a magyart ...***
national anthem	**Himnusz**
National Guard	**Nemzetőrség**
national memorial park	**Pusztaszer**
national	**nemzeti**
nationalization	**államosítás**
Nativity players	**betlehemesek**
Nativity scene	**betlehem**
New Year's Eve	**Szilveszter**
nobility	**nemes(ség)**
numbers' war (game)	**számháború**
nursery rhyme	***Ez elment vadászni ...***
oat	**zab**
oath (of Hungarian nobles)	***Életünket és vérünket!***
occupation	**hódoltság**
October, 23rd (1956)	**október 23.**
October, 6th	**október 6.**
Old Buda, city of	**Óbuda**
once upon a time	***Egyszer volt, hol nem volt ...***
once upon a time	***Hol volt, hol nem volt ...***
onion	**hagyma**
onion	**vöröshagyma**
onion, blue	**kékhagyma**
operetta	**Csárdáskirálynő, a**
operetta, the	**operett**
pain killer	**Algopirin**
painter	**Csontváry Kosztka, Tivadar**
painter	**Munkácsy Mihály**
pallbearer	**gyászhuszár**
pap (in milk)	**tejbegríz**

paprika stew	**paprikás**
parish feast	**búcsú**
pas devant les enfants	***nicht vor dem Kind***
passport	**útlevél**
pasta	**tészta**
pastry horn	**kürtős kalács**
pastry	**cukrászsütemény**
patties	**fasírt**
Peace Treaty, Versailles	**Trianon**
peace-camp	**béketábor**
peasant wedding	**lakodalom (lagzi)**
peasant	**paraszt**
people, group of (in Moldova)	**csángók, a**
people, group of (northern Hungary)	**palóc**
people, group of (Transyalvania)	**székely**
people, of the	**népi**
people, the	**nép**
pepper (red)	**pirospaprika**
pepper, green/ white/red	**paprika**
pessimism	**pesszimizmus**
Pest, city of	**Pest**
Pest, downtown of	**Belváros, a**
Pest, industrial district of	**Angyalföld**
Pest, industrial district of	**Csepel**
Pest, industrial district of	**Kispest**
Pest, industrial district of	**Váci út**
Pest-Buda, cities of	**Pest-Buda**
piano accordion	**tangóharmonika**
pickled vegetables	**savanyúság**
pie	**pite**
pig/swine	**disznó**
pig's funeral feast	**disznótor**
pigkilling	**disznóölés**
pike–perch	**süllő**
pinot gris	**szürkebarát**
pioneer, young	**úttörő**
Plain, the Great (Hungarian)	**Alföld (Nagyalföld)**
play hockey, to	**amerikázni**
plot (of land)	**telek**
poem (quote)	***Hazádnak rendűletlenül légy híve***
poem (quote)	***Repül a nehéz kő ...***
poem (quote)	***Talpra magyar!***
poem	***János vitéz***
poem	***Nemzeti dal***
poem	***Szózat***
poem	***Toldi***
poet	**Ady Endre**
poet	**József Attila**
poet	**Petőfi Sándor**
poet	**Radnóti Miklós**
poet	**Vörösmarty Mihály**
poet, the	**költő**
poetry	**költészet**
Poles, the	**lengyelek, a**
policeman	**rendőr**
Polish market	**lengyel piac**
popinjay	**paprikajancsi**
poppy seed (cone)	**mák**
poppy seed noodles	**mákostészta**
porcelain	**Herend**
porcelain	**Zsolnay**
pork	**sertés**
pork/chicken in breadcrumbs	**rántotthús/csirke**
potato noodles	**krumplistészta**
potato stew	**paprikáskrumpli**
potato	**burgonya**
prefab housing	**panel**
pretzel	**perec**
private (soldier)	**baka**
privatization agency	**ÁPV Rt**
privatization	**privatizáció**
proletarian/proli kid	**proligyerek**
Protestant	**református**
Protestantism	**protestantizmus**
pub	**kocsma**

public radio	**Kossuth Rádió**
pumpkin	**tök**
pumpkin–seeds	**tökmag**
pusta, the	**puszta, a**
putty club/gang	**gittegylet**
Radio Free Europe	**Szabad Európa Rádió**
ratatouille	**lecsó**
red-white-green	**piros-fehér-zöld**
reform	**reform**
region of Hungary	**Bakony**
region of Hungary	**Duna-Tisza Köze**
region of Hungary	**Hortobágy**
region of Hungary	**Nyírség**
region of Hungary	**őrség**
region of Hungary	**Szabolcs megye**
region of Hungary	**Tiszántúl**
regretable events	**sajnálatos események**
relatives/the family	**rokonság**
rent-barracks	**bérkaszárnya**
rent-palace	**bérpalota**
republic	**köztársaság**
residential district of Buda	**Rózsadomb**
restaurant	**kisvendéglő**
revolution, 1848	**forradalom, 1848**
revolution, 1918	**forradalom, 1918**
revolution, 1956	**forradalom, 1956**
revolution, 1956	**november 4. 1956**
river	**Danube**
river	**Lajta**
river	**Rába**
river	**Tisza**
roll	**zsemle (zsömle)**
roll, (walnut/poppy seed)	**beigli**
Roman province	**Pannónia**
Roman province, capital of	**Aquincum**
Romanians, the	**románok, a**
Romany	**roma**
Russia	**Oroszország**
Russian (language)	**orosz (nyelv)**
Russians, the	**oroszok, az**
rye	**rozs**
sailors' blouse	**matrózblúz**
Saint Gerald	**Szent Gellért**
Saint Ladislas	**Szent László**
Saint Luke's Bath	**Lukács-fürdő**
Saint Stephen	**Szent István**
salami	**szalámi**
salami	**téliszalámi**
Santa Claus	**Mikulás**
sausage	**kolbász**
Saxons, the	**szászok**
School, Calvinist	**Sárospatak**
school, Lutheran	**Fasori gimnázium**
school, Pious Fathers'	**Piarista Gimnázium**
scones	**pogácsa**
scouring powder	**VIM**
Scythian	**szittya**
secondary school	**gimnazium**
secret police of the 50's	ÁVÓ
secret police	**három per három**
secret police, member of the	**ávós**
Sekler anthem (quote)	***Maroknyi székely...***
Sekler anthem	**székely himnusz**
Sekler gate	**székelykapu**
Sekler Land	**Székelyföld**
Sekler, the	**székely**
self–service (restaurant)	**önkiszolgáló**
Serbian	**rác**
serenade	**szerenád**
sergeant	**őrmester**
servant	**cseléd**
servus	**szervusz/szerbusz**
Seven Chiefts, the	**Hét vezér, a**
shaman	**táltos**
sheep	**birka**
shopping bag	**cekker**
shopping bag	**háló**
shopping street (of Pest)	**Váci utca**
Siberia	**Szibéria**
singer and movie star	**Karády Katalin**

sir	**uram**
Sir, I've come for my knife…	**Uram, a késemért jöttem…**
six to three (6:3)	**hat-három**
Sixties, the	**hatvanas évek**
Slovak	**szlovák**
Slovak	**tót**
Smith, Mr.	**Kovács úr**
snack bar	**büfé**
snack	**uzsonna**
Social Insurance Center	**SzTK**
socialism	**szocializmus**
socialist	**szocialista**
soldier (Hungarian)	**honvéd**
soldier song	**katonadal**
song (music-hall)	**kuplé**
song (of kuruc insurgents)	**kuruc nóta**
song (student)	***Ballag már a vén diák …***
song (student)	***Gaudeamus igitur***
song	***Akácos út…***
song	***Az a szép, az a szép …***
song	***Boci boci tarka …***
song	***Csak egy kislány van a világon…***
song	***Debrecenbe kéne menni …***
song	***Kossuth-nóta***
song	***Szép vagy, gyönyörű vagy, Magyarország.***
song	***Sződd a selymet, elvtárs …***
song	***Szomorú vasárnap***
Song, Hungarian	**magyar nóta**
song, marching	**induló**
sour/butter milk	**aludt tej**
southern parts, the	**Délvidék**
Soviet Union	**Szovjetunió**
spelling	**helyesírás**
spelling	**Y**
spread	**körözött**
sprinkling (Easter)	**locsolás**
spritzer	**fröccs**
square in Pest	**Rákóczi tér**
square in Pest	**Vörösmarty tér**
stag party	**legénybúcsú**
Stalin statue	**Sztálin-szobor**
Stalin's best Hungarian disciple	**Rákosi Mátyás**
statesman	**Kossuth Lajos**
statesman	**Széchenyi István**
stew	**pörkölt**
stranger to the (working) class	**osztályidegen**
street in Pest	**Markó, a**
street, shopping (in Pest)	**Váci utca**
strudel	**rétes**
sub-Carpathia	**Kárpátalja**
subtenant	**albérlő**
suicide	**öngyilkosság**
Sumero–Hung. family of languages	**sumér-magyar nyelvrokonság**
summer home	**víkendház**
summer kitchen	**nyárikonyha**
Sunday	**vasárnap**
sunflower seeds	**szotyola**
Switzerland	**Svájc**
Symphony (cigarette brand)	**Szimfónia**
Szabó family, The (soap opera)	**Szabó család, a**
tart	**dobos torta**
tart	**rigójancsi**
tart	**zserbó–szelet**
tart, the	**torta**
Tartar invasion	**tatárjárás**
tatties	**krumpli**
tea	**tea**
teacher (elementary school)	**tanító**
team	**kaláka**
telegram	**dísztávirat**

temple/church/ synagogue	**templom**
temporarily stationed	**ideiglenesen itt állomásozó**
tip	**borravaló**
Tokaj (dry)	**szamorodni**
Tokaj (sweet)	**aszú**
Tokaj, wine of	**tokaji**
tongue twister	***mit sütsz kis szűcs ...***
traitor, the	**áruló, az**
Transdanubia	**Dunántúl**
Transylvania	**Erdély**
Transylvania, Prince of	**Rákóczi Ferenc**
travel and ticket office	IBUSZ
tricolor	**nemzetiszín (zászló)**
tumbler	**feles**
tunic, Hungarian-style	**bocskai**
Turks, the	**törökök, a**
uncle	**bácsi (bá')**
uncle	**bátyám**
uniform	**egyenruha**
Upper Hungary	**Felvidék, a**
vacant lot (in a city)	**grund**
vegetable roux	**főzelék**
vegetables	**zöldség**
Versailles Peace Treaty	**Trianon**
victim of show trials	**Rajk László**
Vienna	**Bécs**
village by the Danube	**Nagymaros**
village in the Carpathians	**Verecke**
village	**falu**
voivode/duke	**vajda**
Vojvodina	**Vajdaság**
wall hanging	**falvédő**
Wallach, the	**oláh**
War of Independence	**Szabadságharc**
wedding	**esküvő**
Weinstube	**borozó**
West, the	**Nyugat, a**
wheat	**búza**
whore	**kurva**
wifie	**menyecske**
wine cellar	**talponálló**
wine	**bor**
wine, mulled	**forralt bor**
wine, red	**bikavér**
wine, red	**kadarka**
witch	**Vasorrú bába**
woman/wife	**asszony**
Worker (cigarette brand)	**Munkás**
worker	**dolgozó**
worker	**munkás**
Workers' Militia	**Munkásőrség**
writer	**Jókai Mór**
writer, the	**író**
yellow	**sárga**
you (formal)	**maga**
you (informal)	**te**
you (saying "you")	**tegezés**
you (yourself)	**ön**
your grace	**kegyelmes úr**
your grace	**méltóságos úr**
your honor	**nagyságos úr**
your ladyship	**nagysága**
your ladyship	**nagyságos asszony**

Index of subjects

lángos
lecsó
lekvár
lila hagyma
magyar konyha
mák
mákostészta
margarin
mézeskalács
must
olaj
palacsinta
pálinka
paprika
paprikás
paprikáskrumpli
párizsi
péksütemény
perec
pirospaprika, pite
pogácsa
ponty
pörkölt
rántotthús/csirke
reggeli
rétes
rigójancsi
saláta
savanyúság
sonka
sör
Sport-szelet
spriccer
süllő
sütemény
szalámi
szalonna
szamorodni
szilvapálinka
Szimfónia
szotyola
szürkebarát
saláta
tarhonya
tea
tej
tejbegríz
téliszalámi
tészta
Tibi
tokaji
torta
tök
tökmag
töltöttkáposzta
töpörtyű
törtkrumpli
túró
túróstészta
Unicum
vaj
vattacukor
vöröshagyma
zab
zöldség
zsemle
Zserbó
zserbó-szelet
zsír
zsíroskenyér

geography

Alföld
Amerika
Angyalföld
Ausztria
Bakony
Balaton
Balkán, a
Bécs
Belváros
Buda
Budapest
Csepel
Debrecen
délibáb
Délvidék
Don-kanyar
Duna
Duna-Tisza köze
Dunakanyar
Dunántúl
Dunaújváros
Eger
Erdély
Esztergom
Felvidék
Gellért-hegy
Győr
Hajdúság
Hortobágy
Kárpátalja
Kékes
Kelet Európa
Kispest
Kolozsvár
Komárom
Közép Európa
Kunság
Lajta
Magyarország
Marosvásárhely
Nagymaros
Nyírség
Óbuda
Oroszország
Őrség
Őrvidék
Pannónia
Pécs
Pest
Pozsony
Pusztaszer
Rába
Recsk
Sárospatak
Siófok
Sopron
Sopronkőhida

kényszervállalkozó
Kerepesi úti temető
késés
ki a magyar?
kifőzde
kiskapu
Kispest
kisvendéglő
kocsma
Kohn bácsi
kolóniál
Kossuth Rádió
Kovács úr
Kozma utcai temető
költő
költészet
körút
kunok
kúria
lakás
lakótelep
lengyel piac
lichthóf
Lukács-fürdő
Magyar Honvédség
magyar kártya
magyar nemzet
magyar nóta
magyar nyelv
magyar származású
magyarok
Markó, a
maszek
MÁV
megszólítás
megye
melegek
menedzser
menyasszonytánc
MH
Móricka
MTA, MTK, Mucsa
multik
Munkás
munkás
nagymama
nemzetiszín (zászló)
Nemzetőrség
nép
népies
népköltészet
Népszabadság
Népszava
névmagyarosítás
névnap
New York
nyárikonyha
nyelvújítás
orosz (nyelv)
osztályidegen
ovi
öngyilkosság
önkiszolgáló
őrmester
öröklakás
ötvenes évek
palóc
palotás
panel
Pannonhalma
Pannónia
Papp Laci
paraszt
párttag
párttitkár
Pest
pesszimizmus
Piarista Gimnázium
presszó
privatizáció
proligyerek
protestantizmus
puli
Puskás öcsi
puszi
Rákóczi tér
református
rendőr
rendszerváltás
rokonság
roma
Rózsadomb
Sárospatak
Siófok
sírva vigad a magyar
snóbli
snúrozás
svábok, a
Szabó–család
székely
székelykapu
SZER
SZTK
tabló
tájszólás
talponálló
táncház
tanító
tanya
társasház
társbérlet
te
telek
Teleki tér
temetés
termelőszövetkezet
Trabant
ulti
uzsonna
Újköztemető
útlevél
ügyvéd
Váci út
Váci utca
vadászat
vállalkozó
vásár
vasárnap
vicc